Friends of God and Slaves of Men

Religion and slavery have been connected since the beginning of human history, but their tangled relationship has rarely been dissected and truly understood. This groundbreaking book illuminates how religion has intersected with the institution of slavery, both as a force for its perpetuation and as a catalyst for its abolition. Spanning antiquity to the present day, this book offers a comprehensive overview of how Christianity, Islam, Judaism, Hinduism, Buddhism, and other faiths have variously justified, moderated, restricted, or opposed slavery. Experts Kevin Bales and Michael Rota integrate historical, philosophical, theological, and social scientific perspectives to offer fresh interdisciplinary insights into this crucial social justice issue. Engaging contemporary challenges, the book covers religious justifications for enslavement by ISIS and the role of the caste system in modern bondage. Finally, it highlights faith-based antislavery activism today and asks how religious communities can amplify their efforts to combat the enduring scourge of slavery worldwide.

Kevin Bales is Professor of Contemporary Slavery and co-founder of the Rights Lab, University of Nottingham, and the American NGO Free the Slaves. His book *Disposable People: New Slavery in the Global Economy* has been published in twelve languages. Archbishop Desmond Tutu called the book "a well researched, scholarly and deeply disturbing exposé of modern slavery." The film based on *Disposable People*, which he co-wrote, won the Peabody Award and two Emmys.

Michael Rota is Professor of Philosophy at the University of St. Thomas, Minnesota. He has authored scholarly articles on the definition of slavery and on the relevance of moral psychology to the history of abolition, as well as numerous contributions to the philosophy of religion.

Slaveries since Emancipation

General Editors

Randall Miller, *St. Joseph's University*
Zoe Trodd, *University of Nottingham*

Slaveries since Emancipation publishes scholarship that links slavery's past to its present, consciously scanning history for lessons of relevance to contemporary abolitionism and that directly engages current issues of interest to activists by contextualizing them historically.

Also in this series:

Sophie van den Elzen, *Slavery in the International Women's Movement, 1832–1914: Memory Work and the Legacy of Abolitionism*

Justin Roberts, *Fragile Empire: Slavery in the Early English Tropics, 1645–1720*

Dexter J. Gabriel, *Jubilee's Experiment: The British West Indies and American Abolitionism*

Andrea Nicholson, *Bearing Witness: Contemporary Slave Narratives and the Global Antislavery Movement*

Genevieve LeBaron, Jessica R. Pliley, and David W. Blight, eds., *Fighting Modern Slavery and Human Trafficking: History and Contemporary Policy*

Hannah-Rose Murray, *Advocates of Freedom: African American Transatlantic Abolitionism in the British Isles*

Catherine Armstrong, *American Slavery, American Imperialism: US Perceptions of Global Servitude, 1870–1914*

Elizabeth Swanson and James Brewer Stewart, eds., *Human Bondage and Abolition: New Histories of Past and Present Slaveries*

R. J. M. Blackett, *The Captive's Quest for Freedom: Fugitive Slaves, the 1850 Fugitive Slave Law, and the Politics of Slavery*

Anna Mae Duane, ed., *Child Slavery before and after Emancipation: An Argument for Child-Centered Slavery Studies*

Friends of God and Slaves of Men

Religion and Slavery, Past and Present

KEVIN BALES
University of Nottingham

MICHAEL ROTA
University of St. Thomas

CAMBRIDGE
UNIVERSITY PRESS

Shaftesbury Road, Cambridge CB2 8EA, United Kingdom

One Liberty Plaza, 20th Floor, New York, NY 10006, USA

477 Williamstown Road, Port Melbourne, VIC 3207, Australia

314–321, 3rd Floor, Plot 3, Splendor Forum, Jasola District Centre,
New Delhi – 110025, India

103 Penang Road, #05–06/07, Visioncrest Commercial, Singapore 238467

Cambridge University Press is part of Cambridge University Press & Assessment,
a department of the University of Cambridge.

We share the University's mission to contribute to society through the pursuit of
education, learning and research at the highest international levels of excellence.

www.cambridge.org
Information on this title: www.cambridge.org/9781009631129

DOI: 10.1017/9781009631143

When citing this work, please include a reference to the DOI 10.1017/9781009631143

First published 2026

Printed in the United Kingdom by CPI Group Ltd, Croydon CR0 4YY

A catalogue record for this publication is available from the British Library

A Cataloging-in-Publication data record for this book is available from the Library
of Congress

ISBN 978-1-009-63112-9 Hardback

To the long line of Freedom Fighters and Abolitionists, known and unknown, that stretches back across history, and especially to the powerful women bringing freedom and hope around the world today – Ginny Baumann, Peggy Callahan, Jolene Smith, Zoe Trodd, Supriya Awasthi, Grace Forrest, Caroline Haughey, Julia de Boinville, Eugenie Brooksbank, Katherine Chon, Cathy Turner, Katarina Schwarz, Doreen Boyd, Nicola Wright, Jacqui Clay, Helen Taylor, Karen Eveson, Vicky Brotherton, Jody Sarich, Lois Bosatta, Laoise Ni Bhriain, Urmila Bhoola, Helen McCabe, Lola Young, Sara Thornton, Jessica Leslie, Holly Burkhalter, Alison Friedman, Tari Weiss, Tina Davis, Alison Gardner, Minh Dang, Amelia Watkins-Smith, Helen Spiby, Sara Borelli, Fiona de Hoog, Christine Annerfalk, Susu Thatun, and so many others.
(K. B.)

To my children, amazed at how many books on slavery have been written, and shocked at how many people are still enslaved today.
(M. R.)

Contents

Figures

Acknowledgments

We are grateful to many colleagues and friends for their assistance on this project: Catherine Armstrong shared helpful references to literature on the global history of slavery and material from her courses on the subject at Loughborough University. Nathan Ballantyne directed us to several relevant sources in social and cognitive psychology, and a few in history as well. Karen Batdorf and the staff at the University of St. Thomas library helped us obtain a number of rare reference materials. Ed Freedman and two anonymous referees at the *Journal for Interdisciplinary History* supplied constructive criticism on the material on moral psychology and abolition. James LePree and Matthew Ponesse shared in advance of publication material from their critical edition and translation of Smaragdus' *Via Regia*, and Andrew Rosato assisted in our analysis and translation of a key passage in Smaragdus' text. John Oldfield, James Brewer Stewart, and David Williard guided us in navigating the historical literature. Bernard Freamon's research on slavery and Islam deeply influenced our work on that topic. Jonathan A. C. Brown shared a number of documents on slavery in Islamic contexts, and Amal Ghazal assisted us with some Arabic-language sources. Peggy Callahan and Tawney Bevacqua helped us find several suitable images for Part II, and Anti-Slavery International, Leslie Roberts, Supriya Awasthi, Brian Woods, and Voices4Freedom kindly supplied permission to use their images at no charge. In 2019, Chris Stewart and the team at the Templeton Religion Trust supported a grant application from Bales and Luke de Pulford, "Prosocial Benefits of Religion: The Case of Modern Slavery," which subsequently supported field research that informs our discussion in Chapter 8. A Distinguished Early Career grant and subsequently a sabbatical from the University of St. Thomas facilitated the drafting and completion of Part I. Finally, Samuel Lebens and Randall Miller supplied helpful comments on portions of Part I. We offer our sincere thanks to these individuals and institutions, and to any others we may have forgotten to include.

Introduction

In the summer of 1550, Charles V, the King of Spain, ordered a group of fourteen officials, scholars, and clerics to judge a dispute. The conquest of the Americas had swept on for over half a century, but a debate was stirring within Spain – were the wars in the New World unjust? During a month of meetings, the judges heard and discussed opposing arguments: Juan Gines de Sepulveda, a noted Renaissance scholar, argued that the Spanish could legitimately enslave the Native Americans (or "Indians") because they were "natural slaves," and that the wars of conquest were justified both by the Indians' barbarism and idolatry, and by the imperative to spread Christianity. The Dominican Friar Bartolemé de Las Casas (1474–1566) spoke for five days in defense of the Indians, arguing on both ethical and theological grounds that the conquistadors' conquest and enslavement of the natives was gravely wrong.[1]

Both Sepulveda and Las Casas thought religion was firmly on his side on the slavery question. The same was true of the Jewish Rabbi Morris J. Raphall and his critic Rabbi David Einhorn, in Civil War-era America. Both thought that Judaism was on his side, as Morris defended slavery with religious arguments and Einhorn argued for abolition with religious arguments. And the same was true in the early twentieth century as Muslim thinkers debated whether Islam required that slavery continue or provided an imperative to end it.

From the beginning of human history, slavery and religion have been linked. Slaves have been forced to serve religious hierarchies, even to the

[1] See Lewis Hanke, *The Spanish Struggle for Justice in the Conquest of America* (Philadelphia: University of Pennsylvania Press, 1949), chap. 8.

point of ultimate sacrifice. Religious doctrine has often set out who might be enslaved and justified that slavery. Yet religious ideas and motivations also led people of faith to restrict the scope of slavery and ease the lives of slaves in ages past, and religious groups were at the center of the successful abolitionist movements of the eighteenth and nineteenth centuries. Unknown to many, the tangled and varied connections between religion and slavery continue today. Religious groups play a vital role in the fight against contemporary slavery, yet religious identity is still being used to facilitate enslavement, in many ways and in many countries.

The academic literature on slavery is vast, including thousands of articles and books on slavery as it relates to particular religious traditions in particular periods or societies. Surprisingly, there is no single work that synthesizes this prior work and analyzes the common patterns in the relationship between slavery and religion that appear with a bird's eye view. There is also a sizable literature on contemporary slavery, yet little has been written on the important and fascinating connections between religion and contemporary slavery. In this book we attempt to fill both these gaps, focusing principally on Judaism, Christianity, and Islam, but with some treatment of Hinduism, Buddhism, and several other religions. In Part I, we examine the ways in which religious groups and religiously inspired individuals have responded to slavery in the past. In Part II, we turn to the relationship between religion and slavery in the present.

Part I consists of four chapters, on religious attempts to *justify* slavery, to *ameliorate* or ease the lives of slaves, to *restrict* slavery without at the same time seeking to eradicate it, and to *abolish* slavery. Chapter 2, on the justification of slavery, includes a detailed discussion of religious proslavery arguments, as well as our own critiques of those arguments. Chapter 3 examines attempts by religious groups or individuals to make the lives of slaves better in some way, but without challenging the legitimacy of slavery as such. We organize these attempts into four categories: (i) moral exhortations to treat slaves well, (ii) exhortations to manumit or ransom slaves, (iii) legislation aimed at easing the lives of slaves, and (iv) promulgation of doctrines of spiritual equality and shared eternal destiny that likely promoted the welfare of some slaves. Chapter 4, on restricting slavery, reviews religious attempts to reduce the scope of slavery that fall short of abolition. For example, religious groups at various times have restricted slavery by making it more difficult to turn a free person into a slave, and by making it more difficult to sell slaves, and by placing limits on who could hold a slave of a certain category. In this chapter we also evaluate the influence of religion in the waning of slavery in medieval

Europe. Chapter 5 is an overview of the religious rejection of slavery. We discuss early antislavery voices, such as the Essenes and St. Gregory of Nyssa (c. 335–395 AD), and tell the story of the Christian rejection of slavery in the seventeenth and eighteenth centuries. The chapter closes with an overview of Islamic abolitionism in the nineteenth and twentieth centuries.

Part II focuses on the relationship between religion and slavery in the present and recent past. In Chapter 6, we provide context by sketching the evolution of slavery and the development of antislavery efforts from after the American Civil War until the late twentieth century, including discussions of the antislavery movement focused on the Congo around the turn of the twentieth century, the persistence of slavery in various European colonies, and the use of state-organized slave labor by Axis powers during World War II. Chapter 7 is an examination of the ways in which religion is still being used to facilitate slavery. We describe the use and justification of slavery by the Islamic State of Iraq and Syria (ISIS), *trokosi* slavery in West Africa, and temple slavery in India. We also show how the religious identity and beliefs of victims are sometimes used to trap them in slavery. Finally, in Chapter 8, we show how religious groups are helping in the fight against contemporary slavery, and ask how they might help more.

I.I HOW BAD WAS ANCIENT SLAVERY?

For religious believers, it can be painful to learn how one's own religious tradition has justified the practice of owning and exploiting human beings. A natural response is to wonder just how bad slavery was in the ancient contexts in which the major religions permitted it. Life was hard back then … weren't ancient slaves basically just dependent family members, living a totally different reality than the kidnapped and brutalized Africans worked to death on the sugar plantations of the New World in more recent centuries? In a word, no. While it is certainly true that the slavery of the sugar plantations was particularly brutal, and that in any age slaves have experienced a wide variety of conditions, an examination of historical evidence indicates that for the vast majority of slaves in ancient times, slavery was very harsh indeed. As a scholar of ancient slavery explains:

[T]he widespread use of rewards, the existence of many masters who endeavored to be as kind and forbearing as possible, and the proliferation of slaves who held positions of power and prestige should not lead us to think that slavery was fundamentally a humane institution at the time of the New Testament. It was not—not by a long shot. Life may have been relatively good for some slaves, but "slavery in the Greco-Roman world remained an often exploitative and humiliating institution in which slaves, though recognized in a sense as human beings, were still property or 'things' (*res*), and could be beaten, tortured, or even killed by their owners."[2]

Classicist Richard Saller, speaking of Roman slavery, writes that "The lot of bad slaves was to be beaten and that of good slaves was to internalize the constant threat of a beating."[3] In the words of another historian:

The conditions of life which produced fear of their owners in slaves were thus numerous and all-embracing. … Slaves were never in a position to predict when the wrath of an owner would descend upon them and their lives were thus conditioned by this perennial fear of physical abuse and maltreatment. Within that element of fear lay owners' capacity for the permanent control of their slaves.[4]

Some slaves had it far better than others, but in all but the most exceptional cases, to be a slave was to be controlled by violence or the threat of violence, and exploited as a tool for the benefit of others.

1.2 HOW BAD IS MODERN SLAVERY?

Similarly, it's natural to wonder how bad "modern slavery" really is. When we speak of modern slaves, are we simply talking about people who, because of poverty, find it necessary to work under extremely demanding conditions? Again, the short answer is "no."

In the present moment, though it is hard to imagine, slavery is equally if not more brutal and deadly than it has been in the past. A key reason for this is the complete collapse of the monetary value of slaves. In the mid nineteenth century a healthy young male slave in the United States had an average "sale" price that, in today's money, would be around £40,000/ $50,000. Today, slaves practically cost nothing or very little. The large number of vulnerable people, especially in poorer countries, means that

---

[2] John T. Fitzgerald, "The Stoics and the early Christians on the treatment of slaves," in T. Rasimus, T. Engberg-Pedersen, and I. Dunderberg (eds.), *Stoicism in Early Christianity* (Grand Rapids, MI: Baker Academic, 2010), 141–175, 162. Fitzgerald is quoting J. P. Hershbell, "Epictetus: a freedman on slavery," *Ancient Society*, 26 (1995), 185–204, 188.

[3] Richard Saller, "Corporal punishment, authority, and obedience in the Roman household," in B. Rawson (ed.), *Marriage, Divorce, and Children in Ancient Rome* (Oxford: Clarendon Press, 1991), 144–165.

[4] K. R. Bradley, *Slaves and Masters in the Roman Empire: A Study in Social Control* (Oxford: Oxford University Press, 1987), 137.

men, women, and children are easily lured into bondage – their own desperation pushing them to accept false job offers. Once removed from their community, those lured into slavery are treated as disposable inputs, to be used up and discarded. They can be worked until they collapse, and then they are dumped or killed. Significant numbers of people are enslaved within armed conflict. On the day this is being written, there are fifty-six ongoing conflicts, the largest number since the end of World War II. Most of these conflicts are occuring in Africa and the Middle East, where enslavement in war is most common. Research on conflicts occurring between 1989 and 2016 found several forms of enslavement occurring in 78 percent of all conflicts.[5]

While slavery is illegal in most countries, and very much prohibited by international agreements and United Nations conventions, the efforts of criminals, the deadly impacts of climate change and environmental destruction, the intentional impoverishment of minority groups, and the assaults on the lives and livelihoods of people because of their particular religious or tribal affiliation, can all lead to the loss of freedom and enslavement, if not worse.

As a hidden crime, it is not possible to determine the precise number of people in slavery around the world – but years of work by antislavery organizations and scholars have produced estimates ranging up to 50 million slaves, with the caveat that because slavery is often a hidden crime and occurring in remote areas no estimates are fully precise.

1.3 WHAT DO WE MEAN BY "SLAVERY"?

As discussed in Chapter 6, the League of Nations 1926 Convention to Suppress the Slave Trade and Slavery included a definition of slavery that has proven applicable today: "Slavery is the status or condition of a person over whom any or all of the powers attaching to the right of ownership are exercised." And as explained in the Bellagio-Harvard Guidelines, the right of ownership "should be understood as constituting control over a person in such a way as to significantly deprive that person of his or her individual liberty, with the intent of exploitation through the use, management, profit, transfer or disposal of that person. Usually this

---

[5] Angharad Smith, Monti Narayan Datta, and Kevin Bales, "Contemporary slavery in armed conflict: Introducing the CSAC dataset, 1989–2016," *Journal of Peace Research*, 60:2 (2022): doi.org/10.1177/00223433211065649.

exercise will be supported by and obtained through means such as violent force, deception and/or coercion."[6]

The fundamental fact of slavery, past and present, is that a person is reduced to "property" and may be used, abused, exploited, bought, sold, or killed. Slaves today, because they tend to be much less costly than slaves in the past, are normally treated as disposable inputs in criminal activities.

I.4 USING SLAVERY

In Part I, we examine four major responses by religious groups to human bondage: justifying, ameliorating, restricting, and rejecting slavery. Space constraints inclined us to forgo coverage of a fifth response, *using* slavery, but we say a few words about it here.

Many religious groups have used slave labor to support their material needs. There are many references to Catholic clergy owning slaves in the early medieval period, for example. Buddhist monastic estates and Confucian academies used slaves for food production and the performance of manual labor.[7] Certain Islamic societies made extensive use of slaves within their armies.[8] At several points in history, moreover, religious groups have used slaves for specifically religious purposes. In ancient Sumeria, temple slaves were used "to assist priests" in their functions, and the earliest evidence of Greek slavery includes references to two categories of slaves: those owned by individuals and "slaves of the god."[9] In the religious system of *trokosi* in West Africa, young girls are given as slaves by their families to fetish priests, in atonement for offenses committed by male relatives or ancestors. (As we'll discuss in Chapter 7,

[6] Research Network on the Legal Parameters of Slavery, "Bellagio-Harvard Guidelines on the Legal Parameters of Slavery" (2012), available as Appendix 6 in Jean Allain, *The Law and Slavery: Prohibiting Human Exploitation* (Leiden: Brill, 2015). For a close analysis of several proposed definitions of slavery, see Michael Rota, "On the definition of slavery," *Theoria* (Stockholm) 86:5 (Oct 2020), 543–564.

[7] James B. Palais, *Confucian Statecraft and Korean Institutions* (Seattle: University of Washington Press, 1996), 210. Another example of the religious use of slavery is found in the Catholic Church's use of slavery as a penalty in the early medieval period: The Church punished clerics who violated their vow of celibacy by making their children slaves of the Church. See Christopher J. Kellerman, S. J., *All Oppression Shall Cease: A History of Slavery, Abolitionism, and the Catholic Church* (New York: Orbis Books, 2022), 29 and 34.

[8] See Bernard Freamon, *Possessed by the Right Hand: The Problem of Slavery in Islamic Law and Muslim Cultures* (Leiden: Brill, 2019), 286–293.

[9] Freamon, *Possessed by the Right Hand*, 35 and 50.

this practice has continued into the present day.) Perhaps the most shocking example of the religious use of slaves was as victims in ritual human sacrifice, which was practiced in many ancient societies. Two common motivations were a belief that a dying king or other important person needed attendants in the next life, and a desire to please the gods so that the crop cycle might not cease.[10] In some societies, slaves and war captives were used as the victims.[11] Tribute slaves from north of the Aztec Empire could end up as victims sacrificed to the Aztec gods.[12] In Benin (West Africa), slaves were killed to ward off plague, and in pre-Christian Europe, "Norsemen and Teutons regularly sacrificed war prisoners to their gods."[13] In such cases, the victims satisfy the definition of slavery laid out in the Bellagio-Harvard Guidelines: They were controlled "in such a way as to significantly deprive" them of "individual liberty, with the intent of exploitation through" their use as sacrificial victims. In this case, the "use" was for a specifically religious purpose.

Much more could be written about how religious groups have *used* slavery, but in this book we focus on more explicitly evaluative responses: When have religious groups thought slavery was acceptable, thus *justifying* it, and when have they thought it was wrong, thus *rejecting* it? And when have they recognized its problems without yet rejecting it outright, thus attempting to *ameliorate* the lives of slaves or *restrict* the institution? We begin with the story of the religious justification of slavery.

[10] Nigel Davies, *Human Sacrifice: In History and Today* (New York: Dorset Press, 1981), 16–17.

[11] See Catherine M. Cameron, *Captives: How Stolen People Changed the World* (Lincoln, NE: University of Nebraska Press, 2016).

[12] Davies, *Human Sacrifice*, p. 21; David Eltis and Stanley Engerman, "Dependence, servility, and coerced labor in time and space," in D. Eltis and S. Engerman (eds.), *The Cambridge World History of Slavery: Volume 3, AD 1420—AD 1804* (Cambridge: Cambridge University Press, 2011), 1–21, 8.

[13] Davies, *Human Sacrifice*, 45.

PART I

RELIGIOUS RESPONSES TO SLAVERY – HISTORICAL PATTERNS

2

Justifying Slavery

Before he was elected the twenty-eighth President of the United States (1913–1921), and before he became the thirteenth President of Princeton University, Woodrow Wilson was voted the most popular teacher on the Princeton faculty by the student body, six years in a row.[1] Late in Wilson's life, a friend asked him who had been *his* best teacher. "My father!" Wilson replied, "I got ten times more from my father than I got at college."[2] Joseph Ruggles Wilson (1822–1903) was an outgoing, lively man, with a good sense of humor and a love of conversation. During Woodrow's childhood Joseph would regularly take his son on excursions to sites he thought might interest the boy. Upon returning home Joseph would ask Woodrow to compose an essay about what they had seen. After Woodrow read the essay aloud, his father would say "Now put down your paper and tell me in your own words what you saw." After this was done, Joseph would have Woodrow write down the narration in that shorter, more direct way.[3] Joseph remained an engaged and encouraging father as Woodrow grew, and the two remained exceptionally close

[1] John Milton Cooper, Jr., *Woodrow Wilson: A Biography* (New York: Alfred A. Knopf, 2009), 67.

[2] Stockton Axson, *Brother Woodrow: A Memoir of Woodrow Wilson*, ed. A. S. Link (Princeton: Princeton University Press, 1993), 9. On the life of Wilson's father, Joseph Ruggles Wilson, we have also been helped by Ray Stannard Baker, *Woodrow Wilson: Life and Letters* (New York: Charles Scribner's Sons, 1946), George C. Osborn, *Woodrow Wilson: The Early Years* (Baton Rouge, LA: Louisiana State Press, 1968), and Jan Willem Schulte Nordholt, *Woodrow Wilson: A Life for Peace* (Berkeley: University of California Press, 1991).

[3] Cooper, *Woodrow Wilson*, 20.

throughout their lives. When he died, Woodrow was at his side. Joseph's last intelligible words were "My dear, dear son!" According to Woodrow's brother-in-law and friend,

The love between these two was lifelong, tender, deep and understanding. His father had always been Woodrow Wilson's true hero, for, added to filial affection and the respect which he maintained to the end of his father's life … there was profound admiration for the character and mind of his father.[4]

Joseph Wilson was a Presbyterian minister and a university professor. Although he published little, theological research and sermon-writing were an important component of his work, and on one occasion, at least, he was asked and agreed to publish one of his sermons. That sermon was on slavery, preached in Georgia shortly before the outbreak of the Civil War. Joseph Wilson hoped that it might:

be the means of doing a service to my slaveholding brethren throughout the State, by promoting intelligence upon a momentous subject of practical interest to them and the whole world. It is surely high time that the Bible view of slavery should be examined, and that we should begin to meet the infidel fanaticism of our infatuated enemies upon the elevated ground of a divine warrant for the institution we are resolved to cherish.

The distinguished pastor went on to argue that the slavery of the American South was a positive good – not merely permissible, but righteous:

Does this great, beneficial, civilizing institution of slavery live beneath the light of His face, with no fault to be found with it upon the part of His infinite holiness, except when and wherein it may suffer abuse at the hands of the parties concerned? Surely the Bible is clear enough upon this point to satisfy the most sensitive conscience. Light cannot shine with greater brightness than does the doctrine of the sinlessness – nay, than does the doctrine of the righteousness – of an institution, which, besides being sustained and promoted by a long course of favorable providences, besides being recognized as a prime conservator of the civilization of the world, besides being one of the colored man's foremost sources of blessing, is likewise directly sanctioned by both the utterance and silence of Scripture.[5]

Here, in Part I of this book, we will describe and illustrate four major religious responses to slavery. Joseph Wilson's use of religious arguments

---

[4] Axson, *Brother Woodrow*, 24.

[5] Joseph R. Wilson, *Mutual Relation of Masters and Slaves as Taught in the Bible* (Augusta, GA: Steam Press of Chronicle and Sentinel, 1861), available in the University of North Carolina at Chapel Hill *Documenting the American South* digital collection: docsouth.unc .edu/imls/wilson/wilson.html.

to support slavery was common in the antebellum American South, reaching, as well, into the North. Indeed, the use of religious ideas to justify slavery has occurred all over the world and throughout recorded history. In this chapter we examine the *justification* of slavery by religious groups and by individuals on religious grounds. To "justify" slavery is to assert, argue for, or defend the view that slavery is just, but "just" can be taken in at least two senses. In a weak sense, any action that is morally permissible can be said to be just. In a strong sense, an action needs to be positively good to count as just. Accordingly, we distinguish between strong justifications of slavery, which contend that the social practice of slaveholding is a good, beneficial, and appropriate social practice, and weak justifications of slavery, which hold that slavery is morally permissible without claiming that it is a positive good. Joseph Wilson justifies slavery in the strong sense. An example of a weak justification of slavery is found in the thought of Virginian Thomas Roderick Dew (1802–1844), Professor and later President of the College of William and Mary, who does not deny that slavery is wrong in the abstract, and admits that it is "against the spirit of Christianity" but argues that it cannot be gotten rid of without the production of "greater injury to both the masters and slaves."[6]

The distinction between strong and weak justifications of slavery marks an important difference among defenders of slavery, but (like the distinction between bald and not bald) it is best thought of as a spectrum. The historical record contains intermediate cases – St. Augustine of Hippo (354–430 AD), for example, falls in between the poles of a paradigmatic strong and a paradigmatic weak justification of slavery, holding that slavery is bad in some respects and good in others. With this background in place, we examine the religious justification of slavery in the North American context.

2.1 PROSLAVERY IN NORTH AMERICA

Thornton Stringfellow (1788–1869), an active and influential Baptist minister in Virginia, was known in the antebellum South for his religiously based argument in favor of Negro slavery. Stringfellow contended

---

[6] Thomas R. Dew, "Abolition of Negro Slavery," *American Quarterly Review*, 12 (1832), 189–265, reprinted in Drew Gilpin Faust (ed.), *The Ideology of Slavery: Proslavery Thought in the Antebellum South, 1830–1860* (Baton Rouge, LA: Louisiana State University Press, 1981), 23–77, 61.

that, "The guardianship and control of the black race, by the white, is an indispensable Christian duty, to which we must yet look, if we would secure the well-being of both races."[7] In a widely reprinted piece, Stringfellow argued that slavery was "full of mercy." Those "who feared not God nor regarded men" and were enslaved by the Jews in the time of Abraham, Job, and the Patriarchs, "were surely brought under great obligations to the mercy of God, in allowing such men as these to purchase them, and keep them in their families." And since the founding of Christianity, the institution of slavery

has brought within the range of Gospel influence, millions of Ham's descendants [Africans] among ourselves, who, but for this institution, would have sunk down to eternal ruin; knowing not God, and strangers to the Gospel. In their bondage here on earth, they have been much better provided for, and great multitudes of them have been made the freeman of the Lord Jesus Christ, and left this world rejoicing in hope of the glory of God.[8]

This, which we may call the "Spiritual Blessing Argument," posits that New World slavery benefitted Africans because it provided a means by which enslaved Africans and their descendants could come to the True Faith. As we show below, some Jewish and Islamic thinkers have deployed their own versions of this argument.

The Spiritual Blessing Argument was a common arrow in the quiver of proslavery thinkers, but only one among several. Christians seeking to justify slavery on religious grounds also typically turned to specific passages in the Bible. As a preliminary to their use of these passages, they first had to show that the Hebrew or Greek terms translated as "servant" in then-current English translations of the Bible actually meant "slave." This was not difficult to do. Several texts in the Old Testament make the distinction between a hired servant and a bondservant.[9] Bondservants served their masters for an indefinite period, they were bought and sold for money, their children became bondservants of the master, and they could be physically punished by their masters – in a word they were *property*. If a bondservant died while being beaten by a master, the master was to be punished, but if the servant survived the beating for a day and only died thereafter, the master was not to be punished (Exod 21:20–21).

---

[7] Thornton Stringfellow, *Scriptural and Statistical Views in Favor of Slavery*, 4th ed. (Richmond, VA: J. W. Randolph, 1856), 105.

[8] Thornton Stringfellow, "A brief examination of Scripture testimony on the institution of slavery," *Religious Herald* (1841), reprinted in Faust (ed.), *The Ideology of Slavery*, 166.

[9] See, for example, Lev 25:39–40, Exod 12:43–45, and Job 7:2.

So despite the King James Version of the Bible using "servant" rather than "slave," it was easy enough for antebellum proslavery writers to establish that the bondservants of the Old Testament were slaves. And given the ubiquity of slavery in the Roman Empire, the Roman context of the New Testament made it easy to argue (correctly) that the "servants" (*doulos*) mentioned in the New Testament were also slaves. Language thus clarified, proponents of slavery could turn to several biblical texts to formulate what we might call Arguments from Divine Sanction. It is helpful to distinguish two versions of this approach: The first are Arguments from Divine Permission, which argue in favor of slavery from a claim that God permitted or approved of slavery, and the second are Arguments from Divine Command, which argue in favor of slavery from a claim that God explicitly commanded it.

A common Argument from Divine Permission stated that, before the giving of the Ten Commandments to Moses on Mt. Sinai, God had shown special approval to men who were slaveholders, such as Abraham and Job, and to someone who was closely involved in the buying of slaves, Joseph.[10] God had, for example, declared that "Abraham obeyed my voice and kept my charge, my commandments, my statues, and my laws" (Gen 26:5).[11] Yet Abraham had owned slaves. Thus, it was inferred, owning slaves must not have been contrary to God's laws.[12]

A common Argument from Divine Command began by observing that, in the law given at Mt. Sinai, God himself had explicitly authorized the Jews to buy and hold non-Jews as hereditary slaves:

As for your male and female slaves whom you may have: you may buy male and female slaves from among the nations that are round about you. You may also buy from among the strangers who sojourn with you and their families that are with you, who have been born in your land; and they may be your property. You may bequeath them to your sons after you, to inherit as a possession for ever; you may make slaves of them, but over your brethren the people of Israel you shall not rule, one over another, with harshness. (Lev 25:44-46)

[10] See especially Gen 24:35–36, Gen 47:18–25, and Job 1:1–3. For a statement of this argument, see Stringfellow, "A brief examination of Scripture testimony on the institution of slavery," 140–149.

[11] Unless otherwise indicated, translations from the Bible are from *The Holy Bible: containing the Old and New Testaments*, Revised Standard Version, Catholic Edition (San Francisco: Ignatius Press, n.d.)

[12] This particular version of the argument is given by Raymund Harris, on whom see Section 2.4.4.

The anonymous author of an important essay appearing in 1850 used this and other passages to argue that slavery was merely not sinful, but a positive good:

[A]t a time when the Israelites had no slaves, but were themselves, in a manner, fugitive slaves, and when they had no use for slaves, being wanderers in a wilderness, and fed by God's own hand, he [God] provided laws for bringing in, buying, inheriting and governing, slaves, in the land unto which they were to be brought at the end of forty years. He made laws recognizing the right of property, in man and in his descendants, forever ... To any man, who admits that the Bible is given by inspiration from God, they prove that, in buying, selling, holding and using slaves, there is no moral guilt. Like all the institutions of the Deity, the holding of slaves may become criminal, by abuse of the slave; but the relation, in itself, is good and moral.[13]

Similarly, in a letter to the English antislavery activist Thomas Clarkson, the Governor of South Carolina James Henry Hammond (1807–1864), himself a wealthy slaveholder, concluded from an examination of Exod 20:17 and Lev 25 that "American slavery is not only not a sin, but [is] especially commanded by God through Moses."[14]

A third scriptural argument in favor of slavery focused on the first passage in the Bible to mention slavery: the story of Ham related in Genesis 9:18–27. Noah, in response to a transgression committed against him by his son Ham, curses Ham's son Canaan: "Cursed be Canaan, a slave of slaves shall he be to his brothers" (v. 25). Reading this text together with a long-standing tradition (based on Gen 10) that Ham was the progenitor of Black Africa, proponents of American slavery sometimes argued that Black slavery had been decreed by God through Noah. Thus Benjamin Morgan Palmer (1818–1902), an influential Presbyterian pastor in New Orleans:

Upon Ham was pronounced the doom of perpetual servitude ... Accordingly, history records not a single example of any member of this group [African peoples] lifting itself, by any process of self-development, above the savage condition. From first to last their mental and moral characteristics, together with the guidance of Providence, have marked them for servitude ...[15]

---

[13] "Slavery and the Bible," *De Bow's Review*, 9 (Sept. 1850), 281–286, reprinted in Paul Finkelman (ed.), *Defending Slavery: Proslavery Thought in the Old South, A Brief History with Documents* (Boston: Bedford/St Martin's, 2003), 113.

[14] James Henry Hammond, "Letter to an English abolitionist," Jan. 28, 1845, in Faust (ed.), *The Ideology of Slavery*, 175.

[15] Benjamin Morgan Palmer, "National responsibility before God," a homily preached Jun. 13, 1861, quoted in Stephen R. Haynes, *Noah's Curse: The Biblical Justification of American Slavery* (Oxford: Oxford University Press, 2002), 132.

And in the more succinct words of another Southern writer: "The blacks were originally designed to vassalage by the Patriarch Noah."[16] Because these arguments make the claim that God explicitly decreed the institution of slavery, they can be classified as Arguments from Divine Command.

Fourth, proslavery thinkers made much of the apostolic teaching in the New Testament that slaves should be submissive to their masters. St. Paul's Letter to the Ephesians 6:5–7 reads:

Slaves, be obedient to those who are your earthly masters, with fear and trembling, in singleness of heart, as to Christ; not in the way of eye-service, as menpleasers, but as slaves of Christ, doing the will of God from the heart, rendering service with a good will as to the Lord and not to men …

The same teaching is given elsewhere by Paul (Col 3:22–25, 1 Tim 6:1–6, Titus 2:9), and by Peter (1 Pet 2:18–24). And in Paul's letter to Philemon we have a recorded instance in which Paul sent a fugitive slave, Onesimus, back to his master Philemon.[17] Based on these passages James Henry Hammond concluded that "American slavery" was "approved by Christ through his apostles."[18] Interpreting the apostolic commands that slaves obey their masters and that masters treat their slaves justly and fairly as a divine provision for the perpetuation of slavery, Joseph Wilson was yet more emphatic:

[I]t is remarkable, to say the least, that the institution of compulsory slavery, as it existed throughout the Roman Empire, although often referred to in the New Testament, is never once condemned, never once even discountenanced. On the contrary, provision is made for its perpetuation, by means of the rules which are given for its regulation and improvement. So far from Scripture appearing as the destroyer, it appears as the upholder, of an institution, which, under proper management, by christian people, is represented as an element in domestic completeness, whose presence is a benefit and a blessing.[19]

This brief review of Christian proslavery arguments should not be taken to imply that religiously based arguments were the only arguments used to justify American slavery, or even that they were the most important

---

[16] J. J. Flournoy, *A reply, to a pamphlet, entitled "Bondage …"* (Athens, GA, 1838), 16, quoted in David M. Goldenberg, *The Curse of Ham: Race and Slavery in Early Judaism, Christianity, and Islam* (Princeton: Princeton University Press, 2003), 1.

[17] As we'll argue in the following chapter, this way of describing Paul's action is technically accurate but highly misleading. Antislavery thinkers would have a much different interpretation of Paul's actions.

[18] Hammond, "Letter to an English abolitionist," in Faust (ed.), *The Ideology of Slavery*, 175.

[19] Wilson, *Mutual Relation of Masters and Slaves as Taught in the Bible*, 11–12.

such arguments. Historian Larry Tise's careful examination of proslavery thought reveals the extensive use of economic arguments (e.g. in a slave economy "labor becomes capital, equalizing the interests of master and slave"), political arguments (e.g. slave societies are protected from radical movements), arguments relating to supposed Negro history or character (e.g. the life of Blacks in Africa was already degraded, or Blacks "are happier enslaved than free"), and arguments relating specifically to the American experience (e.g. American slavery is a particularly mild form of slavery, and an essential ingredient to American success).[20] Indeed, abolitionists were more likely to invoke religion in their attacks on slavery than were proslavery thinkers in their defense of slavery.[21] Still, religious justifications of slavery in the antebellum United States reinforced all of the other proslavery arguments.[22] And these religious justifications were not merely the product of a fanatical fringe. Among those who justified slavery on religious grounds were influential men, such as Joseph Wilson, well regarded by their peers. Proslavery views were taken seriously enough that, as the sectional conflict between North and South increased, several major Christian denominations split over their views on the morality of slavery – the Presbyterian Church in 1838, the Methodist Church in 1844, and the Baptists in 1845.[23]

Turning now to weak justifications of slavery in the North American context: in addition to Bible-based Arguments from Divine Permission, the Massachusetts judge and slaveholder John Saffin (1626–1710), writing in 1701, provided an argument linking the theological to social inequality. Responding to an antislavery tract penned by his fellow

---

[20] Larry E. Tise, *Proslavery: A History of the Defense of Slavery in America, 1701–1840* (Athens, GA: The University of Georgia Press, 1987). See especially chap. 5. See also Lacy K. Ford, *Deliver Us from Evil: The Slavery Question in the Old South* (Oxford: Oxford University Press, 2009).

[21] Rodney Stark, *For the Glory of God: How Monotheism Led to Reformations, Science, Witch-Hunts, and the End of Slavery* (Princeton: Princeton University Press, 2003), 344–345. Particularly striking is the differential frequencies at which antislavery and proslavery writers made reference to experiential religiosity. In a linguistic analysis of the writings (including letters and diaries) of 101 slaveholders, eleven proslavery clergymen, and fifty abolitionists (of whom fifteen were clergyman) in English-speaking North America, John Auping found that the rate at which abolitionists mentioned an experience of God per page of text was more than seventy times higher than the rate at which slaveholders and proslavery clergyman did so (John A. Auping, *Religion and Social Justice: The Case of Christianity and the Abolition of Slavery in America* [Mexico City: Universidad Iberoamericana, 1994], chap. 9, esp. 151).

[22] A point suggested to us by Randall Miller, personal communication, Jan. 27, 2024.

[23] Auping, *Religion and Social Justice*, 104–108.

Massachusetts judge Samuel Sewall (1652–1730), Saffin attempted to rebut Sewall's claim that all men have an equal right to liberty and the outward comforts of life, by means of an appeal to God's providential ordering of the world:

[God] hath Ordained different degrees and orders of men, some to be High and Honourable, some to be Low and Despicable; some to be Monarchs, Kings, Princes and Governours, Masters, and Commanders, others to be Subjects, and to be Commanded; Servants of sundry sorts and degrees, bound to obey; yea, some to be born Slaves, and so to remain during their lives ... So God hath set different Orders and Degrees of Men in the World.[24]

Over a century later, South Carolina Baptist clergyman Richard Furman (1755–1825) would rely on a similar claim about God's providence. Furman acknowledged that slavery "is undoubtedly an Evil; and, as I conceive a Natural and Political evil; but frequently combined with Moral evil or Sin."[25] Yet, he contended, "such is the order of providence that a considerable portion of the human race must necessarily move in a humble sphere and be generally at the disposal of their fellow men."[26] While Saffin and Furman do not formalize this argument carefully, one might reconstruct their reasoning in three steps:

(1) God has intentionally arranged human affairs in such a way that some are permanent slaves while others are masters.

(2) It is not unjust to accept God's intentional arrangement of human affairs.

(3) Thus, it is not unjust to accept permanent slavery.

Call this the Argument from Divine Providence.

The use of religious ideas to justify slavery was of course limited neither to the United States nor to Christianity. In this and the following three sections we discuss the justification of slavery in Hinduism, Buddhism, Judaism, Christianity, and Islam.[27]

---

[24] John Saffin, *A Brief and Candid Answer to a Late Printed Sheet, Entitled, The Selling of Joseph*, partially available in George H. Moore, *Notes on the History of Slavery in Massachusetts* (New York: Appleton & Co., 1866), 251–256, and at: nationalhumanitiescenter.org/pds/becomingamer/ideas/text3/slaverychristian.pdf.

[25] From a letter of Richard Furman to Dear Sir [Rev. W. Mg. (?)], Jun. 29, 1807, quoted in Tise, *Proslavery*, 39.

[26] Furman to Dear Sir, Jun. 29, 1807, quoted in Tise, *Proslavery*, 40.

[27] Due to length constraints, we focus on key figures and texts, rather than attempting to provide a comprehensive survey.

2.2 THE JUSTIFICATION OF SLAVERY IN HINDUISM AND BUDDHISM

Slavery is accepted as a given in early Hindu and Buddhist texts. The Hindu religious epic *Mahābhārata*, composed sometime between the third century BC and the third century AD, assumes the existence of slaves and mentions "the customary rule of conquest on the field of battle" by which conquered warriors are enslaved.[28] The roughly contemporaneous *Manu-smrti*, an influential legal and religious text, accepts without comment seven types of *dāsas* [servants or slaves], including those who are bought, sold, inherited, or enslaved from birth. The *Narada-smrti*, another influential text of religious law of similar age, acknowledges fifteen categories of bondage, and states that slaves in the first four categories (those born in the house, purchased, gifted, or inherited) "cannot be released from bondage, except by the favour of their owners."[29] Buddhist ethics, for its part, tends to focus on the path to enlightenment and "rarely on the organization of society or the legal regulation of conduct within the society,"[30] and so perhaps it is not surprising that "there is almost no indication in any premodern Buddhist source, scriptural or documentary, of opposition to, or reluctance to participate in, institutions of slavery."[31] Until modern times, Buddhist monasteries throughout Asia owned many slaves.[32]

The more the existence of slavery is taken for granted, the less pressure is exerted on slaveholders to legitimize the practice. Still, we do see some arguments justifying slavery in Hindu and Buddhist sources. The *Manu-smrti* presents an Argument from Divine Sanction for the

---

[28] *The Mahabharata of Krishna-Dwaipayana Vyasa*, book 3, section CCLXX, trans. Pratap Chandra Roy, vol. 3 (Calcutta: Oriental Publishing Co., no date), 580.

[29] *Narada-smrti* V.30, translation from *The Minor Law-Books, Part I: Narada, Brihaspati*, trans. Julius Jolly (Oxford: Clarendon Press, 1889). See v.25–43, and cf. Dev Raj Chanana, *Slavery in Ancient India: As Depicted in Pali and Sanskrit Texts* (New Delhi: People's Publishing House, 1960), 115.

[30] Michael Barnhart, "Buddhist ethics and social justice," in R. Bontekoe and M. Stepaniants (eds.), *Justice and Democracy: Cross-Cultural Perspectives* (Honolulu: University of Hawai'i Press, 1997), 327–341, 327.

[31] Jonathan A. Silk, "Slavery," in R. E. Buswell (ed.), *The Encyclopedia of Buddhism* (New York: Thomson Gale, 2004), vol. 2, 780. A notable exception is the Buddha's command that lay followers should not engage in trading slaves, on which see Chapter 4, n. 8.

[32] See Silk, "Slavery," 780; Gregory Schopen, "Liberation is only for those already free: reflections on debts to slavery and enslavement to debt in an early Indian Buddhist monasticism," *Journal of the American Academy of Religion*, 82:3 (2014), 606–635; Sung-Eun Thomas Kim, "Perception of monastic slaves by scholar-officials and monks in the late Koryo and early Choson Periods," *Journal of Korean Religions*, 7:1 (2016), 5–34.

conclusion that Brahmins (the highest caste) may justly exact forced labor from Shudras (the lowest of the four Aryan castes):

But a Shudra, whether bought or unbought, [a Brahmana/Brahmin] may compel to do servile work; for he [the Shudra] was created by the Self-existent to be the slave [*dāsa*] of a Brahmana. A Shudra, though emancipated by his master, is not released from servitude; since that is innate in him, who can set him free from it? There are slaves of seven kinds, (viz.) he who is made a captive under a standard [= in war], he who serves for his daily food, he who is born in the house, he who is bought and he who is given, he who is inherited from ancestors, and he who is enslaved by way of punishment. A wife, a son, and a slave, these three are declared to have no property; the wealth which they earn is (acquired) for him to whom they belong.[33]

Traditional Hindu beliefs about caste can strengthen the hands of those wishing to justify slavery. Hindu societies exhibit two overlapping caste systems (*varna* and *jati*). The first specifies the four *varnas* described in the oldest surviving Hindu text, the *Rigveda*: Brahmin (priests), Kshatriya (warriors), Vaishya (farmers or merchants), and Shudra (laborers and artisans). The Candalas (untouchables, now referred to as Dalits) are a fifth group considered to be outside the *varnas* and of the lowest social position. The second system specifies thousands of smaller units, the *jatis*. Classifications in both systems are hereditary and rely heavily on occupational distinctions. The quotation from the *Manu-smrti* (above) might lead one to assume that every Shudra was a slave, but this was by no means the case. Yet being of low caste and being enslaved were strongly correlated: Shudras and individuals of certain low *jatis* were much more likely to be enslaved than individuals from high *varnas* and *jatis*.[34] This was true centuries ago, and it remains true even today.[35]

The doctrines of reincarnation and *karma*, central to both Hinduism and Buddhism, are also relevant to the justification of slavery. According to the *Brihadaranyaka Upanishad* (composed c. ninth–sixth century BC), "When a person dies, it is only the physical body that dies; that person lives on in a nonphysical body, which carries the impressions of his past

---

[33] *The Laws of Manu: Translated with Extracts from Seven Commentaries*, trans. G. Buhler (Oxford: Clarendon Press, 1886), VIII.413–417, 326–327.

[34] Dharma Kumar, "Colonialism, bondage, and caste in British India," in Martin A. Klein (ed.), *Breaking the Chains: Slavery, Bondage, and Emancipation in Modern Africa and Asia* (Madison, WI: The University of Wisconsin Press, 1993), 112–130, cf. 113–115; Hillary P. Rodrigues, *Introducing Hinduism*, 2nd ed. (New York: Routledge, 2017), 75–81.

[35] Kevin Bales, *Disposable People: New Slavery in the Global Economy*, rev. ed. (Berkeley: University of California Press, 2004), 202.

life. It is these impressions that determine his next life."[36] While those who attain Self-realization are freed from the cycle of birth and rebirth, all others are reincarnated, in a better or worse state depending on their actions in previous lives. This in turn implies that one's state of life in the present is due to one's earlier actions, as a contemporary scholar of Hinduism explains:

[T]he inexplicable causes for the present circumstances of one's life are also attributed to *karma*. If one is beautiful or intelligent, born into a wealthy home, or gifted with talents, these are regarded as the fruits produced from previously sown karmic seeds. Similarly, *karma* is also regarded as responsible for misfortune.[37]

Some scholars explicitly assert that the doctrine of *karma* was used to justify "one's birth in a *Jati* or *varna* and for the privileges and disabilities attached to it."[38] But if that is so, and given that being born into a despised *jati* greatly increased the chance that one would be enslaved, then it would not be surprising if the doctrine of *karma* has sometimes been used to justify enslavement as well. We have not found explicit examples of this for Hinduism, but have found examples in Buddhist sources. In an early Buddhist text (c. 300 BC–400 AD), the Buddha tells a story in which *karma* is invoked to explain the suffering of a slave:

In the sorrow which the slave Bijaka now suffers he receives the fruit of sins which he formerly committed. That sin is melting away since he is devoted to moral virtue, but let him not enter into Kassapa's devious paths.[39]

And in the nineteenth century, a didactic Cambodian Buddhist poem asserts that wealthy slaveholders possess slaves as a result of their good deeds in former lives:

> The wealth you have is commensurate
> to your generosity in previous lives;
> now having taken birth in this life,

[36] *Brihadaranyaka* IV.9, translation from *The Upanishads*, 2nd ed., trans. Eknath Easwaran (Nilgiri Press, 2007).

[37] Rodrigues, *Introducing Hinduism*, 63–65.

[38] Surabhi Sheth, "Equality and inequality in the Hindu Scriptures," in R. Siriwardena (ed.), *Equality and the Religious Traditions of Asia* (New York: St. Martin's Press, 1987), 21–50, 44.

[39] *The Jataka, Or: Stories of the Buddha's Former Births*, vol. 6, trans. E. B. Cowell and W. H. D. Rouse (Cambridge: Cambridge University Press, 1907), 119 (Jataka 544). The ascetic Kassapa denied *karma*, implying that Bijaka's good deeds would bring him no respite in a future life. On *karma* as justification for slavery, see Chanana, *Slavery in Ancient India*, 61–62, and 10.

your wealth is determined by past cause.
If you have a high position,
possessing wealth and slaves,
keep your thoughts aimed at what is upright
and in future lives, you will obtain them again.[40]

This assertion implies that the law of *karma* (conceived as a principle of cosmic *justice*) endorses the fact that those in a high position have slaves. Sadly, the use of *karma* to justify slavery is no mere relic of the past, as the testimony of a Thai teenager enslaved in commercial sexual exploitation in the 1990s illustrates: "When I met Siri, she had just crossed the invisible line between resistance and submission. Though only fifteen she was reconciled to life as a prostitute. She explained it was her fate, her karma, and each day she prayed to Buddha for acceptance."[41]

2.3 JUDAISM AND THE JUSTIFICATION OF SLAVERY

From the time of the Bronze Age (3300–1200 BC) most, if not all, Mediterranean cultures had settled into an acceptance of slavery as a natural and reasonable institution – especially when slaves could be and were acquired through conflict. Conquest meant enslavement for those conquered. This was codified, as in the Code of Hammurabi, and rarely if ever questioned. The ancient Jews, like their neighbors, accepted slavery, and the Torah explicitly permitted it. As noted above, Lev 25:44–46 allowed Jews to purchase non-Jewish slaves and hold them in perpetual slavery:

[Y]ou may buy male and female slaves from among the nations that are round about you. You may also buy from among the strangers who sojourn with you and their families that are with you, who have been born in your land; and they may be your property. You may bequeath them to your sons after you, to inherit as a possession for ever.

The statement that slaves may be handed on to heirs "for ever" suggests that the offspring of non-Jewish slaves were typically designated as slaves from birth. Whether or not the text literally implies that those born to

---

[40] Anne Ruth Hansen, *How to Behave: Buddhism and Modernity in Colonial Cambodia, 1860–1930* (Honolulu: University of Hawai'i Press, 2011), 53. See also 68–69: "In regard to slavery, efforts by French colonials and modern-minded Siamese reformists to abolish slavery challenged implicit Buddhistic assumptions on which society rested, including the idea that social life was structured by a *kammic* ordering of people based on their moral histories in the cosmos."

[41] Bales, *Disposable People*, 63.

non-Jewish slave parents inherit their parents' slave status, this was the traditional understanding in Jewish law. Besides purchase and birth to slave parents, the Torah also authorized the acquisition of slaves via warfare against distant cities:

When you draw near to a city to fight against it, offer terms of peace to it. And if its answer to you is peace and it opens to you, then all the people who are found in it shall do forced labor for you and shall serve you. But if it makes no peace with you, but makes war against you, then you shall besiege it; and when the Lord your God gives it into your hand you shall put all the males to the sword, but the women and the little ones, the cattle, and everything else in the city, all its spoil, you shall take as booty for yourselves. (Deut 20:10–14)

In a subsequent text (Deut 21:10–14), the instruction is given that female war captives taken as wives (or concubines – the language is ambiguous) cannot subsequently be sold; they must either be kept or freed.

Given the presence of these texts in the Hebrew Bible, it is not surprising that in antiquity and in the medieval period the vast majority of Jewish sources discussing slavery assume rather than argue for its permissibility. Still, some justifications for slavery can be found in the history of Jewish thought. One example is provided by the philosopher and scriptural interpreter Philo of Alexandria (fl. early first century AD), who advanced the theory that in some cases slavery was a benefit to the slave:

[T]he law-book of the Jews ... tells of two brothers [Jacob and Esau], one wise and temperate, the other incontinent, how the father of them both [Isaac] prayed in pity for him who had not attained to virtue that he should be his brother's slave. He held that slavery, which men think the worst of evils, was the best possible boon to the fool, because the loss of independence would prevent him from transgressing without fear of punishment, and his character would be improved under the control of the authority set above him.[42]

Philo's position is not that slavery is a positive good in general, since he recognizes that persons of the highest virtue (who are thus not natural slaves) can "through adverse blows of fortune" lose "the freedom to which they were born."[43] But he does assert that slavery is a good in some cases – those in which the character of the enslaved would render their freedom a mere means to bad choices.

---

[42] Philo, "Every good man is free," 57, in Peter Garnsey, *Ideas of Slavery from Aristotle to Augustine* (Cambridge: Cambridge University Press, 1996), 164–165.

[43] Philo, "Every good man is free," 17–19, in Garnsey, *Ideas of Slavery from Aristotle to Augustine*, 158.

In the modern era, Jewish thinkers could be found on either side of the abolitionist question. Rabbi Morris J. Raphall (1798–1868), of New York, offered a weak justification of slavery on the eve of the Civil War. While declaring himself no friend of slavery, Raphall gives an Argument from Divine Permission for the conclusion that "slaveholding is no sin."[44] His argument leans heavily on the claim that the Ten Commandments prescribe the coveting of the slave of one's neighbor – which Raphall interprets as a divine permission to hold slaves as property – and on the observation that Abraham, Isaac, Jacob, and Job were slaveholders.

In yet more recent times, as moral censure of slavery became nearly universal, believing Jews increasingly faced the question of how divine revelation could include permission of the evil of slavery. One approach was to argue that the slavery of the ancient Israelites was comparatively mild, and even a benefit for non-Israelite slaves, given the likely alternatives. Thus Rabbi Ben Zion Meir Hai Uziel (1880–1953), the first Sephardic Chief Rabbi of the State of Israel, contended that the acquisition of Canaanite slaves:

was not permitted other than regarding those who were already sold to their brothers under the same conditions. And even so, it was not permitted to exploit their bodies. Rather, even if one should damage a major human limb, this slave goes free, even for a tooth or an eye … From here you see that the acquisition of a Canaanite slave that the Torah permits is for the good of the slave himself, to save him from his Canaanite brothers so that he should not be enslaved cruelly and physically exploited to the point of death.[45]

Rabbi Joseph H. Hertz (1872–1946), Chief Rabbi of the British Empire from 1913 to 1946, takes a similar approach, arguing that the "system of slavery which is tolerated in the Torah was fundamentally different from the cruel systems of the ancient world."[46] Rabbi Naftali Zevi Yehudah Berlin (1816–1893) gives a version of the Spiritual Blessing Argument, seeing the enslavement of ancient Canaanites by Israelites as a pathway for idolaters to share, to a limited extent, in Israel's covenantal relationship with God.[47]

---

44 Morris J. Raphall, *The Bible View of Slavery: A Discourse* (New York: Rudd & Carleton, 1861), text available at: www.jewish-history.com/civilwar/raphall.html.

45 R. Ben-Zion Meir Hai Uziel, *Mikhmannei Uziel* (Tel Aviv, 1939), 263, quoted in Gamliel Shmalo, "Orthodox approaches to Biblical slavery," *The Torah U-Madda Journal* 16 (2012–2013), 1–20, 6.

46 From his commentary on Lev 25:46, quoted in Shmalo, "Orthodox approaches to Biblical slavery," 7.

47 See Shmalo, "Orthodox approaches to Biblical slavery," 8–11.

2.4 CHRISTIANITY AND THE JUSTIFICATION OF SLAVERY

2.4.1 Early Christianity

Early Christians included both slaves and slaveholders, and the early Church did not demand that Christian slaveholders free their slaves. This is not to say that the teachings of Jesus cannot be applied to the morality of slaveholding – Christian abolitionists would eventually argue that the Golden Rule (Matt 7:12) and the commandment to love one's neighbor as oneself imply that slaveholders should free their slaves. Yet the texts of the New Testament assert neither "masters, free your slaves," nor "slaves, flee your masters," but something closer to "everyone, become slaves to one another, voluntarily, out of love."[48] Thus Jesus, speaking about the dynamics of power, says:

You know that those who are supposed to rule over the Gentiles lord it over them, and their great men exercise authority over them. But it shall not be so among you; but whoever would be great among you must be your servant, and whoever would be first among you must be slave of all. For the Son of man also came not to be served but to serve, and to give his life as a ransom for many.

(Mark 10:42–45)

Paul writes of himself in a similar fashion, "For though I am free from all men, I have made myself a slave to all, that I might win the more" (1 Cor 9:19). And in another text he makes this attitude normative for all believers: "For you were called to freedom, brethren, only do not use your freedom as an opportunity for the flesh, but through love be servants [δουλεύετε] of one another" (Gal 5:13).

The verb here translated as "be servants" is derived from the word for slave (δοῦλος), and the final clause could just as correctly be translated "through love be slaves to one another." Paul even explicitly commands masters to serve their slaves, in an easily overlooked text that immediately follows Paul's directives to slaves:

Slaves, be obedient to those who are your earthly masters, with fear and trembling, in singleness of heart, as to Christ; not in the way of eye-service, as men-pleasers, but as slaves of Christ, doing the will of God from the heart, rendering service with a good will as to the Lord and not to men, knowing that whatever good any one does, he will receive the same again from the Lord, whether he is a slave or free. Masters, *do the same to them*, and forebear threatening, knowing

---

[48] On this topic, see Jennifer Glancy, *Slavery as Moral Problem: In the Early Church and Today* (Minneapolis: Fortress Press, 2011), 23–27.

that he who is both their Master and yours is in heaven, and that there is no partiality with him. (Eph 6:5–9, italics added)[49]

With the imperative "do the same to them [slaves]," Paul commands Christian slaveholders to "render service" to their slaves with a good will as though they were serving the Lord. Paul's injunctions to masters appear to amount to this: don't relate to your slaves as slaves, but instead act as servants to them.[50]

Still, early Christians had ample grounds to assume that their Church accepted slaveholding as morally permissible. Paul commanded slaves to obey their masters. The Church did not require of Christian slaveholders that they free their slaves. Early Christians did not condemn slavery as an institution (with the notable exception of Gregory of Nyssa). And when the question of a religious case for slave flight or revolt was broached, the Church's reaction was negative. According to a decree of the Council of Gangra in Asia Minor (340 AD):

If anyone, on the pretext of religion, teaches another man's slave to despise his master, and to withdraw from his service, and not to serve his master with good will and all respect, let him be anathema.[51]

While this was the work of a local rather than an ecumenical Church council, the theologian Gratian (fl. at Bologna in the twelfth century AD) later included the decree in his influential work of canon law known as the *Decretum*, which makes it likely both that it was considered important before Gratian's time and that it was influential long after.

2.4.2 Augustine

After the New Testament authors, Augustine may well be the single most influential Christian theologian in history. His views on slavery present a

---

[49] Scholars debate whether Paul was the author of several letters which traditionally have been ascribed to him, including Ephesians, Colossians, 1 Timothy, and Titus, all of which include instructions relating to slaves and masters. For the purposes of our argument, it is not crucial to take a position on the authenticity of these letters, since even if they were not in fact written by Paul, they were nonetheless written by one or more members of the early Christian community whose writings were subsequently influential within Christianity, and therefore express early, authoritative Christian views on slavery.

[50] For this interpretation of Paul, see Andrew Wilson, "The best argument for a trajectory hermeneutic – and where it goes wrong," *Think*, March 6, 2013: thinktheology.co.uk/blog/article/the_best_argument_for_a_trajectory_hermeneutic_and_where_it_goes_wrong.

[51] Canon 3. *C. J. C. Decreti Gratiani*, II, C.XVIII, Q. IV, c. 37, quoted in John Francis Maxwell, *Slavery and the Catholic Church: The History of Catholic Teaching Concerning the Moral Legitimacy of the Institution of Slavery* (Chicester and London: Barry Rose Publishers, 1975), 30.

puzzle. On the one hand, he clearly held that slaveholding is morally permissible. He considers a master's ownership of slaves as no less legitimate than a person's ownership of other types of property – both are legitimated by human law made by the appropriate political authority.[52] On the other hand he called for masters to recognize their slaves as brothers, to love them as the masters love themselves, and even to "serve those whom they seem to command" with "mercy in providing for others," out of a sense of "dutiful concern for others" rather than a lust to dominate.[53] It might be thought that a master who viewed his slave as a brother and loved his slave as himself would conclude that he should free his slave. Yet that is not the conclusion that Augustine draws.

Pinpointing Augustine's position on the spectrum between strong and weak justification of slavery is not easy. He never goes so far as Joseph Wilson or those others who call slavery a blessing, nor even as far as Aristotle (384–322 BC) who considers the condition of enslavement to be natural and entirely fitting for some. Yet in an oft-quoted text, he asserts that enslavement is a just punishment for sin – either the slave's personal sin or original sin:

[T]he condition of slavery is justly imposed on the sinner. . . . The prime cause of slavery, then, is sin, so that man was put under man in a state of bondage; and this can be only by a judgment of God, in whom there is no unrighteousness, and who knows how to assign divers punishments according to the deserts of the sinners.[54]

This text has been interpreted by some scholars to mean that, according to Augustine, every enslaved person deserves enslavement due to his or her sins.[55] Yet an overlooked passage elsewhere in Augustine's work challenges this interpretation:

[52] See *In Johannis Evangelium tractatus* 6.25. While Augustine did object to and work against the illegal enslavement of free persons, he accepted the legal slavery of his time. On the former point, see Gervase Corcoran, *Saint Augustine on Slavery* (Rome: Institutum Patristicum Augustinianum, 1985), 24–25.

[53] Sermon 58.2.2 (PL 38, 393); *Sermon on the Mount* 1.19.59; *City of God*, 19.14. The quoted phrases are from Augustine, *The City of God against the Pagans*, vol. 6, trans. William Chase Greene (Cambridge, MA: Harvard University Press, 1960), 185–187.

[54] *City of God*, 19.15.

[55] As in Ilaria L. E. Ramelli, *Social Justice and the Legitimacy of Slavery: The Role of Philosophical Asceticism from Ancient Judaism to Late Antiquity* (Oxford: Oxford University Press, 2016), 154 and 156, and Kellerman, *All Oppression Shall Cease*, 18.

Either iniquity or adversity made man a slave to man: iniquity, as it was said, *Cursed is Canaan; he shall be slave to his brothers*; or adversity, as happened to Joseph himself, in that he was sold by his brothers to become the slave of a foreigner.[56]

What is more, Augustine counts some slaves among the righteous.[57] So Augustine says in the *City of God* that man does not fall under the dominion of man except by a judgment of God – which suggests that the condition of being enslaved is in every case a punishment for the guilt of the slave – yet in other works he contrasts those slaves who become slaves because of their sin with those slaves who become slaves because of an adverse course of events, and he says that some slaves are righteous – which suggests that the condition of being enslaved is in some cases the result of the sins of others rather than the sins of the slave. Toward harmonizing these disparate statements, note that Augustine says that sin is the "prime" or "first" (*prima*) cause of slavery, but does not say that sin is the *only* cause of slavery, which is consistent with Augustine's holding that not every case of slavery is due to the sin of the enslaved. One who says that smoking causes lung cancer is not thereby committed to holding that every case of lung cancer was caused by smoking. Similarly, Augustine may have held that slavery first entered the world because of the sin of the enslaved, and that for the most part slavery is a punishment for sin, but not that all slaves are justly enslaved because of their sin.

It has been asserted that Augustine "was convinced that slavery is decreed by God, and therefore good ..."[58] But from the mere fact that Augustine thought God permitted or commanded slavery as punishment for sin it does not thereby follow that Augustine thought slavery was good. For in his worldview, death is a divinely instituted punishment for sin (original sin),[59] but he does not take that to imply that death is good. Again, Augustine asserts in *City of God* 19.15 that when the just side loses in a war, and the (relatively) just are enslaved for the sake of correcting their sins, this is according to a just judgment of God, but he would not have taken that to imply that the waging of that war by the unjust against the just was itself a good thing.

---

[56] Questions on the Heptateuch (*Questiones in Heptateuchum*), 1.153, in Augustine, *The Works of Saint Augustine: Volume 14: Writings on the Old Testament*, trans. Joseph T. Lienhard and Sean Doyle (New York: New City Press, 2016), 75–76.

[57] *Expositions on the Psalms* 124:7–8, in P. Schaff (ed.), *A Select Library of the Nicene and Post-Nicene Fathers of the Christian Church, Volume 8, Saint Augustin: Expositions on the Book of Psalms* (Buffalo, NY: Christian Literature Publishing Co., 1888).

[58] Ramelli, *Social Justice and the Legitimacy of Slavery*, 156.

[59] See the *Unfinished Commentary on the Epistle to the Romans*, 10, in *Augustine on Romans*, trans. Paula Fredriksen Landes (Chico, CA: Scholars Press, 1982), 65.

In the final analysis, Augustine represents an intermediate case between those who justify slavery in the strong sense and those who justify it only in the weak sense, holding that slavery was good in some respects while bad in others. In his view, slavery is contrary to God's original intention, a moral hazard for masters, and a dangerous opportunity for the unrighteous to dominate others. But he accepted from Cicero that slavery was "useful for some"[60] and justified slavery by asserting that it was a just punishment for sin.

2.4.3 Aquinas

Thomas Aquinas (c. 1225–1274) has on occasion been presented as an antislavery figure. In a treatment of the role of Christianity in the abolition of slavery, sociologist Rodney Stark asserts, "in the thirteenth century, Saint Thomas Aquinas deduced that slavery was a sin ... Based on the immense authority vested in Aquinas by the Church, the official view came to be that slavery is sinful."[61] This is incorrect. While Aquinas did enunciate principles which could have led to the conclusion that enslaving another is wrong,[62] he himself did not draw such a conclusion. On the contrary, Aquinas explicitly asserts that slaveholding is compatible with justice. In his commentary on Titus 2:9 ("Bid slaves to be submissive to their masters ..."), he notes that the same exhortation is found in 1 Pet 2:18, Col 3:22, and Eph 6:5. Why, he asks,

does the Apostle exhort this so frequently? I respond that not without cause. For heresies began among the Jews that the servants of God ought not obey men, and from this it was derived among the Christian people that, having been made sons of God through Christ, they should not be the slaves of men. But Christ through faith did not come to take away the order of justice; rather, through faith in Christ justice is kept. Now, *justice makes some men subject to others*, but such service regards the body. For now through Christ we are freed from slavery regarding the soul but from neither slavery nor corruption of the body. However, in the future, we shall also be freed from both bodily slavery and bodily corruption.[63]

Aquinas follows Augustine in conceiving of slavery as something outside of God's original intention for human beings, and looks forward to a

---

[60] *City of God*, 19.21.　　[61] Stark, *For the Glory of God*, 329–330.

[62] See, for example, Aquinas' commentary on the *Sentences* of Peter Lombard (*Super Sent.*) II.44.1.3, in which Aquinas observes that one human being is not subordinated to another as a mere means to the other's good.

[63] *Commentary on the Epistle to Titus*, ch. 2, l. 2, n.64, in Thomas Aquinas, *Commentaries on St. Paul's Epistles to Timothy, Titus, and Philemon*, trans. Chrysostom Baer (South Bend, IN: St. Augustine's Press, 2007), 178. Italics added.

future state in which slavery will be no more. He recognizes that the state of being enslaved is bound to involve suffering, and that freedom is "an inestimable good."[64] And on occasion he underlines the elements of the Judaeo–Christian tradition which tend toward the amelioration of slavery. He prefaces his commentary on Philemon, for example, with a quotation from the deuterocanonical Book of Sirach: "If thou have a faithful servant, let him be to thee as thy own soul: treat him as a brother," and goes on to comment: "The use of a slave is that he may be treated as a brother, for he is a brother, both as regards the generation of nature ... and as regards the generation of grace ..."[65] Aquinas also argues on philosophical grounds for certain limitations on a master's power over his or her slaves:

[T]he positive law arises out of the natural law, and consequently slavery, which is of positive law, cannot be prejudicious to those things that are of natural law. Now just as nature seeks the preservation of the individual, so does it seek the preservation of the species by means of procreation; wherefore even as a slave is not so subject to his master as not to be at liberty to eat, sleep, and do such things as pertain to the needs of his body, and without which nature cannot be preserved, so he is not subject to him to the extent of being unable to marry freely, even without his master's knowledge or consent.[66]

Nevertheless, Aquinas adopts the common view of his time that some slavery is morally permissible. While kidnapping (the stealing of a human being) deserves the death penalty,[67] a person born to a slave mother is a legitimate slave.[68] In the course of arguing for the conclusion that a

---

[64] *Summa theologiae* (ST) I.96.4 and *Super Sent.* IV.36.1.3 ad 1. At ST I.96.4, Aquinas notes: "someone has dominion over another as a slave [*servus*] when the one who has dominion looks to the one over whom he has dominion for his usefulness to himself, i.e., to the one who has dominion. And since everyone desires his own good and consequently finds it deplorable to have to give exclusively to someone else a good that ought to have been his own, it follows that this sort of dominion cannot exist without suffering ..." Translation is slightly adapted from that of Alfred Freddoso: www3.nd.edu/~afreddos/ summa-translation/TOC.htm. See also *De perfectione* 14, where Aquinas calls slavery "civil death."

[65] Translation from Aquinas, *Commentaries on St. Paul's Epistles to Timothy, Titus, and Philemon*, trans. Chrysostom Baer, 197.

[66] ST *Tertia pars supplementum* 52.2. Translation from Thomas Aquinas, *Summa Theologica*, vol. 5, trans. Fathers of the English Dominican Province (Westminster, MD: Christian Classics, 1981).

[67] ST II-II.66.6 ad 2.

[68] ST *Tertia pars supplementum* 52.4. Aquinas most likely accepted other traditional forms of "just title" to a slave, such as capture in a just war, voluntary self-sale, and purchase of a slave already held with just title.

master can beat his slave, Aquinas accepts as a premise the claim that the authority of master over slave is a *legitimate* authority:

Beating someone is not lawful except for the person who has some authority over the one who is beaten. And since the son is subject to the authority of the father, and the slave [is subject to] the authority of the master, the father is lawfully able to beat his son, and the master [is lawfully able to beat] his slave, for the sake of correction and discipline.[69]

Aquinas' commentaries on certain passages of Aristotle and Paul which treat of slavery also indicate that he accepted the institution.[70] We can thus classify Aquinas as a justifier of slavery in the weak sense.

2.4.4 Later Thinkers

The position that chattel slavery was morally acceptable in many common circumstances continued to be a mainstream view among Christian and Jewish theologians until the nineteenth century. Here are a few examples of different types of justifying arguments.

A version of the Spiritual Blessing Argument can be found in the writings of the fifteenth-century Italian Giovanni Pontano (1426–1503), who contended that the purchase of Christian slaves living in lands overrun by non-Christians was a virtuous act, since it removed them (the Christian slaves) from the danger of lapsing into unbelief. Pontano applied the same reasoning to argue that it was virtuous to buy non-Christian slaves, so as to bring them to Christianity.[71]

An appeal to Divine Sanction is found in the work of Juan Ginés de Sepúlveda (1490–1573), a Spanish humanist and theologian best known for his defense of the legitimacy of Spanish military conquest in the Americas:

[D]ivine and natural decree and law ... commands that the most perfect and powerful should rule over the imperfect and unequal ... By this law, wild beasts are tamed and subjected to man's domination. By this law, the man rules over the woman, the adult over the child, the father over his children, that is to say, the most powerful and most perfect over the weakest and most imperfect. The same thing is seen among men, with some being masters by nature, and other being slaves. Those who exceed others in prudence and intelligence, if not in physical

---

[69] Aquinas, ST II-II.65.2c, Latin text from: corpusthomisticum.org. Translation is Rota's.

[70] See Aquinas' commentaries on Aristotle's *Politics* I, and on Eph 6:5, Titus 2:9, 1 Tim 6:1–2, and Philemon.

[71] Giovanni Pontano, *De obedientia*, cited in Iris Origo, "The domestic enemy: the Eastern slaves in Tuscany in the fourteenth and fifteenth Centuries," *Speculum*, 30 (July 1955), 321–366, 335.

strength, are by nature masters; those, on the other hand, who are mentally slow and lazy, though they may have the physical strength to fulfill all their necessary obligations, are by nature slaves, and it is just and useful that they be, and we even see this sanctioned by divine law itself. For it is written in the Book of Proverbs: "He who is foolish shall serve the wise man" [Prov 11:29]. Such are the uncivilized and barbaric peoples, strangers to civil life and peaceful customs. And it will always be just and in accordance with natural law that such peoples be subjected to the rule of more cultured and civilized princes and nations …"[72]

Sepúlveda's views on the enslavement of Native Americans were hotly contested in his time (indeed, the book in which the above quotation appears was banned).[73] In Chapter 4 we consider the thought of his principal opponent, and the founder of what may be described as the first antislavery campaign, the Dominican Friar Bartolemé de Las Casas.

Whereas Sepúlveda tends toward a strong justification of slavery, other thinkers used an Argument from Divine Sanction as a weak justification of slavery. Thus British proslavery advocate James Griffith, writing in 1823:

If once it can be shewn that the Almighty ever did sanction the possession of bond servants or Slaves, the following unanswerable syllogism must be deduced … God never can or could sanction anything [in] itself unjust or wicked; But God did sanction the possession of slaves, with Abraham and among the Jews … Therefore, it must necessarily follow, that, the Possession of Slaves cannot, in itself, be either unjust or wicked.[74]

The same logic can be found more succinctly in Richard Watson (1737–1816), Bishop of Llandaff: "God cannot authorise injustice; but he did authorise slavery amongst the Jews; therefore slavery is not opposite to justice."[75]

---

[72] Juan Ginés de Sepúlveda, *Democrates secundus* (1547), section translated in Jon Cowans, *Early Modern Spain: A Documentary History* (Philadelphia: University of Pennsylvania Press, 2003), 58–59.

[73] Derek Hughes (ed.), *Versions of Blackness: Key Texts on Slavery from the Seventeenth Century* (Cambridge: Cambridge University Pres, 2007), 285. For the ban on Sepúlveda's *Democrates secundus*, see Eduardo Andujar, "Bartolome de Las Casas and Juan Gines de Sepulveda: moral theology versus political philosophy," in Kevin White (ed.), *Hispanic Philosophy in the Age of Discovery*, Studies in Philosophy and the History of Philosophy, vol. 29 (Washington, DC: The Catholic University of America Press, 1997), 70.

[74] "'Philalethes' [James Griffith] to the editor of the Bath and Cheltenham Gazette, July 4, 1823," National Library of Jamaica, Kingston, MS 723a, f. 3, quoted in Michael Taylor, "British proslavery arguments and the Bible, 1823–1833," *Slavery & Abolition*, 37:1 (2016), 139–158, 145.

[75] Richard Watson, *Anecdotes of the Life of Richard Watson, Bishop of Llandaff; Written by Himself at Different Intervals and Revised in 1814* (London, 1817), 454, quoted in Taylor, "British proslavery arguments and the Bible," 145.

This chapter opened with a discussion of proslavery arguments in North America. Proslavery thinkers in Britain and the British West Indies employed the same sorts of arguments (economic, political, and racial, as well as religious) as did their counterparts in the United States.[76] A particularly interesting piece of religious proslavery reasoning appears in a much-debated pamphlet published in 1788 and written by one "Raymund Harris," who gave an extended argument that the slave trade was compatible with the principles of justice revealed in Scripture, and that it had "the positive sanction of God in its support."[77] Though based in Liverpool, a center of the British slave trade, Harris was in fact Don Raymondo Hormaza (c.1750–c. 1789), a Spanish ex-Jesuit.[78] In his pamphlet, he gives particularly clear formulations of most of the scriptural arguments mentioned above and several more besides, and then closes with a consideration of an objection to his position based on the Golden Rule:

All things whatsoever, says our Blessed Saviour, ye would that men should do to you, do ye even so to them; for this is the Law and the Prophets [Matt 7:12]: whatsoever things therefore we would not, that men should do to us, we are not even so to do to them; but no person whatever would certainly wish, that a fellow-creature should reduce him to the condition of a Slave; therefore no person whatever is to reduce a fellow-creature to that condition.[79]

Harris' reply to this was that parallel reasoning would lead to an absurd conclusion:

It is an Axiom in Logic, that An argument that proves too much, proves nothing: the above is just such a one: for, by the same manner of reasoning, one might equally conclude ... that not only Slavery, but every other kind of subordination of one man to another, ought not to be suffered to continue in the world. – The argument, if conclusive in the former case, must be equally so in the latter ... : whatsoever things therefore we would not that men should do to us, we are not even so to do to them; but every person would naturally wish not to be controlled by a fellow-creature, not to be under any subjection to him, but to be absolute

---

[76] See Tise, *Proslavery*, 75–96.

[77] R. Harris, *Scriptural researches on the licitness of the slave-trade, shewing its conformity with the principles of natural and revealed religion, delineated in the sacred writings of the word of God* (London: John Stockdale, 1788), 20. The text is available online through the University of Michigan Digital Library: name.umdl.umich.edu/N17436 .0001.001.

[78] See David Brion Davis, *The Problem of Slavery in the Age of Revolution, 1770–1823* (Ithaca: Cornell University Press, 1975), 542–550.

[79] Harris, *Scriptural researches...*, 72.

master of his own actions; no person therefore ought to keep a fellow-creature under any control or subjection whatever.[80]

2.5 ISLAM AND THE JUSTIFICATION OF SLAVERY

Slavery was a prominent feature in most Islamic societies until the late nineteenth or early twentieth century. In contrast to the plantation slavery of the New World, the use of slavery for intensive commodity production was the exception rather than the rule in Islamic contexts, where slaves tended to be domestic workers, concubines, soldiers, and eunuchs, as well as producers of commodities in certain times and places. The emphasis on domestic services and concubinage rather than plantation labor explains the fact that for every three slaves taken West from Africa across the Atlantic to the New World, roughly two were male, while for every three slaves taken North or East out of sub-Saharan Africa via the slave trade to the Islamic world, roughly two were female.[81] As will be detailed in the chapters to follow, the responses of Muslims to slavery have been various; here we consider Muslim justifications of slavery.

In Islamic sources predating the modern era, the moral permissibility of enslavement and slaveholding tends to be assumed rather than argued for. The Qur'an, for example, explicitly permits Muslim men to have sexual relations with their female slaves (23:6, 4:3, 4:24, and cf. 66:1). But this particular permission assumes a more general permission to own slaves in the first place. If it were impermissible to hold slaves at all, then only by a

[80] Harris, *Scriptural researches…*, 72–73. In reply to Harris, it should be noted that some subordination (e.g. young child to parent) is such that the superordinated person who switched positions with the subordinated person (but somehow retained full information) would not reasonably want the subordination removed. So the Golden Rule doesn't imply that all sorts of subordination should be opposed. Other types of subordination (e.g. of a subject to tyrant) are such that if the powerful person switched positions with the subordinated (and retained full information), he or she would want the subordination removed – these are the cases the Golden Rule opposes. Harris' critique of an antislavery argument based on the Golden Rule can thus be parried by replacing the following argument for the version Harris criticizes: (i) What we would reasonably wish others to not do to us if our positions were reversed (while we retained full information), we should not do to them. (ii) We would reasonably wish (enslavable) others not to enslave us if our positions were reversed (but we retained full information). Thus (iii), we should not enslave others.

[81] Ronald Segal, *Islam's Black Slaves: The Other Black Diaspora* (New York: Farrar, Straus and Giroux, 2001), 4.

very tortured logic could it somehow be permissible to have sexual relationships with them.

Early Muslims also regularly enslaved non-Muslims captured in war. Qur'an 8:41 regulates the distribution of "the spoils of war," which at the time was understood to include war captives (see also 8:67 and 33:50). Indeed, Muhammad himself obtained via this route three Jewish women, Juwayriya, Saffiyah, and Rayhana. According to a well-attested Hadith,

the Prophet – may God bless him and grant him peace – raided the Banu al-Mustaliq [a Jewish tribe] at a time when they were off guard and their herds were being watered. He slaughtered their warriors and captured their offspring. That day he obtained Juwayriya.[82]

Other ancient texts supply the additional details that after the battle (in which her husband was killed), Juwayriya had been received as war booty by a Muslim soldier who then sold her to Muhammad after she accepted Muhammad's proposal of marriage.[83] Similarly, Safiyyah was captured after the Battle of Khaybar (her father was executed at Muhammad's direction).[84] While Juwayriya and Safiyyah were freed and married by Muhammad, Rayhana may have remained a slave-concubine.[85] The eminent twelfth-century Andalusian philosopher and jurist Ibn Rushd (Averroes, 1126–1189), in agreement with earlier sources, tells us that "The Prophet himself would in some cases slay captives outside the field of battle, while he would pardon them in others. Women he used to enslave."[86] Muhammad was not the only Muslim to take slaves from among the female prisoners of war, as is evidenced by the fact that

[82] John Hunwick and Eve Troutt Powell (eds.), *The African Diaspora in the Mediterranean Lands of Islam* (Princeton: Markus Wiener Publishers, 2002), 6–7. Translation is by John Hunwick, from the Arabic text of *al-Jami al-sahih* of al-Bukhari.

[83] Muhammad Ibn Ishaq, *The Life of Muhammad: A Translation of Ibn Ishaq's Sirat Rasul Allah*, trans. A. Guillaume (Oxford: Oxford University Press, 1967), 490–493; Freamon, *Possessed by the Right Hand*, 142 and the commentary on 33:50 in Seyyed Hossein Nasr (ed.), *The Study Quran: A New Translation and Commentary* (New York: HarperOne, 2015).

[84] See Ma'mar ibn Rashid, *The Expeditions: An Early Biography of Muhammad*, trans. Sean W. Anthony (New York: NYU Press, 2015), 56 and *The Study Quran*, commentary on 33:50.

[85] *The Study Quran*, commentary on 33:50; *Sahih al-Bukhari* 7.62.98, available at: www .sahih-bukhari.com/Pages/Bukhari_7_62.php. On Rayhana, see Ibn Ishaq, *The Life of Muhammad*, 466, and Jonathan A. C. Brown, *Slavery & Islam* (London: Oneworld Academic, 2019), 163.

[86] Averroes, *Bidayat al-mudjtahid*, translated in Rudolph Peters, *Jihad in Mediaeval and Modern Islam: The Chapter on Jihad from Averroes' Legal Handbook "Bidayat al-mudjtahid"* (Leiden: Brill, 1977), as excerpted in Andrew G. Bostom (ed.), *The Legacy*

Juwayriya was first the property of a Muslim soldier before being bought by Muhammad. What Ibn Rushd almost certainly means in saying "Women he used to enslave" is not merely that Muhammad himself took some women as slaves, but that he authorized the general policy by which formerly free female captives could be enslaved and distributed as war booty. Ibn Rushd also tells us that the Companions of the Prophet, after his death, "reached unanimity about the rule that the People of the Book [=Jews and Christians, primarily] both male and female, might be enslaved."[87] The enslavement of war captives provides a second indication that slavery was assumed to be permissible by early Muslims.

For devout Muslims, Muhammad's own words and behavior are normative in a strong sense. As Jonathan Brown explains, "According to the consensus of Muslim scholars across fourteen centuries ... stating that the Prophet committed a grave sin (*kabira*) or unambiguously belittling his moral judgment would be unbelief (*kufr*) that removed someone from Islam."[88] For this reason additional aspects of Muhammad's behavior and moral judgments regarding slaves are relevant to Islamic justifications of slavery. Besides taking the war captive Rayhana as a slave-concubine, the founder of Islam also received a second slave-concubine, Mariya, who was a gift from the Patriarch of Alexandria. Strong evidence indicates that Mariya remained a slave-concubine until Muhammad's death.[89] Muhammad also owned fifteen male slaves, "all of whom he eventually freed."[90] Of his many statements on slavery in the Hadith (reports about Muhammad's words and actions, put down in writing in the first several centuries after his death), three are especially noteworthy regarding the justification of slavery.

The first contains both an exhortation to good treatment of slaves and the claim that God has in some way actively placed slaves under the control of the Muslim slaveholders to whom Muhammad was speaking:

Your slaves are your brothers, whom God has put under your control. Feed them from what you eat, clothe them from what you wear, and do not burden them with work that overwhelms them. If you give them more than they can do, then assist them.[91]

---

of *Jihad: Islamic Holy War and the Fate of Non-Muslims* (Amherst, NY: Prometheus Books, 2005), 149.

[87] Ibid.   [88] Brown, *Slavery & Islam*, 198.

[89] See Brown, *Slavery & Islam*, 163 and 294–298.   [90] Brown, *Slavery & Islam*, 163.

[91] This Hadith, or a variation, is found in the collections of Bukhari, Muslim, Abu Dawud, and Ibn Majah. Translation is from Brown, *Slavery & Islam*, 71.

The assertion that God has put slaves under the slaveholders' control naturally suggests an Argument from Divine Providence – that is, (i) God has put these slaves under your control, (ii) it is not wrong to cooperate with God's ordering of human affairs, thus (iii) it is not wrong to have these slaves under your control. And since the key premise is explicitly asserted by Muhammad, whose teachings are authoritative in Islam, it is a short step to generate from this Hadith an Argument from Divine Sanction offering at least a weak justification of slavery.

Second, Muhammad is reported to have taught that faithful slaves will receive an extra reward from God: "If a slave is faithful to his owner and worships his Lord truly, he will receive his reward [from God] twice over."[92] And a third Hadith has it that a runaway slave's prayers will not be accepted.[93] While these last two claims do not logically entail that holding slaves is justified, it is easy to see how they could provide support for the conclusion that Allah in some way sanctions slavery.

By medieval times, the consensus opinion among Islamic legal scholars was that in certain circumstances it was permissible to reduce formerly free people to slavery. On the enslavement of war captives, Ibn Rushd writes:

Damage inflicted upon the enemy may consist in damage to his property, injury to his person or violation of his personal liberty, i.e., that he is made a slave and is appropriated. This may be done, according to the *Consensus* (*idjmā*) to all polytheists: men, women, young and old, important and unimportant.[94]

Similarly, in his treatment of the laws of war the Hanbali jurist and theologian Ibn Qudama (1147–1223) explains:

The chief of state decides on the fate of the men who are taken as prisoners: he can have them put to death, reduce them to slavery, free them in return for a ransom or grant them their freedom as a gift. He must choose the solution most in keeping with the common good of the Muslims.[95]

Again, an authoritative fourteenth-century Egyptian legal text reads:

The imam [i.e. the Muslim ruler conducting the *jihād*] should look into the fate of adult male prisoners, and take whichever of the following options he considers

---

[92] Hunwick and Powell (eds.), *The African Diaspora in the Mediterranean Lands of Islam*, 7, translating from the Arabic text of *al-Jami al-sahih* of al-Bukhari.

[93] Brown, *Slavery & Islam*, 72.

[94] Averroes, *Bidayat al-Mudjtahid*, translated in Bostom (ed.), *The Legacy of Jihad*, 149. See also 163.

[95] Bostom (ed.), *The Legacy of Jihad*, 162.

most beneficial: to put them to death, to release them without penalty, to ask ransom for them, to demand capitation tax (*jizya*), or to enslave them.[96]

Besides the enslavement of war captives, the purchase of slaves from non-Muslim slavetraders was also widely considered permissible by Muslim jurists before the twentieth century.[97]

Those who benefit from slavery are most likely to undertake explicit efforts to legitimize it when they feel the presence of a strong challenge to the practice, whether that challenge arises internally, from conscience or private reflection, or externally, from someone else questioning the legitimacy of slavery.[98] The most strident justifications of slavery seem to arise when slavery is challenged forcefully by others. Thus one would expect to find both the strong justification and the weak justification of slavery in the early nineteenth century, when Western powers began to pressure Islamic societies to abolish slavery. And this is in fact what one does find: while some Muslims jurists and theologians responded with calls to restrict or abolish slavery, others took a primarily defensive stance:

Numerous ulama [scholars of the holy law of Islam] accepted no more than rectifications in the law of slavery, to bring it in line with underlying principles. Regulations pertaining to servitude accounted for a large proportion of the sharia [the holy law of Islam], and scholars were uneasy about jettisoning too much of what their illustrious predecessors had elaborated. Property rights were guaranteed in holy law, and the Prophet and his companions had owned slaves. Those released from bondage might become vagrants, or otherwise undermine social order. Slavery was necessary to gain merit from manumission, and was effective in bringing infidels to Islam.[99]

Like the Christian proslavery thinkers profiled above, Muslim justifiers of slavery have used both generic theological arguments and arguments tied to particular passages from authoritative texts. Bernard Lewis, Professor of Near Eastern Studies at Princeton, asserts that the Spiritual Blessing Argument was common: "The notion that slavery is a divine boon to mankind, by means of which pagan and barbarous peoples are brought to Islam and civilization, occurs very frequently in later writers."[100]

---

[96] From the *Mukhtasar* of Khalil b. Ishaq al-Jundi, translated and quoted in Hunwick and Powell (eds.), *The African Diaspora in the Mediterranean Lands of Islam*, 23.

[97] See Brown, *Slavery & Islam*, 237–238.

[98] See Tise, *Proslavery*, 78–79 and 392 n.29.

[99] William Gervase Clarence-Smith, *Islam and the Abolition of Slavery* (Oxford: Oxford University Press, 2006), 129.

[100] Bernard Lewis, *Race and Slavery in the Middle East: An Historical Enquiry* (Oxford: Oxford University Press, 1990), 42. For similar arguments in older sources, see the citations listed in Brown, *Slavery & Islam*, 387 n.129.

An example from the early twentieth century is that of the influential Palestinian scholar Yūsuf al-Nabhānī. Writing in 1908 and aware of European criticism of slavery in Islamic societies, al-Nabhānī employed both socioeconomic and religious considerations to argue that slavery, when practiced according to Islamic law (*shari'a*), was a positive good. Al-Nabhānī contended that the distinction of rich and poor was natural and that the rich needed slaves to accomplish work. Slaves, in turn, needed someone to provide for them and protect them, which masters living according to the *shari'a* would do, "since noble people would treat their slaves the same way they would treat their own children, following the example of the Prophet."[101] Masters and slaves needed each other and were "a blessing to each other."[102] After giving this socioeconomic argument, al-Nabhānī then gave a version of the Spiritual Blessing Argument: enslavement by Muslim masters was a good for non-Muslim slaves, because it provided a path to knowledge of God and an opportunity to convert to Islam.[103]

A second Islamic proslavery argument depends on a particular aspect of Islamic law concerning penalties for wrongdoing. The Qur'an calls for the freeing of a slave in atonement for certain sins, for example involuntary manslaughter:

Never should a believer kill another believer, except by mistake. If anyone kills a believer by mistake he must free one Muslim slave and pay compensation to the victim's relatives, unless they charitably forgo it; if the victim belonged to a people at war with you but is a believer, then the compensation is only to free a believing slave ... Anyone who lacks the means to do this must fast for two consecutive months ... (Qu'ran 4:92)[104]

Given that the freeing of a slave was enshrined in the Qur'an as the principal route to atonement for certain sins, some Islamic jurists came to the conclusion that the integrity of Islamic law was inconsistent with

---

[101] Yūsuf al-Nabhānī, *Sa'ādat al-anām fi ittibā' dīn al-islām wa tawḍīḥ al-farq baynahu wa bayna dīn al-naṣara fī al-'aqā'id wa al-aḥkām* [*Happiness in Following the Religion of Islam and Clarifying the Difference between Islam and Christianity in Terms of Beliefs and Rules*], (no publisher, 1908), 42, quoted in Amal N. Ghazal, "Debating slavery and abolition in the Arab Middle East," in Behnaz A. Mirzai, Ismael Musah Montana and Paul E. Lovejoy (eds.), *Slavery, Islam, and Diaspora* (Trenton, NJ/Asmara, Eritrea: Africa World Press, 2009), 139–154, 142.

[102] Yūsuf al-Nabhānī, *Sa'ādat al-anām...*, 42, quoted in Ghazal, "Debating slavery and abolition in the Arab Middle East," 143.

[103] Ghazal, "Debating slavery and abolition in the Arab Middle East," 143.

[104] Similarly, see Qur'an 58:3 and 5:89. Unless otherwise indicated, all translations of the Qu'ran in this chapter are from M. A. S. Abdel Haleem (ed. and trans.), *The Qur'an, English Translation and Parallel Arabic Text* (Oxford: Oxford University Press, 2010).

the abolition of slavery. Muhammed Rāghib, writing in 1911, argued on these grounds that slavery could not be abolished. Historian Amal Ghazal summarizes his reasoning:

Because manumission was part and parcel of a coherent legal system in which the sinner could be punished by being ordered to free his slave(s) – as in cases of breaking an oath or accidental death – slavery, Rāghib insisted, could not be abolished.[105]

Speaking in the late twentieth century, Muhammad Nasir al-Din Albani appears to make a similar argument, contending that the *shari'a* provides "rulings valid until the end of time that assume slavery" in its precepts regarding expiation for oath-breaking and manslaughter.[106]

A much earlier justification of slavery can be found in the work of al-Qādī 'Abd al-Jabbār (935–1024), a major Muslim theologian from Persia. In a brief text Al-Jabbār appears to present an Argument from Divine Command; at the least he presents the main premise of such an argument: "'Abd al-Jabbār states explicitly that since God permitted and even commanded slavery on occasion, slavery must be 'good,' that is, it must serve some human interest."[107]

While al-Jabbār goes so far as to claim that God commanded slavery (on occasion), other proslavery Islamic thinkers focus on an Argument from Divine Permission: No one can allow what is prohibited by God or prohibit what has been made lawful by God. But slavery has been made lawful by God. Thus, no one can prohibit slavery. Evidence offered for the second premise (slavery has been made lawful by God), includes texts from the Qu'ran as well as sayings and deeds of Muhammad. Thus argues Sultan 'Abd al-Rahman of Morocco (r. 1822–1859), writing in 1842 in reply to British diplomat John Drummond Hay's antislavery communications:

As to what regards the making of Slaves and Trading therewith, it is confirmed by our Book as also by the *Sunna* of Our Prophet, on whom be the blessing and the peace of God – and furthermore there is not any controversy between the Oolamma [Ulama] on that subject, and no one can allow what is prohibited or prohibit that which is made lawful. By whomsoever innovation be attempted

---

[105] Ghazal, "Debating slavery and abolition in the Arab Middle East," 143–144. Rāghib's article appeared an Arabic-language journal published in Syria: *Al-Haqā'iq*, 10 (1911), 369ff.

[106] Quoted in Brown, *Slavery & Islam*, 241.

[107] Sherman A. Jackson, *Islam and the Problem of Black Suffering* (Oxford: Oxford University Press, 2009), 184 n.90. Jackson cites 'Abd al-Jabbār's multi-volume work *al-Mughnī fī abwāb al-tawḥīd wa al-'adl*, ed. A. F. al-Ahwānī and I. Madkūr, 15 vols. (Cairo: al-Mu'assasah al-Misrīyah al-Āmmah li al-Ta'līf wa al-Tarjamah wa al-Tibā'ah wa al-Nashr, 1960–1969), 13:465–466.

contrary to it (the Law) the same shall be rejected, inasmuch as our sacred religion is not regulated by mens' counsel or deliberation, for it proceeds out of Inspiration from the Lord of all creatures, through the tongue of our Faithful Prophet, on whom be the Peace and Blessing of God![108]

A fourth relevant line of thought found in several Islamic sources is the idea that slavery is a punishment for unbelief. Sa'd al-Dīn Masūd ibn Umar ibn Abd Allah al-Taftāzānī (1322–1390) writes:

[Slavery] was established as a punishment for unbelief, for since unbelievers have disdained worship of God Most High and made themselves as one with animals in failing to examine and reflect upon the message of divine unity, God Most High has punished them by making them slaves of His slaves, living in degradation with the status of animals.[109]

And, similarly, the jurist Ahmad Baba (1556–1627) of Timbuktu:

You should be aware that the cause of enslavement is unbelief, and the unbelievers of the *sudan* are like any other unbelievers in this regard—Jews, Christians, Persians, Berbers, or others whose persistence in unbelief rather than Islam has been established ... Whoever is enslaved in a state of unbelief may rightly be owned, whoever he is, as opposed to those of all groups who converted to Islam first ... They are free Muslims who may not be enslaved under any circumstance.[110]

As is apparent, the idea that slavery is a punishment for unbelief could be deployed both to argue against the enslavement of Muslims by other Muslims, and to justify the enslavement of non-Muslims.

2.6 RELIGION AND THE JUSTIFICATION OF SLAVERY: REASONING OR RATIONALIZATION?

It is puzzling that thoughtful people could have arrived at the conclusion that slavery is actually a good thing. While in most religious traditions

---

[108] Sultan 'Abd al-Rahman to John Drummond Hay, Mar. 18, 1842, quoted in Lewis, *Race and Slavery in the Middle East*, 156. See also Clarence-Smith, *Islam and Abolition of Slavery*, 139 and 159; Y. Hakan Erdem, *Slavery in the Ottoman Empire and Its Demise, 1800–1909* (New York: St. Martin's Press, 1996), 92; and Paul E. Lovejoy, *Transformations in Slavery: A History of Slavery in Africa* (Cambridge: Cambridge University Press, 1983), 264.

[109] From the *al-Talwih bi-kashf haqaiq al-Tanqih*, quoted by Muhammad Bayram al-Khamis (1840-1889), in Hunwick and Powell (eds.), *The African Diaspora in the Mediterranean Lands of Islam*, 16. See also Brown, *Slavery & Islam*, 178 for a similar statement by the thirteenth-century Muslim scholar al-Babarti.

[110] Quoted in John Hunwick, "Islamic law and polemics over race and slavery in North and West Africa (16–19th Century)," in Shaun E. Marmon (ed.), *Slavery in the Islamic Middle East* (Princeton: Markus Wiener Publishers, 1999), 43–68, 49–50.

there is support for the view that slavery is permissible (or at least, that slavery of a certain sort was permissible in the past), the religious arguments contending that slavery is a positive good are nowhere near strong enough to support the sort of confidence in the rightness of slavery that authors like Joseph Wilson exhibit. Justifications of slavery built on Arguments from Divine Command involve a series of inferences, from a specific sacred text or texts to the intermediate conclusion that God decreed or commanded a particular sort of slavery in a particular context in the past, to the further conclusion that slavery of that sort in that context was a positive good, to the final conclusion that the slavery of the proslavery author's own time and context is a positive good. But each of these inferences is subject to serious objections. Taking them in reverse order, assume for the sake of argument that, for example, the Old and New Testament texts cited by Hammond (above) really do imply that slavery in the ancient Mediterranean world was commanded by God and a positive good. How would it follow that slavery in Hammond's nineteenth-century South Carolina was also commanded by God and a positive good? As Jonathan Edwards had noted over a century before Hammond, from a special injunction to Israel one cannot infer an "Established Rule" in support of Christians holding slaves, any more than God's permission to Israel to take goods from the Egyptians at the time of the Exodus (Deut 15:6) is equivalent to "Establishing it as a rule that his People might borrow & not pay in all ages."[111] Hammond asserts that "American Slavery is … especially commanded by God through Moses, and approved by Christ through his apostles."[112] The claim that God commanded *American* slavery, or that Christ approved *American* slavery, hundreds of years before it came into existence requires additional argumentative support, to say the least.[113]

[111] Quoted in Kenneth P. Minkema, "Jonathan Edwards on slavery and the slave trade," *The William and Mary Quarterly*, 54:4 (Oct 1997), 823–834, 827. The same argument was made in the popular biblical commentary of John Brown, *A Dictionary of the Holy Bible … Forming a Sacred Commentary; a Body of Scripture History, Chronology, and Divinity* (Pittsburgh, PA: 1807), and quoted by George Bourne in *The Book and Slavery Irreconcilable* (Philadelphia: J. M. Sanderson & Co., 1816).

[112] Hammond, "Letter to an English abolitionist," in Gilpin Faust (ed.), *The Ideology of Slavery*, 175.

[113] It might be objected that Lev 25:46 institutes slavery among the Jews in perpetuity ("You may bequeath them [your slaves] to your sons after you, to inherit as a possession for ever"), and therefore that this one text, at least, warrants an inference from what God decreed in the past to what God wills in the present. To reply: At best, this objection would only authorize Jews (and not those of other religions) to continue to hold as slaves

Next, assume for the sake of argument that God commanded a particular sort of slavery in a particular context in the past. Why would it follow that even *that* sort of slavery in that context was a positive good, as opposed to a necessary evil?

Finally, it should be asked whether the texts cited in Arguments from Divine Command really do imply that God commanded slavery, when they may only be evidence (for those accepting the divine origin of the texts) that God tolerated or permitted it. Compare Jesus' attitude to the Old Testament allowance for divorce. A text in Deuteronomy presupposes that if a man "takes a wife and marries her" but "she finds no favor in his eyes because he has found some indecency in her," then he may "write her a bill of divorce" (Deut 24:1). Jesus asserts that divorce was an evil tolerated for a specific reason:

They said to him, "Why then did Moses *command* one to give a certificate of divorce, and to put her away?" He said to them, "For your hardness of heart Moses *allowed* you to divorce your wives, but from the beginning it was not so." (Matt 19:7-8, italics added)

Similarly, sacred texts in which God appears to decree that slavery be practiced may indicate only that there was some sufficient reason for God to permit slavery, and not that God commanded it. Writing in 1773, Benjamin Rush (1746–1813) makes just this argument: "although the chief Design of rendering the Slavery of the Heathens perpetual, was to prevent the Jews from intermarrying with them [so that God's plan that they remain a distinct people might be accomplished], yet this Evil like the Divorces spoken of by our Saviour, was permitted amongst them, upon the Account of the 'Hardness of their Hearts.'"[114] In the same year, the Anglican Granville Sharp (1735–1813) makes a similar argument.[115] In the background for both is the ancient notion of divine pedagogy or progressive revelation – the claim that God had fitted his revelation to the developing condition of the recipients. As the teacher gives a different lesson to a beginner than

---

persons descended from those slaves that Jews at the times of Moses held. But no such persons can be identified.

[114] Benjamin Rush, *A Vindication of the Address to the Inhabitants ...*, in Roger Bruns (ed.), *Am I Not a Man and a Brother: The Antislavery Crusade of Revolutionary America, 1688–1788* (New York: Chelsea House Publishers, 1983), 233.

[115] Granville Sharp, *An Essay on Slavery, Proving from Scripture Its Inconsistency with Humanity and Religion* (Burlington: Isaac Collins, 1773), 18-20.

to an advanced student (Augustine's analogy), God revealed his will in stages as humanity progressed.[116]

Note also that although Hammond uses Lev 25:44–46 as a basis for his Argument from Divine Command, the text can be read as divine permission rather than divine command:

As for your male and female slaves whom you may have: you *may* buy male and female slaves from among the nations that are round about you. You *may* also buy from among the strangers who sojourn with you ... You *may* bequeath them to your sons after you, to inherit as a possession for ever ... [italics added]

New Testament texts in which slaves are instructed to obey their masters are similarly ambiguous. Even on the supposition that God opposed slavery, He still might inspire the New Testament authors to instruct slaves to obey their masters, if, for example, that was good practical advice at a time and place in which running away from a slaveholder left a fugitive slave vulnerable to grave dangers and nonviolent slave resistance had no chance of long-term success.

Indeed, we question whether the New Testament texts entail even so much as the moral permissibility of slavery. Andrew Wilson argues that they do not. Paul's statement that slaves should obey their masters was equivalent to the conditional "If you are a Christian slave, then you should obey your master." But Wilson notes that this conditional does not necessarily imply an acceptance of slavery:

To tell someone what to do if X takes place is not to condone X, but merely to recognize that X happens sometimes, as all pastors know full well ... If I urge someone who has been wrongfully dismissed to react without malice, I am not signing off on the wrongful dismissal, or saying that it doesn't matter ...[117]

Similarly, when Jesus counsels his followers not to resist one who is evil, but to turn the other cheek when struck (Matt 5:38–41), he is not implying that battery is morally permissible.[118]

---

[116] See R. S. Crane, "Anglican apologetics and the idea of progress, 1699–1745," *Modern Philology*, 31:3 (1934), 273–306, and Davis, *The Problem of Slavery in the Age of Revolution*, 532–537. Nicholas Stokman has pointed out to us the relevance here of John 16:12–13.

[117] Wilson, "The best argument for a trajectory hermeneutic – and where it goes wrong."

[118] What of Paul's directive to Christian slaveholders to "treat your slaves justly and fairly, knowing that you also have a Master in heaven" (Col 4:1)? It could be argued that since Paul is not ordering slaveholders to free their slaves, Paul must have thought it was possible to both own a slave and treat that slave justly, which implies that Paul must have thought owning slaves was not necessarily unjust and thus was morally permissible. This is certainly possible, but the argument is not as compelling as it first appears. Col

So while a plausible explanation of Paul's directives on slavery is that
he thought slavery was morally permissible and that slaves had a moral
duty to accept their role, other explanations are also possible. Paul could
have been unsure about the morality of slavery or even opposed to it as
practiced, but also thought that it was good prudential advice for
Christian slaves to obey their masters, either because (i) this would on
the whole safeguard the physical well-being of slaves, or (ii) counseling
rebellion or flight or would have encouraged a situation in which the
nascent Christian church was persecuted and both slaves and free would
therefore have been less able to live out the Christian life, or (iii) Paul's
belief that the end of the world was imminent reduced in his mind the
urgency of reforming corrupt social practices, or (iv) Paul thought that a
Christian slave who accepted his plight in the right way might spark
conversion in his master, or (v) some combination of the above.[119]

4:1 should be read together with a similar passage, Eph 6:9: "Masters, do the same to
them [slaves], and forebear threatening, knowing that he who is both their Master and
yours is in heaven, and that there is no partiality with him." When Paul commands
masters to "do the same to them," he is referring to what he has just told slaves to do vis-
à-vis masters: "Slaves, be obedient to those who are your earthly masters, with fear and
trembling, in singleness of heart, as to Christ; not in the way of eye-service, as men-
pleasers, but as slaves of Christ, doing the will of God from the heart, rendering service
with a good will as to the Lord and not to men, knowing that whatever good any one
does, he will receive the same again from the Lord, whether he is a slave or free" (Eph
6:5–8). When we examine these verses, the meaning of the injunction that masters
should "do the same to them" in v. 9 is nothing short of astounding. Minimally, Paul
is telling Christian slaveholders to serve their slaves with a good will as though they were
serving the Lord. It is plausible, then, to read Paul's injunctions to masters as amounting
to this: don't relate to your slaves as slaves but instead act as servants to them. So while
Paul didn't teach "masters, free your slaves," he did teach "masters, serve your slaves,"
radically subverting the typical master–slave relationship. Given this, it may be that Paul
thought that having slaves was not necessarily unjust, but only because he was envis-
aging the monumentally atypical situation in which masters and slaves were mutually
serving one another. This interpretation is supported by Paul's letter to Philemon, master
of the slave Onesimus, in which Paul suggests to Philemon that he treat Onesimus "no
longer as a slave but more than slave, as a beloved brother" (Phlm v. 16). In sum, Paul
may have thought that the typical way slaveholders treat slaves is unjust, and that the
typical manner of slaveholding was such as to make it unjust, but that a radically altered
situation in which slaves and masters serve each other voluntarily out of religious duty is
permissible. See Wilson, "The best argument for a trajectory hermeneutic – and where it
goes wrong."

[119] Possibilities (i) and (ii) are put forward by Bourne, *The Book and Slavery Irreconcilable*,
178, quoting David Rice, *Slavery Inconsistent with Justice and Good Policy* (Lexington,
Kentucky, 1792). On (iii), see Glancy, *Slavery as Moral Problem*, 45–46. On the
conversion of masters (iv), see the commentaries of Ambrosiaster (fl. fourth century)
on Eph 6:6–8 and 1 Tim 6:1 (Ambrosiaster, *Commentaries on Galatians–Philemon*,

Next, the curse of Ham tradition was used in some Christian contexts to provide a justification for the enslavement of Blacks (and in some Islamic contexts as well).[120] But the text of Genesis does not warrant this, as Goldenberg notes: "In the Bible Ham is the father of four sons: three (Misrayim/Egypt, Put, Kush) who became the ancestors of various dark-skinned African people, and Canaan. Only Canaan, the nonblack ancestor of the Canaanites, was cursed with slavery."[121]

The interpretation that uses Gen 9–10 to associate blackness and slavery does not appear till the seventh century AD.[122] While an alternate, nonbiblical genealogy dating at the second century BC has Canaan as the progenitor of the Ethiopians and the Egyptians, the link between blackness and slavery only emerges, gradually, from the third century AD, more than 1,000 years after the writing of Genesis.[123] Solid rebuttals of the proslavery interpretation of the curse of Ham appear from the early eighteenth century.[124]

Turning to the Qur'an, 'Abd al-Jabbār's claim that God has on occasion commanded slavery is unwarranted. The Qur'an does permit slavery, but there is no text in which Allah clearly commands slaveholding.[125] Islamic arguments justifying slavery from Divine Command are thus questionable.[126]

---

    trans. and ed. Gerald L. Bray [Downers Grove, IL: InterVarsity Press, 2009], 60–61 and 138).

[120] See Goldenberg, *The Curse of Ham*, 170.   [121] Goldenberg, *The Curse of Ham*, 169.

[122] Goldenberg, *The Curse of Ham*, 170.

[123] Goldenberg, *The Curse of Ham*, 171–174.

[124] See Samuel Sewall, *The Selling of Joseph a Memorial* (Boston, 1700), reprinted in Bruns (ed.), *Am I Not a Man and a Brother*, 12; Anonymous, *Arguments against Making Slaves of Men* (1715) in Bruns (ed.), *Am I Not a Man and a Brother*, 28; Samuel Hopkins, *A Dialogue Concerning the Slavery of the Africans* (Norwich: Judah P. Spooner, 1776), 27.

[125] Some would disagree: 47:4 commands the taking of captives, and this has been interpreted as a command to take slaves, as in Lamin O. Sanneh, *The Jakhanke Muslim clerics: A Religious and Historical Study of Islam in Senegambia* (Lanham, MD: University Press of America, 1989), 218. For a different reading, see our discussion in Chapter 5.

[126] Regarding Arguments from Divine Permission, meant to support a weak justification of slavery as morally permissible, it could perhaps be argued that the passages from the Qur'an and Hadith permitting slavery were intended as temporary toleration of evil, and thus do not strictly imply that slavery was morally permissible, even when it was allowed. (That is, it could be held that early Muslims were permitted to do something morally wrong.) This approach faces somewhat greater difficulties than the corresponding approach with Christian texts, however, because adherence to Islam has traditionally required an acceptance of the view that Muhammad committed no serious sins, and Muhammad himself enslaved formerly free war captives, and bought and owned slaves

Moving on from scripturally based Arguments from Divine Sanction, the more general Spiritual Blessing Argument is seriously flawed. The argument moves from the premise that (1) The enslavement of a non-believer by a believer will benefit the nonbeliever by providing him or her with an opportunity to embrace the True Faith, to the conclusion that (2) Enslavement of nonbelievers by believers is a good practice.

But (2) does not follow from (1), given that there are alternative ways to give nonbelievers equally good (or better) opportunities to embrace the True Faith, and given that the enslavement of nonbelievers typically involves serious harm to them. Suppose that a patient with a gangrened leg needed an amputation, and although anesthetics were available, the presiding physician chose not to use them in order to increase his profit. It would be fallacious for the doctor to argue that because the painful surgery benefitted the patient by providing him or her with an opportunity to remain alive, it was a good thing to do surgery without anesthetics. Yes, the good of continued life outweighs the pain of the unanesthetized surgery, but that same good (continued life) could have been achieved without the pain. Similarly, the good of an opportunity to embrace the True Faith could be given to the nonbeliever without permanently enslaving him or her and his or her offspring. Moreover, as Samuel Sewall notes in response to the Spiritual Blessing Argument, in an antislavery argument from 1700, "Evil must not be done, that good may come of it. The extraordinary and comprehensive Benefit accruing to … Joseph … did not rectify his Brethren's Sale of him [a reference to Gen 37–45]."[127]

Finally, consider the general Argument from Providence: (1) God has intentionally arranged human affairs in such a way that some are permanent slaves while others are masters. (2) It is not unjust to accept God's intentional arrangement of human affairs. (3) Thus, it is not unjust to accept permanent slavery.

The fact that human affairs have a certain feature does not imply that God has intentionally arranged for human affairs to have that feature. Compare the prevalence of commercial sexual exploitation in human history … few religious thinkers would infer that God has intentionally arranged human affairs so as to include sexual exploitation. This casts (1)

______

(see Brown, *Slavery & Islam*, 198). We discuss Muslim efforts to reject slavery in Chapter 5.

[127] Sewall, *The Selling of Joseph a Memorial*, in Bruns (ed.), *Am I Not a Man and a Brother*, 13. Similarly see Anonymous, *Arguments against Making Slaves of Men* (1715) in Bruns (ed.), *Am I Not a Man and a Brother*, 28.

into doubt in the absence of a specific revelation asserting or implying (1). In the case of Islam, Muhammad's claim to a group of Muslim slave-holders that God had put their slaves under their control[128] does supply special grounds for those particular Muslims for something like (1), but a further premise is required to conclude that Muslim slaveholders in later times had their slaves as a result of God's intentional action.

The puzzling combination of (a) the magnitude of the injustice involved in slavetrading and slaveholding, (b) the weaknesses in the religious arguments attempting to strongly justify slavery, and (c) the confidence on the part of the proponents of those arguments raises the question of how the religious justifiers of slavery (in the strong sense) could have so thoroughly failed to perceive the wrongness of slavery. While some of those justifying slavery on religious grounds may have been insincere in their assertion that slavery was a divinely sanctioned good, we think it plausible that most religious justifiers of slavery were convinced of their position. A better explanation of the surprising failure of these thinkers to grasp the evils of slavery has to do with the human proclivity for rationalization, or motivated reasoning – a proclivity that research by experimental psychologists has begun to elucidate. As psychologists Jonathan Haidt and Fredrik Bjorklund summarize:

People are extremely good at finding reasons for whatever they have done, are doing, or want to do in the future. In fact, the human tendency to search only for reasons and evidence on one side of a question is so strong and consistent in the research literature that it might be considered the chief obstacle to good thinking.[129]

In Chapter 5, we explore further the idea that the phenomenon of motivated reasoning may help to explain how the justifiers of slavery could have gotten it so wrong.

---

[128] See Brown, *Slavery & Islam*, 71.

[129] Jonathan Haidt and Fredrik Bjorklund, "Social intuitionists answer six questions about moral psychology," in W. Sinnott-Armstrong (ed.), *Moral Psychology, Volume 2, The Cognitive Science of Morality: Intuition and Diversity* (Cambridge, MA: The MIT Press, 2008), 181–254, 190. For more on the application of the psychology of moral judgment to the history of abolition, see Michael Rota, "Moral psychology and social change: the case of abolition," *The Journal of Interdisciplinary History*, 49:4 (2019), 567–590.

3

Ameliorating Slavery

Paul was in prison – not in the harshest sort of Roman prison, but in military custody. This allowed him to receive food and visitors but also meant being chained, at least with leg-irons or manacles. During Paul's imprisonment, a man named Onesimus had become a Christian disciple with Paul's guidance. Onesimus was a slave who had either run away from, or had in some other way antagonized, his owner Philemon. Philemon was himself a Christian known to Paul, likely brought into the new religious movement by the Apostle. These details emerge from an examination of the shortest of Paul's letters in the New Testament, Philemon.[1] In this letter, written in the 50s or early 60s AD, Paul intercedes with Philemon on behalf of Onesimus.

Onesimus would have appreciated such intercession. To be a runaway slave in the Roman Empire was perilous. In Roman law, slaves were classified as things or property rather than persons, and runaway slaves were held to be guilty of stealing valuable property from their masters, namely themselves. Punishments for a fugitive slave ranged from beating, branding, flogging, and the imposition of metal collars, all the way up to death by being fed to wild animals or by crucifixion (in cases where runaway slaves took up arms).[2] And even if Onesimus was not in fact a

---

[1] See Richard J. Cassidy, *Paul in Chains: Roman Imprisonment and the Letters of St. Paul* (New York: The Crossroad Publishing Company, 2001) and David W. Pao, *Colossians and Philemon: Zondervan Exegetical Commentary Series on the New Testament* (Grand Rapids, MI: Zondervan, 2012).

[2] P. R. Coleman-Norton, "Paul and the Roman law of slavery," in P. R. Coleman-Norton (ed.), *Studies in Roman Economic and Social History in Honor of Allan Chester Johnson* (Princeton: Princeton University Press, 1951), 155–177, 172–177; John G. Nordling,

runaway (some commentators have suggested that Philemon might have sent him to assist Paul in prison), he was nonetheless in a vulnerable position. Playing on the meaning of the name Onesimus ("Handy" or "Useful"), Paul writes to Philemon: "Formerly he was useless to you, but now he is indeed useful to you and to me" (v. 11). And later Paul alludes to actual or perceived wrongdoing by Onesimus: "If he has wronged you at all, or owes you anything, charge that to my account" (v. 18). Paul's phrasing, without technically implying that Onesimus had done something wrong, makes it clear that Philemon was seriously displeased with him. That would have been enough to give Onesimus cause for fear. Roman law and custom at the time granted immense power to slaveholders, allowing them to punish slaves by flogging and torture, and to separate slave families by selling or giving away one member of a family but not others.[3]

The socially expected relationship between a master and a slave was one of dominance and submission. But Paul urges Philemon to radically reconceive his relationship with Onesimus: "So if you consider me your partner, receive him [Onesimus] as you would receive me" (v. 17). How would Philemon have received Paul? With respect, love, even deference, and certainly not with punishment or command. Paul refers to Philemon as his "beloved fellow worker" (v. 1) and his "brother" (v. 7), and refers to other Christians mentioned in the letter as "fellow workers" (v. 23). For Paul to ask Philemon to receive Onesimus as Philemon would receive Paul is, minimally, to ask that Philemon relate to Onesimus primarily as to a fellow worker in the Faith. In other words, Onesimus' identity as Philemon's fellow Christian is supposed to eclipse, in some sense, his identity as Philemon's slave.

What precisely Paul is asking of Philemon is left vague, however. Some commentators have understood Paul to be asking only that Philemon forgive Onesimus, others have taken Paul to be asking that Philemon give Onesimus his freedom, and others that Philemon give Onesimus his freedom so that he can support Paul in the missionary work of the Church.[4]

"Onesimus fugitivus: a defense of the runaway slave hypothesis in Philemon," *Journal for the Study of the New Testament*, 41 (1991), 97–119; Laurie Venters, "Recovering runaways: slave catching in the Roman world," Master's thesis (Leiden University: 2019): studenttheses.universiteitleiden.nl/handle/1887/74843.

[3] Jane F. Gardner, "Slavery and Roman law," in K. Bradley and P. Cartledge (eds.), *The Cambridge World History of Slavery: Volume 1, The Ancient Mediterranean World* (Cambridge: Cambridge University Press, 2011), 414–437, 431–432 and 425.

[4] See Pao, *Colossians and Philemon*, 347–348, and Calvin's commentary on Philemon, in John Calvin, *Calvin's New Testament Commentaries: A New Translation*, vol. 10, eds.

We can glimpse more about Paul's intentions by noting five features of the short communication.[5] First, Paul addresses the letter not only to Philemon but also to two other named persons and to the whole assembly of Christians who apparently met for religious services at Philemon's home (v. 2). The letter would likely have thus been read to the whole Christian community of which Philemon was a part, creating social pressure for Philemon to heed Paul's exhortation.

Second, Paul subtly deflects a common rationalization of slaveholders, viz., the argument that slavery was good for slaves because it restrained them from acting badly. We find this view expressed in a near contemporary of Paul, the Jewish philosopher Philo:

> [T]he law-book of the Jews … tells of two brothers [Jacob and Esau], one wise and temperate, the other incontinent, how the father of them both [Isaac] prayed in pity for him who had not attained to virtue that he should be his brother's slave. He held that slavery, which men think the worst of evils, was the best possible boon to the fool, because the loss of independence would prevent him from transgressing without fear of punishment, and his character would be improved under the control of the authority set above him.[6]

One rebuttal of this defense of slavery is the observation that good action springing from a person's free will is more valuable than good action that is compelled. Paul invokes this very thought, but does so indirectly by applying the principle to Philemon rather than Onesimus:

> I would have been glad to keep him [Onesimus] with me, in order that he might serve me on your behalf during my imprisonment for the gospel; but I preferred to do nothing without your consent in order that your goodness might not be by compulsion but of your own free will (vv. 13–14).

It's possible to see here a subtle invitation to Philemon to follow Paul's example and allow Onesimus' goodness to "not be by compulsion" but by his own free will.

D. Torrance and T. Torrance (Grand Rapids, MI: Eerdmans, 1972). It has even been suggested that Paul was hinting that Philemon might send Onesimus back to Paul, to serve as Paul's slave. Yet this is belied by the text: in v. 16 Paul suggests that Philemon receive Onesimus not as a slave but as a brother, and at v. 17 Paul asks Philemon to receive Onesimus as he would receive Paul himself. But Onesimus would not suppose he could treat Paul as property transferable to another.

[5] In attending to the letter's rhetorical nuances, I'm helped by Andy Crouch, *Culture Making: Recovering Our Creative Calling* (Downers Grove, IL: InterVarsity Press, 2008), 213–214.

[6] Philo, "Every good man is free," 57, in Garnsey, *Ideas of Slavery from Aristotle to Augustine*, 164–165.

Third, Paul suggests that God's providential plan is that Philemon relate to Onesimus as to a brother and *not* as to a slave:

Perhaps this is why he [Onesimus] was parted from you [Philemon] for a while, that you might have him back for ever, no longer as a slave but more than a slave, as a beloved brother, especially to me but how much more to you, both in the flesh and in the Lord (vv. 15–16).

This has seemed to many commentators to be a hint from Paul that Philemon should manumit Onesimus.

Fourth, despite his earlier rhetoric ("though I am bold enough in Christ to command you to do what is required, yet for love's sake I prefer to appeal to you" vv 8–9), Paul lays a heavy hand on Philemon near the end of the letter:

If he has wronged you at all, or owes you anything, charge that to my account. I, Paul, write this with my own hand, I will repay it – to say nothing of your owing me even your own self. Yes, brother, I want some benefit from you in the Lord. Refresh my heart in Christ. Confident in your obedience, I write to you, knowing that you will do even more than I say (vv. 18–21).

The phrase "even more than I say" might be a second hint that Philemon should manumit Onesimus. Finally, Paul gently puts Philemon on notice that he may be checking up on Philemon's behavior in person: "At the same time, prepare a guest room for me, for I am hoping through your prayers to be granted to you" (v. 22).

What was Philemon's response to Paul's letter? We don't know, but history has left some evidence that Philemon did free Onesimus. A fourth-century text states that worthy slaves who have been freed by their masters can be ordained to ecclesiastical office, mentioning as an example "our Onesimus."[7] And Ignatius of Antioch, writing around the turn of the second century praises the bishop of Ephesus, one "Onesimus."[8]

No one could call Paul a vocal critic of slavery. In many passages he encourages slaves to obey their masters, either because he believed this was the slave's moral duty, or because he considered one's state in this life to be of little importance compared to one's eternal salvation, or because he feared the effect of promoting antislavery policies on the nascent

---

7 *Constitutions of the Holy Apostles*, 8.47.82, in Alexander Roberts and James Donaldson (eds.), *The Ante-Nicene Fathers*, *Volume VII*, rev. A. C. Coxe (Grand Rapids, MI: Eerdmans, 1982), 387–505, 505.

8 Ignatius of Antioch, *Epistle to the Ephesians*, in Roberts and Donaldson (eds.), *The Ante-Nicene Fathers*, *Volume I*, rev. A. C. Coxe (New York: Charles Scribner's Sons, 1913), 49–58.

Christian movement's prospects for growth, or perhaps simply because he knew that slave resistance or flight was so likely to end badly for slaves. But in *Philemon* we see another side to Paul's response to slavery, in his effort to improve the situation of a particular slave. In this regard Paul exemplifies the response to slavery that is the focus of this chapter: ameliorating slavery.

"What moral instruction do we get from the God of Abraham on [the subject of slavery]?" asks the prominent critic of religion Sam Harris. "Consult the Bible, and you will discover that the creator of the universe clearly expects us to keep slaves ..."[9] Relying on passages in the Torah that permit slavery and Paul's injunctions in the New Testament that slaves should obey their masters, Harris emphasizes the Bible's justification of slavery in service of a wider argument against Christianity. Speaking of the Qur'an, Harris writes that "the most straightforward reading of scripture suggests that Allah advises jihadists to take sex slaves from among the conquered ..."[10] Given the historical frequency of religious justifications for slavery, one might well conclude that specific religions, or even religion in general, have in the main supported slavery. But this would be inaccurate. What is accurate is that almost all religions have, for the vast majority of their histories, *allowed* some forms of slavery. But the religious permission of slavery is only one part of a larger story. Religious communities, individuals, and texts have also helped to ease the lives of slaves, to restrict the scope of slavery, and to lead and inspire eighteenth- and nineteenth-century efforts to criminalize slavetrading and slaveholding.

In this chapter we examine attempts to ameliorate slavery by religious groups and by individuals inspired by their religious beliefs. To "ameliorate slavery," as we use that phrase, is to make the lives of slaves better in some way (e.g. by easing the harsh conditions accompanying slavery or by promoting manumission, even liberation), but without challenging the legitimacy of the system of slavery as such. In the next chapter we will consider the response of restricting slavery – limiting the class of those who are held to be legitimately enslaveable or restricting the possible pathways into slavery. While the amelioration of slavery is a distinct response from justification or restriction of slavery, attempts to ameliorate slavery can co-occur with either of these other responses. That

---

[9] Sam Harris, *Letter to a Christian Nation* (New York: Alfred A. Knopf, 2006), 14.
[10] Sam Harris and Maajid Nawaz, *Islam and the Future of Tolerance: A Dialogue* (Cambridge, MA: Harvard University Press, 2015), 67.

is, one and the same religiously inspired individual might seek both to defend the moral permissibility of slavery and to ease the lot of suffering slaves (justify and ameliorate), or one and the same religious community might seek to ease the lot of slaves and to restrict the scope of "legitimate" slavery (ameliorate and restrict). Indeed, it is possible to engage in all three of those responses: justify, ameliorate, and restrict. But for the sake of analytical clarity, we distinguish these responses, and here discuss the amelioration of slavery.

The many ways in which religious groups or individuals have tended to ameliorate slavery can be organized into four categories. First, various religions have exhorted their adherents to treat slaves well (in ways not directly tied to freeing them). Second, religious leaders have given their flocks moral exhortation to free slaves (this includes both the manumission of one's own slaves and the ransom of slaves owned by others) and have sometimes provided legal pathways to facilitate manumission or ransom. Third, religious groups have promoted specific legal requirements regarding the treatment of slaves that tended to make life better for some slaves. And fourth, various religions have espoused doctrines of human spiritual equality and shared eternal destiny which provided slaveholders with additional reasons to adopt a more humane attitude to slaves and which may have given believing slaves a greater sense of worth, purpose, and hope for the future.

3.1 MORAL EXHORTATIONS TO TREAT SLAVES WELL

3.1.1 Islam

According to a well-established Muslim tradition, the last words of Muhammad were "Prayer, prayer; fear Allah about those whom your right hands possess."[11] In his final moments the thoughts of the founder of Islam turned to Muslim slaveholders and their slaves. This would not have been particularly surprising to his followers – over the course of his life, he had spoken frequently of slavery, often urging gentle treatment of slaves. Both the Hadiths (reports about Muhammad's words and actions, put down in writing in the first several centuries after his death) and the Qur'an itself express norms regarding slavery. One such norm is the

---

[11] *Sunan Abi Dawud* 5156, English translation from sunnah.com/abudawud/43, chap. 134.

command to be virtuous to "those whom your right hands possess," that is, to one's slaves:

> Worship God, and ascribe not partners unto Him. And be virtuous toward parents and kinsfolk, toward orphans and the indigent, toward the neighbor who is of kin and the neighbor who is not of kin, towards the companion at your side and the traveler, and toward those whom your right hands possess. (4:36)[12]

In a well-attested Hadith, Muhammad encouraged his followers to think of their slaves as their brothers, to provide for their material needs accordingly and to refrain from overworking them:

> Your slaves are your brothers, whom God has put under your control. Feed them from what you eat, clothe them from what you wear, and do not burden them with work that overwhelms them. If you give them more than they can do, then assist them.[13]

And in other Hadiths, Muhammad enjoins clemency in response to a slave's (perceived) failures, and warns of eternal judgment upon those who mistreat their slaves:

> A man came to the Prophet and asked: Messenger of Allah! how often shall I forgive a servant? He gave no reply, so the man repeated what he had said, but he still kept silence. When he asked a third time, he replied: Forgive him seventy times daily.[14]
>
> One who is a bad owner [of slaves] will not enter Heaven.[15]

While the explicitly formulated doctrine that bad slaveholders will not enter Heaven appears unique to Islam, other religions encouraged good treatment of slaves as well.

3.1.2 Buddhism

The Buddha recognized the great suffering that attended the life of a slave and encouraged masters to serve their slaves by providing adequate food, assigning work according to their ability, tending them when sick, sharing

---

[12] Unless otherwise indicated, translations from the Qur'an in this chapter are from Nasr (ed.), *The Study Quran.*

[13] This Hadith, or a variation, is found in the collections of Bukhari, Muslim, Abu Dawud, and Ibn Majah. Translation is from Brown, *Slavery & Islam,* 71.

[14] *Sunan Abi Dawud* 5164, English translation from sunnah.com/abudawud/43, chap. 134.

[15] Found in the collection of Ibn Majah and other sources, cited and translated in Brown, *Slavery & Islam,* 72.

delicacies, and granting time off of work.[16] Discussing the proper uses of wealth, he taught that the noble disciple "makes his wife and children, his slaves, workers, and servants happy and pleased and properly maintains them in happiness."[17] In another passage, the Buddha refers to the Hindu ritual of sacrifice at the household fire (*agnihotra*) and invites his Brahmin audience to consider service to their dependents, including slaves, as an analogous (or higher?) form of sacrifice: "O Brahmin, you have sons, wives, slaves, messengers, and servants. It is they who constitute the household fire. Therefore, you should revere, respect, worship this household fire."[18] In the third century BC, Ashoka, the Buddhist ruler of the massive Mauryan Empire (r. c. 268–232 BC), had inscriptions carved on rock pillars, boulders, and cave walls, all promoting *Dharma* (righteous conduct). Several of these edicts include exhortation to treat slaves well, for example:

There is no gift that can equal the gift of Dharma, the establishment of human relations on Dharma, the distribution of wealth through Dharma, or kinship in Dharma. That gift consists in proper treatment of slaves and servants, obedience to mother and father, liberality to friends, acquaintances, relatives, priests and ascetics, and abstention from the slaughter of animals.[19]

And in a list of precepts for *upasaka* (lay followers of Buddhism) translated into Chinese in the fifth century AD, we read: "If an *upasaka* who has taken the precepts beats or scolds his slaves, servants, or other people for the sake of his own wealth and life, he commits a grave offense."[20] According to a scholar of slavery in Thailand:

Buddhism, as well as other customary ideas and practices, had a mitigating effect on possible abuses of persons, slave and free, and ... these are reflected to some extent in laws and reforms, in a way comparable to the effect of Christianity on medieval European slavery.[21]

---

[16] *Long Discourses: A faithful translation of the Digha Nikaya*, vol. 3, trans. Bhikkhu Sujato (Eastwood, Australia: SuttaCentral, 2018), DN 31.13, p. 157. Cf. v. 1, DN 2, 4.3.2.4, 75.

[17] *Anguttara Nikya* 4:61, trans. from Bhikku Bodhi (ed.), *In the Buddha's Words: An Anthology of Discourses from the Pali Canon* (Somerville, MA: Wisdom Publications, 2015), 126.

[18] *Anguttara Nikaya Atthakatha* vii-v-44, quoted in Chanana, *Slavery in Ancient India*, 164 n.184.

[19] *The Edicts of Asoka*, ed. and trans. by N. A. Nikam and Richard McKeon (Chicago: University of Chicago Press, 1959), Rock Edict XI, 44–45.

[20] *The Sutra on Upasaka Precepts: Translated from the Chinese of Dharmaraksa*, trans. Bhiksuni Shih Heng-ching (Berkeley: Numata Center for Buddhist Translation and Research, 1994), chap. 14, 81–82.

[21] Andrew Turton, "Thai institutions of slavery," in James L. Watson (ed.), *Asian & African Systems of Slavery* (Berkeley: University of California Press, 1980), 251–292, 287.

3.1.3 Judaism

The Hebrew Bible distinguishes Jewish and non-Jewish slaves and attempts to restrict the enslavement of Jews by Jews in various ways (to be discussed in the following chapter). In the case of Jews who have sold themselves into slavery to other Jews in order to avoid destitution, the Torah counsels owners to treat them as hired servants rather than as slaves, and to refrain from ruling over them "with harshness" (Lev 25:39–43). Hebrew Scripture contains few if any exhortations toward kind treatment of non-Jewish slaves.[22] Still, some later commentators urged gentle treatment on religious grounds, as does Philo of Alexandria, interpreting the Torah:

There is also, I think, this third suggestion, that men should absolutely abstain from putting any oppressive burden upon anyone else. For if the different parts of the earth which cannot share in any sensations of pain or pleasure yet have to be given respite, how much more must this be the case with men who not only possess the sense which is common also to the irrational animals but even the special gift of reason through which the painful feelings caused by toil and labour stamp and record themselves in mental pictures, more vivid than mere sensation! Let so-called masters therefore cease from imposing upon their slaves severe and scarcely endurable orders, which break down their bodies by violent usage and force the soul to collapse before the body.[23]

So, too, Maimonides (1138–1204) in his concluding remarks after a lengthy compilation and summary of Jewish laws on slavery:

It is permissible to have a Canaanite slave perform excruciating labor.[24] Although this is the law, the attribute of piety and the way of wisdom is for a person to be merciful and to pursue justice, not to make his slaves carry a heavy yoke, nor cause them distress. He should allow them to partake of all the food and drink he serves. This was the practice of the Sages of the first generations who would give their slaves

---

[22] Sirach 33:30–31 may be an exception, but the Book of Sirach is not considered canonical within Judaism.

[23] Philo, *On the Special Laws*, 2.89–90, in Philo, *Philo: Volume VII, On the Decalogue. On the Special Laws, Books 1–3*, Loeb Classical Library 320, trans. F. H. Colson (Cambridge, MA: Harvard University Press, 1937). Philo appears to be commenting on Exod 23:10–13.

[24] In the category of "Canaanite slave," Maimonides includes any Gentile captured in war by other Gentiles and subsequently sold to a Jew. He defines excruciating labor as "labor that has no limit, or labor that is unnecessary and . . . asked of the servant with the intent to give him work so that he will not remain idle." Moses Maimonides, *Mishneh Torah*, book 12 (The Book of Acquisition), Hilchot Avadim (The Law of Slaves), 1.6 and 9.4, English translation by Eliyahu Touger, available at: www.chabad.org/library/article_cdo/aid/1362853/jewish/Avadim.htm

from every dish of which they themselves would partake. And they would provide food for their animals and slaves before partaking of their own meals. And so, it is written Psalms 123:2: "As the eyes of slaves to their master's hand, and like the eyes of a maid-servant to her mistress' hand, so are our eyes to God."

Similarly, we should not embarrass a slave by our deeds or with words, for the Torah prescribed that they perform service, not that they be humiliated. Nor should one shout or vent anger upon them extensively. Instead, one should speak to them gently, and listen to their claims. This is explicitly stated with regard to the positive paths of Job for which he was praised Job 31:13, 15: "Have I ever shunned justice for my slave and maid-servant when they quarreled with me ... Did not He who made me in the belly make him? Was it not the One who prepared us in the womb?"

Cruelty and arrogance are found only among idol-worshipping gentiles. By contrast, the descendants of Abraham our patriarch, i.e., the Jews whom the Holy One, blessed be He, granted the goodness of the Torah and commanded to observe righteous statutes and judgments, are merciful to all.

And similarly, with regard to the attributes of the Holy One, blessed be He, which He commanded us to emulate, it is written Psalms 145:9: "His mercies are upon all of His works." And whoever shows mercy to others will have mercy shown to him, as implied by Deuteronomy 13:18: "He will show you mercy, and be merciful upon you and multiply you."[25]

3.1.4 Christianity

It was not uncommon for Stoic philosophers of late antiquity to urge kind treatment of slaves. Thus Seneca (c. 4 BC–65 AD), emphasizing the common humanity of slaves and masters:

Kindly remember that he whom you call your slave sprang from the same stock, is smiled upon by the same skies, and on equal terms with yourself breathes, lives, and dies. It is just as possible for you to see in him a free-born man as for him to see in you a slave ... I do not wish to involve myself in too large a question, and to discuss the treatment of slaves, towards whom we Romans are excessively haughty, cruel, and insulting. But this is the kernel of my advice: Treat your inferiors as you would be treated by your betters. And as often as you reflect how much power you have over a slave, remember that your master has just as much power over you. "But I have no master," you say. You are still young; perhaps you will have one.[26]

---

[25] Maimonides, *Mishneh Torah*, book 12, (The Law of Slaves), 9.8.

[26] Seneca, *Epistula* 47.10–12, translation from Seneca, *Epistles 1–65*, Loeb Classical Library 75, trans. Richard M. Gummere (Cambridge, MA: Harvard University Press, 1917). Interestingly, Stoic doctrine on slavery had a theological element: As Miriam Griffin argues, "The principal philosophical dogma in Seneca's thought on slavery is that there are no natural slaves: all men share in the divine reason and thus may claim the gods as ancestors" (M. T. Griffin, *Seneca: A Philosopher in Politics* [Oxford: Clarendon Press,

Whereas Seneca invokes here the thought that one who is a slaveholder now might have a master in the future, his contemporary Paul invokes the thought that one who is a slaveholder now has a master *now*, a Master who cares about justice:

Masters, treat your slaves justly and fairly, knowing that you also have a Master in heaven. (Col 4:1)

Slaves, be obedient to those who are your earthly masters ... doing the will of God from the heart, rendering service with a good will as to the Lord and not to men, knowing that whatever good any one does, he will receive the same again from the Lord, whether he is a slave or free. Masters, do the same to them, and forbear threatening, knowing that he who is both their Master and yours is in heaven, and that there is no partiality with him. (Eph 6:5–9)

In the centuries that followed, Christian theologians repeated and sometimes amplified Paul's counsel to slaveholders. The otherwise unknown author of the early Christian text known as the *Didache* cautions Christian slaveholders to avoid anger toward their slaves, lest they harm their slaves' relationship with God:

Do not give orders to your male or female slave – to those who hope in the same God – when you are angry, so that they do not lose respect for God [who is over you] both. For [God] does not come to summon according to status, but those whom the spirit has made ready.[27]

The same teaching is contained in chapter 19 of the *Epistle of Barnabas*, a noncanonical Christian text likely written in the first or second century. In a commentary on Paul's Letter to the Ephesians, Ambrosiaster (fl. late fourth century AD) applies the Golden Rule to the question of what masters should ask of slaves, and reinforces the teaching with a reference to God's future judgement:

Earthly masters should recognize that God is the common Lord of everyone and therefore should demand only such service as they would be prepared to perform if it were demanded of them. In this matter, the measure they give is the measure they will get. The Lord is a just judge who decides according to the cases, not according to the status of the persons involved.[28]

1976], 257). See also Seneca, *Epistle* 31.11, and Fitzgerald, "The Stoics and the early Christians on the treatment of slaves."

[27] *Didache: The Teaching of the Twelve Apostles* 4.10, trans. Clayton N. Jefford (Salem, OR: Polebridge Press, 2013).

[28] Ambrosiaster, *Commentary on Ephesians* 6:9, in Ambrosiaster, *Commentaries on Galatians-Philemon*, 61.

And in his commentary on Paul's letter to Philemon, Ambrosiaster writes that "Whoever loves Christ must demonstrate this in the way he treats his slaves ..."[29]

The Archbishop of Constantinople John Chrysostom (c. 347–407 AD), in his commentary on Eph 6:9, warns slaveholders to fear God "lest He one day accuse you for your negligence toward your slaves." Chrysostom continues:

Think not ... that what is done towards a servant, He will therefore forgive, because done to a servant. Heathen laws indeed, as being the laws of men, recognize a difference between these kinds of offenses. But the law of the common Lord and Master of all, as doing good to all alike and dispensing the same rights to all, knows no such difference.

But should any one ask, whence is slavery, and why it has found entrance into human life, (and many I know are both glad to ask such questions, and desirous to be informed of them,) I will tell you. Slavery is the fruit of covetousness, of degradation, of savagery ... Well, but Abraham, you will say, had servants. Yes, but he used them not as servants ... So, saith he [Paul], ye also in like manner, as being yourselves servants [of God], shall be kind and indulgent.[30]

While permitting female slaveholders to strike their female slaves, Chrysostom rebukes those who do this "to such a degree, that the bruises will not disappear with the day."[31] In another homily, he contends that the chaining and bruising of slaves is inconsonant with the identity of a Christian:

Hast thou ordered thy slave to be put in bonds, and wast thou angry, and exasperated? Remember Paul's bonds, and thou wilt straightway stay thine anger; remember that we are of the bound, not the binders, of the bruised in heart, not the bruisers.[32]

---

[29] Ambrosiaster, *Commentary on Philemon*, in Ambrosiaster, *Commentaries on Galatians-Philemon*, 161.

[30] John Chrysostom, *Homilies on Ephesians*, XXII, in Philip Schaff (ed.), *A Select Library of the Nicene and Post-Nicene Fathers of the Christian Church, Volume XIII: Saint Chrysostom: Homilies on Galatians, Ephesians, Philippians, Colossians, Thessalonians, Timothy, Titus, and Philemon* (Grand Rapids, MI: Eerdmans, 1979). Ambrosiaster also attributes the origin of slavery to human wrongdoing: "God did not create slaves and freemen, but made everyone free-born. However, by the wickedness of the world it came about that when one group invaded the territory of another it took free people captive ... This is how the present state of affairs came into being, for some were redeemed from captivity but others remained slaves" [Commentary on Col 4:1, Ambrosiaster, *Commentaries on Galatians-Philemon*, 98].

[31] Chrysostom, *Homilies on Ephesians*, XV, in Schaff (ed.), *A Select Library of the Nicene and Post-Nicene Fathers of the Christian Church, Volume XIII*.

[32] Chrysostom, *Homilies on Colossians*, XII, in Schaff (ed.), *A Select Library of the Nicene and Post-Nicene Fathers of the Christian Church, Volume XIII*.

As noted in the previous chapter, Augustine urged masters to recognize their slaves as brothers, to love them as the masters love themselves, and even to "serve those whom they seem to command" out of concern for others rather than a desire to dominate.[33] Such examples of early Christian counsel on the treatment of slaves could be multiplied.

3.2 EXHORTATIONS TO FREE SLAVES

Of all the major religions, Islam exhibits the most frequent exhortations to manumit and ransom slaves. The Qur'an lists the freeing of a slave as the first illustration of the "steep path" of righteousness:

Did We not give him [mankind] two eyes, a tongue, two lips, and point out to him the two clear ways [of good and evil]? Yet he has not attempted the steep path. What will explain to you what the steep path is? It is to free a slave, to feed at a time of hunger an orphaned relative or a poor person in distress, and to be one of those who believe and urge one another to steadfastness and compassion. (90:8–17)[34]

And similarly:

It is not piety to turn your faces toward the east and west. Rather, piety is he who believes in God, the Last Day, the angels, the Book, and the prophets; and who gives wealth, despite loving it, to kinsfolk, orphans, the indigent, the traveler, beggars, and for [the ransom of] slaves; and performs the prayer and gives the alms; and those who fulfill their oaths when they pledge them, and those who are patient in misfortune, hardship, and moments of peril. (2:177)

While the translator supplies "the ransom of" here, it is not clear whether this passage refers to the use of one's wealth to free or ransom someone else's slave as opposed to freeing one's own slaves; it could refer to both, or either.

Another important Qur'anic passage addresses the situation of a slave requesting a contract for manumission:

And as for those among the ones whom your right hands possess who seek a contract [of emancipation] with you, contract with them if you know of any good in them, and give unto them from the Wealth of God, which He has given you. (24:33)

At the time of this passage's promulgation, it was already an established practice for a slaveholder to sometimes enter into a contract with one of

---

[33] *Sermon* 58.2.2 (PL 38, 393); *Sermon on the Mount* 1.19.59; *City of God*, 19.14. The quoted phrases are from Augustine, *The City of God against the Pagans*, vol. 6, 185–187.

[34] Trans. from Haleem, *The Qur'an*.

his or her slaves, by which a price would be fixed and the slave would work to gradually pay down the sum, at which point he or she would be freed. Slaves freed by these contracts, and their descendants in perpetuity, were obligated to continue working for their former master after having been freed, but this could itself be an "inestimable advantage in the reality of a highly compact social structure."[35] That is, had freed slaves simply been cut loose from their former masters, they might well have found their social position precarious and the securing of adequate employment difficult. What is more, the transition from slavery to freedom carried many substantial benefits to freed slaves, including the legal ability to own property, testify in court, and the guarantee that their children would not be slaves by birth.[36] Since verse 24:33 naturally reads as a command, it could have been revolutionary, giving all slaves "with any good in them" a route to freedom upon request. But while a few commentators "understood this as a requirement for owners," the "vast majority of Muslim scholars saw it only as a recommendation."[37] The recommendation, furthermore, was qualified according to the condition mentioned in the Qur'anic text ("if you know of any good in them"). Jonathan Brown writes that this condition was most commonly interpreted as referring to "the slaves having the capacity to earn a living once they were freed," and it seems to have applied primarily or even exclusively to Muslim slaves. Brown continues:

Ibn Qudama [d. 1223] wrote that, 'What is recommended is manumitting those who are religious and have the capacity to earn a living and would thus benefit from manumission.' ... In addition, if the owner felt that it was likely that the freed slave would return to non-Muslim lands (*dar al-harb*), apostatize from Islam or do some other harm, then it was disliked (*makruh*) to free the person. And if any of these was very probable ... then it was prohibited.[38]

---

[35] R. Brunschvig, "'Abd," in P. Bearman, Th. Bianquis, C. E. Bosworth, E. van Donzel, and W. P. Heinrichs (eds.), *Encyclopaedia of Islam, Second Edition* (Brill, 2012): dx.doi.org/10.1163/1573-3912_islam_COM_0003. Something similar was true in Roman and Germanic contexts: Manumitted slaves were often placed under obedience to their former masters, and the descendants of the manumitted slave might remain subordinated in various ways to the successor of the master for generations (see Marc Bloch, "How and why ancient slavery came to an end," in *Slavery and Serfdom in the Middle Ages*, trans. William R. Beer [Berkeley: University of California Press, 1975], 1–31, 16–17). In Byzantium, the laws of Justinian may have provided more independence to the freedman. See Rosemary Morris, "Emancipation in Byzantium: Roman law in a medieval society," in M. L. Bush (ed.), *Serfdom and Slavery: Studies in Legal Bondage* (London and New York: Longman, 1996), 130–143, 135–136.

[36] See Brunschvig, "'Abd," sections 3(j) and 3(k).   [37] Brown, *Slavery & Islam*, 87.

[38] Brown, *Slavery & Islam*, 181.

Despite these caveats, it should be noted that no similar prescription is found in any other major religious Scripture, and the *mukataba* contracts (as they came to be known) recommended in 24:33 contributed to the relatively high frequency of manumission among Muslim slaveholders.

From its beginning, Islam has required mandatory charitable giving – the *Zakat* or alms-tax. Free Muslims are generally required to contribute 2.5 percent of their capital wealth once per year.[39] The use of these funds is specified in the Qur'an, which lists eight classes of persons who are permitted to benefit from distribution of *Zakat*:

The charitable offerings are only for the poor, and the indigent, and those working with them, and those whose hearts are [to be] reconciled, and for [ransoming] slaves and for debtors, and in the way of God, and for the traveler: a duty from God. (9:60)

Distribution of mandatory alms for slaves was typically directed to those slaves working to pay off *mukataba* contracts, allowing them to attain freedom sooner than they otherwise could have on their own.[40] So the institution and distribution of the alms-tax facilitated manumission.

Lastly, with respect to Muslim slaves in particular, Islam exhorts believers with the highest incentive of all: reward in the afterlife. Thus Muhammad is reported to have said:

Whoever frees a Muslim slave, Allah will save all the parts of his body from the Fire as he has freed the body-parts of the slave.[41]

Any man who frees a Muslim man, [that freed slave] will be his freedom from the Fire. And any woman who frees a Muslim woman, she will be her freedom from the Fire.[42]

Turning now to other religions: According to Nandadeva Wijesekera, in early medieval Buddhist Sri Lanka, freeing a slave was considered "an act conducive to great merit for oneself as well as for all others."[43] Lev 25:47–55 encourages Jews to redeem fellow Jews who have sold themselves into slavery. The Babylonian Talmud (c. 500 AD) designates the ransoming of captives as a religious duty for which public funds can be used.[44] According to Maimonides' interpretation, the enslaved person's relatives are obligated

---

[39] Freamon, *Possessed by the Right Hand*, 154 and 135–136.

[40] Brown, *Slavery & Islam*, 70 and 358 n.7.

[41] *Sahih al-Bukhari* 2517, translation from: sunnah.com/bukhari/49.

[42] *Sunan Abi Dawud*, translation from Brown, *Slavery & Islam*, 72.

[43] Nandadeva Wijesekera, "Slavery in Sri Lanka: Presidential address delivered on 20-12-74," *Journal of the Sri Lanka Branch of the Royal Asiatic Society*, 18 (1974), 1–22, 11.

[44] *The Talmud of Babylonia* (Baba Batra 1.3; Neusner, ed. 22A:8), cited by Youval Rotman, *Byzantine Slavery and the Mediterranean World* (Cambridge, MA: Harvard University Press, 2009), 216 n.40.

to redeem him "so that he will not become assimilated among the gentiles."
If they do not do so, the obligation to redeem then falls on "every Jew."[45] This
view did not remain in the realm of theory: There is evidence of Jews pooling
their resources to redeem large numbers of their coreligionists from slavery in
the Mediterranean world of antiquity and the Middle Ages.[46]

Among Christians we also find practical efforts aimed at the redemption of coreligionists, as well as the idea that manumission of one's own
slaves is a meritorious act. An example of the latter is found in a writ of
manumission authored by Pope Gregory the Great (r. 590–604 AD), in
which Gregory formally frees two slaves belonging to the Roman Church:

Our Redeemer, the source of all creation, was willing to assume human flesh to
save us for this end, that by the grace of his divinity, breaking the bond of
servitude with which we were held captive, he might restore us to our previous
freedom. And so, it is a salutary act if human beings, whom nature first bore as
free men, but whom the law of nations has subjected to the yoke of slavery, should
be restored to that freedom in which they were born through the gift of manumission. Therefore, moved by regard for piety and through consideration of this
matter, from this day we hereby free you, Montana and Thomas, servants of the
Holy Roman Church, which we serve with God's authority, and we hereby make
you Roman citizens and release to you all of your property [*peculium*].[47]

This perspective appears to have been widespread in the Western Church;
in his influential work of Church Law, the *Decretum*, the medieval jurist
Gratian reproduced this passage from Gregory, and other medieval canonists include formulas of manumission expressing the idea that God will
reward those who free their slaves.[48]

A few early Christian theologians took a yet stronger stance. Thus
Chrysostom, arguing in a homily that those with several slaves should free
them:

For why hast thou many servants? Since as in our apparel we ought to follow our
need only, and in our table, so also in our servants. What need is there then? None
at all. For, in fact, one master need only employ one servant; or rather two or three
masters one servant ... For God hath made men sufficient to minister unto

---

45 Maimonides, *Mishneh Torah*, book 12 (The Law of Slaves), 2.7. See also 1.4.
46 See David Brion Davis, *Slavery and Human Progress* (Oxford: Oxford University Press,
   1984), 85–86, and Rotman, *Byzantine Slavery*, 44–45 and 51–52.
47 Gregory the Great, *Epistle* 6.12 (Sept. 595 AD), in John R. C. Martyn (trans. and ed.),
   The Letters of Gregory the Great, vol. 2 (Toronto: Pontifical Institute of Mediaeval
   Studies, 2004), 410–411.
48 Robert W. Carlyle and Alexander J. Carlyle, *A History of Mediaeval Political Theory in
   the West, Volume II: The Political Theory of the Roman Lawyers and the Canonists,
   from the Tenth Century to the Thirteenth Century* (New York: Barnes & Noble,
   1909–1936), 134–135.

themselves, or rather unto their neighbor also. . . . For to that end did God grant us both hands and feet, that we might not stand in need of servants. Since not at all for need's sake was the class of slaves introduced, else even along with Adam had a slave been formed; but it is the penalty of sin and the punishment of disobedience. But when Christ came, He put an end also to this. "For in Christ Jesus there is neither bond nor free." (Gal. iii. 28.) So that it is not necessary to have a slave: or if it be at all necessary, let it be about one only, or at the most two . . . But if thou collect many, thou dost it not for humanity's sake, but in self-indulgence. Since if it be in care for them, I bid thee occupy none of them in ministering to thyself, but when thou hast purchased them and hast taught them trades whereby to support themselves, let them go free. And I know that I am giving disgust to my hearers. But what must I do? For this I am set, and I shall not cease to say these things, whether any thing come of them or not.[49]

Formulas of manumission in tenth and eleventh-century Italy often referred to God's will: "It is the will of God that all men be free. . . . God created all men free and it was war that made them slaves."[50] Perhaps the most striking single example of theologically inspired manumission in medieval Christendom is provided by the people of Bologna, who in 1256 purchased every slave living within the diocese in order to free them. More than 6,000 slaves were thus manumitted in remembrance of God's redemption of the human race from "the bonds of the slavery by which we were held captive" and "in honor of our redeemer, Jesus Christ."[51] Chrysostom's strong exhortation to manumit and the mass emancipation of Bologna were, to be sure, the exception rather than the rule, but private manumissions in Christendom seem to have been fairly common, especially at the time of death. Speaking of Europe in the early Middle Ages, Chris Wickham writes that "The pious freed their unfree dependents very frequently, as we can see in countless wills and post-mortem donations, in particular in Gaul/Francia and Italy."[52]

Christians – laity and clerical, as individuals and as groups – also sometimes engaged in efforts to ransom fellow Christians who had been

[49] Chrysostom, *Homily on First Corinthians* XL.6, in Philip Schaff (ed.), *A Select Library of the Nicene and Post-Nicene Fathers of the Christian Church, Volume XII: Saint Chrysostom: Homilies on the Epistles of Paul to the Corinthians* (Grand Rapids, MI: Eerdmans, 1979).

[50] Rotman, *Byzantine Slavery*, 135 and 248 n.30.

[51] John T. Noonan, Jr., *A Church That Can and Cannot Change: The Development of Catholic Moral Teaching* (Notre Dame, IN: University of Notre Dame Press, 2005), 51, citing Francesco Gatta and Giuseppe Plessi (eds.) *Liber Paradisus* (Bologna, 1956), 5.

[52] Chris Wickham, *Framing the Early Middle Ages: Europe and the Mediterranean, 400–800* (Oxford: Oxford University Press, 2005), 564.

enslaved. There is evidence from the first through third centuries of the presence of public cash boxes in Christian churches (and synagogues as well) for the collection of funds used to free slaves.[53] As Bishop of Milan, Ambrose (r. 374–397) on at least one occasion melted down gold vessels belonging to the Church in order to ransom Christian captives.[54] The liquidation of Church property for the same purpose is attested in several other early Church leaders, including Cyril of Jerusalem, Chrysostom, Hilary of Arles, and others.[55] A law of Justinian authorized the Church to sell lands (lands that would otherwise have been inalienable) in order to use the money to ransom captives.[56] The collector of alms for the ransoming of slaves was a familiar figure in early modern Europe, and contributions to that cause were encouraged at every level of the Catholic Church:

Each year at Lent ... priests in the Catholic world were ordered by Rome to stress the need to give. In the larger cities, clerics especially skilled in sermonizing would give whole cycles of sermon cycles on successive Lenten Sundays, all of them hammering on the theme that parishioners should *Remember the Poor Slaves*.[57]

From the twelfth century through the sixteenth century (and likely continuing to some extent through the eighteenth century), Christian efforts to ransom fellow believers were widespread on the Iberian peninsula. In the context of frequent wars, raids, and piracy resulting in the capture of Christians by Muslims (and vice versa), Christian laity and clerics alike saw the giving of alms for the redemption of captives as an important work of mercy.[58] Catholic religious orders such as the Trinitarians (late twelfth century) and the Mercedarians (early thirteenth century) were

---

53 James Albert Harrill, *The Manumission of Slaves in Early Christianity* (Tubingen: Mohr-Sieback, 1995), chap. 4, cited in Rotman, *Byzantine Slavery*, 216 n.41.

54 Ambrose, *De officiis: Volume I, Introduction, Text, and Translation*, ed. and trans. Ivor J. Davidson (Oxford: Oxford University Press, 2001), 2.28.136–143, 343–345.

55 See Ambrose, *De officiis: Volume II, Commentary*, ed. and trans. by Ivor J. Davidson (Oxford: Oxford University Press, 2001), 789.

56 Rotman, *Byzantine Slavery*, 31. Cf. also 177.

57 Robert C. Davis, *Holy War and Human Bondage: Tales of Christian–Muslim Slavery in the Early-Modern Mediterranean* (Santa Barbara, CA: ABC CLIO, 2009), 263.

58 Thus James William Brodman, *Ransoming Captives in Crusader Spain: The Order of Merced on the Christian-Islamic Frontier* (Philadelphia: University of Pennsylvania Press, 1986), 10: "For those [captives] unable to afford the cost of redemption, twelfth-century society devised a second method, organized by the Church. This was accomplished by elevating ransoming from a work of civic importance to an act of religious charity that was meritorious in God's eyes." See also Davis, *Holy War and Human Bondage*, 52, 263–270.

established with an explicit focus on the work of redeeming captives held by Muslims. This work included both the gathering and distribution of alms, and journeys to Islamic territories to negotiate redemptions.

Historically, these exhortations to ransom or manumit slaves focused on coreligionists, with the most concern expressed for those within one's own religion who were enslaved by those of a different religion. When a slaveholder had a slave of a different religion, manumission was much less likely. Indeed, Maimonides held that it was "forbidden for a person to free a Canaanite [i.e. gentile] slave," and, as noted above, Muslim jurists sometimes prohibited the manumission of even a Muslim slave if the slave was likely to return to non-Muslim lands or apostatize from Islam.[59] *A fortiori*, we may assume, such jurists also prohibited the manumission of Christian slaves who were likely to return to non-Muslim lands. While this focus on the religious in-group is disappointing from today's vantage point, a case can be made that concern directed toward coreligionists played an important role in the eventual development of a broader anti-slavery sentiment in eighteenth and nineteenth centuries – a point to which we return in the next chapter.

3.3 AMELIORATING LEGISLATION

Beyond mere exhortations, legal requirements which aimed to ease the lives of slaves were also promoted by several major religions. Laws aren't always followed, needless to say, and even when the letter of the law is followed, the spirit might not be. Despite Islamic law's prohibition on castrating slaves, for example, Islamic societies imported significant numbers of eunuchs over the centuries, outsourcing the job of castration to non-Muslims. Still, laws do affect social practice and the ameliorating laws discussed below accomplished some good.

Hindu legal codes contained some regulations aimed at easing the lives of slaves. While *The Laws of Manu* allow the beating of a wife, son, pupil, younger brother, or slave "with a rope or a split bamboo ... on the back part of the body" if the individual had committed a fault, they also lay down a severe punishment for those who beat their dependents in any other way.[60] The Dharmasutra of Apastamba (likely from the third century BC or before) directs that, regarding the distribution of food, a

---

[59] Maimonides, *Mishneh Torah*, book 12 (The Law of Slaves), 9.6.
[60] *The Laws of Manu*, 8.299–300, 306.

man "may deprive himself, his wife, or his son, but never his slaves or workers ..."[61] And in the Arthashastra (c. 300 BC or later) we find a number of ameliorating regulations, for example: a slave cannot be given ritually unclean work; a female slave who is in debt bondage and is raped by one who has control over her work, is released from debt bondage and the master must pay a fine; selling a slave under eight years old in a foreign land carries a fine; and "when a child is begotten on a female slave by her master, both the child and its mother shall at once be recognised as free."[62] However in the case of the Arthashastra, the ameliorating regulations may have applied only to those held in debt bondage, and not to individuals held in more absolute forms of slavery that existed at the time.[63]

Hebrew Scripture lays down a few legal protections for Gentile slaves: A slaveowner who kills his slave is to be punished (Exod 21:20), and a slaveowner who destroys an eye or tooth of his slave must set him free (Exod 21:26–27). When a Gentile woman captured in war is taken as a wife or concubine, she cannot subsequently be sold (Deut 21:10–14). For Jewish slaves a right to a day of rest on the Sabbath is added to this list (Exod 20:10 and Deut 5:14), and this may have applied to Gentile slaves as well. (Exod 23:12 says that the alien is to be refreshed on the Sabbath.) While not a particularly expansive list, this was an improvement compared to the laws of early Rome and Babylon, which allowed a slaveowner the power of life and death over his slaves.[64] Surprisingly, Deuteronomy also commands that runaway slaves *not* be returned to their masters:

You shall not give up to his master a slave who as escaped from his master to you; he shall dwell with you, in your midst, in the place which he shall choose within one of your towns, where it pleases him best; you shall not oppress him. (Deut 23:15–16)

---

[61] *Dharmasutras: The Law Codes of Apastamba, Gautama, Baudhayana and Vasistha,* trans. Patrick Olivelle (Oxford: Oxford University Press, 1999), *Apastamba* 2.9.11, p. 52

[62] Kautilya, *Kautilya's Arthasastra,* trans. R. Shamasastry (Mysore: Mysore Printing and Publishing House, 1960), book 3, chap. 13, 206–208. Cf. book 4, chap. 12.

[63] Uma Chakravarti, "Of Dasas and Karmakaras: servile labour in ancient India," in Utsa Patnaik and Manjari Dingwaney (eds.), *Chains of Servitude: Bondage and Slavery in India* (Madras: Sangam Books, 1985), 35–75, 39–40, 50, and 61–62.

[64] On Rome, see Gaius, *Institutes* 1.52–3; William L. Westermann, *The Slave Systems of Greek and Roman Antiquity* (Philadelphia: The American Philosophical Society, 1955), 75–76; and Andrew T. Fede, *Homicide Justified: The Legality of Killing Slaves in the United States and the Atlantic World* (Athens, GA: University of George Press, 2017), 16. On Babylon, see Freamon, *Possessed by the Right Hand,* 48.

Whether this applies only to slaves fleeing to Israel from foreign nations or whether it also applied within Israel is unclear.[65]

Later scholars of the Torah filled in a number of details left vague or unmentioned in Scripture itself. On Maimonides' interpretation, Jewish law provided a number of ameliorating rules applying to Jewish slaves held by Jewish masters. Jewish slaves could not be put to excruciating labor, defined as "labor that has no limit, or labor that is unnecessary and … asked of the servant with the intent to give him work so that he will not remain idle."[66] They were to be given food, drink, clothing and living quarters equal in quality to what the master enjoyed. "On this basis," Maimonides adds, "our Sages said: 'Whoever purchases a Hebrew servant purchases a master for himself.'" And further: "A master must treat his [Jewish] servant with brotherly love."[67] The master must also provide sustenance for the Hebrew wife and children of his Hebrew slave, though he is not entitled to proceeds from the labor of the wife and children.[68] And as noted above, the Rambam interprets a text in Leviticus allowing for the redemption of Jews who have sold themselves to Gentiles as grounds for an obligation for Jews to redeem Jewish slaves of Gentiles.[69]

Christianity was the official religion of the Roman Empire from the fourth century, the Byzantine Empire could naturally be described as a Christian polity throughout its existence, and numerous European states of the Middle Ages were Christian states in some substantial sense. The legal codes of these states included laws that eased the lives of slaves, limiting for example the rights of owners to mutilate or kill slaves and prohibiting the prostitution of female slaves.[70] Still, from the fact that a particular law of a Christian state ameliorated slavery, it does not follow that that law was inspired by Christianity or had an origin in religious belief or practice. The ameliorating influence of Christianity is fairly clear

---

[65] Maimonides relates that Gentile slaves who have fled from the Diaspora to the Land of Israel should not be returned to their master, citing this passage (*Mishneh Torah*, book 12 [The Law of Slaves], 8.10–11).

[66] Maimonides, *Mishneh Torah*, book 12 (The Law of Slaves), 1.6.   [67] Ibid., 1.9.

[68] Ibid., 3.1–2.   [69] Ibid., 1.4 and 2.6–7.

[70] See Westermann, *Slave Systems*, 76, 114–115; Rotman, *Byzantine Slavery*, 139 and 169; Brown, *Slavery & Islam*, 361 n.50; *Novella Theodosia II* 18 in Clyde Pharr (trans. and ed.), *The Theodosian Code: And Novels and the Sirmondian Constitutions* (Princeton: Princeton University Press, 1952), 504; *Las Siete Partidas* 4.22.4 in *Las Siete Partidas, Volume 4: Family, Commerce, and the Sea: The Worlds of Women and Merchants*, trans. Samuel Parsons Scott, ed. by R. I. Burns, S. J. (Philadelphia: University of Pennsylvania Press, 2001).

in some cases, however. First, the Church tended to back up laws protecting slaves by adding its own ecclesiastical penalties to the contravention of those laws, and sometimes by assisting with enforcement.[71] Second, the Church's prohibition of labor on Sundays (explicitly noted as applying to slaves in the sixth-century Council of Macon) put pressure on slaveholders to exempt their slaves from labor on fifty-two days of the year, and there is record of several early medieval states repeating the prohibition in their own laws.[72] Third, Christianity had a positive effect on the legal recognition of and social respect accorded to slave marriages.[73] According to historian Ross Samson, "There is every reason to believe that the impact made by the Church in these areas [rest on the Sabbath and marriage] was sufficiently great that there was measurable effect on the nature of master-slave relations."[74] In classical Roman law, it was not possible for slaves to enter into a legally recognized marriage. Male and female slaves were often permitted to enter into long-term unions, but in early Rome slaves had little protection against being separated from their partners or children. Roman laws were inherited by the Byzantine Empire (which in its origin was simply the Eastern Roman Empire), and the Byzantine Emperor Justinian (r. 527–565 AD) did not alter the law that slaves could not marry. Yet "he also turned this law on its head, decreeing that anyone who had received the Christian sacrament of marriage was now legally free."[75] Justinian's policy that all those in Christian marriages were *ipso facto* free created a conflict between the Church's promotion of sacramental marriage and the interests of slaveholders. This conflict was addressed by the Byzantine Emperor Alexius I (r.1081–1118), who in the late eleventh century ruled that slaves could be married without ceasing to be slaves and rendered Christian marriage the sole legitimate conjugal union between two Christian slaves. The same legislation "obliged masters to consent to the Christian unions of their slaves: slaves to whom

---

[71] See Carlyle and Carlyle, *A History of Mediaeval Political Theory in the West, Volume II*, 129–131.

[72] Ross Samson, "The end of early medieval slavery," in A. J. Frantzen and D. Moffat (eds), *The Work of Work: Servitude, Slavery, and Labor in Medieval England* (Glasgow: Cruithne Press, 1994), 95–124, 114–115.

[73] On slave marriages, we draw on Westermann, *Slave Systems*, 81, 114 n.83, and 147; Rotman, *Byzantine Slavery*, 121, 141–144; and Carlyle and Carlyle, *A History of Mediaeval Political Theory in the West, Volume II*, 131–132.

[74] Samson, "The end of early medieval slavery," 115.

[75] Jeffrey Fynn-Paul, "Empire, monotheism and slavery in the greater Mediterranean region from antiquity to the early modern era," *Past & Present*, 205 (Nov 2009), 3–40, 20 n. 43.

Christian marriage was not granted would be freed."[76] Given Alexius I's legislation, Christian marriage was no route to freedom for Byzantine slaves, but marriage did afford some protection against being separated from one's spouse and children. Since Christian marriage was indissoluble, masters attempting to separate married slaves could face legal action.[77]

In Western Europe not long after, the Benedictine monk Gratian argued in the *Decretum*, his influential work of canon law, that slaves were eligible for sacramental marriage provided their masters gave consent. Writing in the early twelfth century, Gratian relied on earlier Church councils to provide support for this conclusion, which was at odds with Roman law. A generation later, Pope Adrian IV (r. 1154–1159) went an important step further, decreeing that marriages between slaves were valid even if their masters opposed the union.[78] We find Aquinas, writing a century after this, giving a philosophical justification of the position staked out by Adrian and Alexius:

[T]he positive law arises out of the natural law, and consequently slavery, which is of positive law, cannot be prejudicious to those things that are of natural law. Now just as nature seeks the preservation of the individual, so does it seek the preservation of the species by means of procreation; wherefore even as a slave is not so subject to his master as not to be at liberty to eat, sleep, and do such things as pertain to the needs of his body, and without which nature cannot be preserved, so he is not subject to him to the extent of being unable to marry freely, even without his master's knowledge or consent.[79]

Alfonso X, King of Castile (r. 1252–1284), enshrined the same position in his influential legal treatise *Las Siete Partidas*, which affirmed a slave's right to marry and prohibited the separation of married slaves:

Slaves can marry one another, and although their masters oppose it, the marriage will be valid ... where several men own two slaves, who were married, and it becomes necessary to sell them, it should be done in such a way that they can live together, and serve those who purchase them. They cannot be sold, one in one country and one in another, because they would have to live apart.

Where two slaves who are married [to each other] have two masters, one in one country and the other in another, and they are so far apart that where they serve their masters they cannot join one another and live together, the church can then compel one of the masters to buy the slave of the other. Where they are unwilling to do this, whichever one of them the church may select can be compelled to sell his slave to some man who is a resident of the town or community where the

---

[76] Rotman, *Byzantine Slavery*, 143–144. [77] See Rotman, *Byzantine Slavery*, 142.
[78] Noonan, *A Church That Can and Cannot Change*, 54–55.
[79] Thomas Aquinas, *Summa theologiae, Tertia pars supplementum* 52.2.

master of the other slave resides, and if no one wishes to buy him, the church should do so, in order that the husband and wife may not be separated.[80]

Called "the Blackstone of Latin America," *Las Siete Partidas* would go on to inform law throughout Central and South America. In the New World, slave marriage was accordingly protected in Catholic Latin America more than in Protestant North America.[81] To sum up, the recognition by Christians of the validity of slave marriage secured for many slaves within many Christian states both the right to marry and some protection against familial dissolution.

Fourth, Christianity played a role in securing a set of protections relating to the law of asylum (or sanctuary). The First Council of Orange (441), held in the Western Roman Empire, granted slaves the right to obtain refuge in a church. In the next century the First Council of Orleans (511), convened by Clovis I, King of the Franks, makes clear a key qualification: If the master swore an oath not to harm the slave, the slave was to be given up.[82] The Church thus seems to have played a role in mediating between masters and slaves in certain extreme cases.[83] A more significant protection for slaves appears to have been afforded by Justinian, who – breaking with Church precedent – gave a slave the right to join a monastery or enter the clergy against the will of his or her master, provided that the slave had not harmed the master other than by flight. It is not clear how long this law had effect, but for some time at least the power of the state and the Church joined to provide at least one possible means by which a slave might escape an untenable situation.[84]

[80] *Las Siete Partidas*, 4th partida, title 5, laws 1–2, in *Las Siete Partidas*, trans. Samuel Parsons Scott, 901–902.

[81] Auping, *Religion and Social Justice*, 13–14.

[82] See Geoffrey Nathan, *The Family in Late Antiquity: The Rise of Christianity and the Endurance of Tradition* (London: Routledge, 2000), 174–175; and Charles Joseph Hefele, *A History of the Councils of the Church, From the Original Documents*, vol. 3 (Edinburgh: T & T Clark, 1883) and vol. 4 (Edinburgh, T & T Clark, 1895). See *Codex Theodosianus* 9.45.5 in Pharr, *The Theodosian Code*, 266.

[83] A letter of Pope Gregory the Great in the late sixth century provides an example (Epistle III.1). For more on rights of asylum, see Carlyle and Carlyle, *A History of Mediaeval Political Theory in the West, Volume II*, 132–134, and Samson, "The end of early medieval slavery", 115–117.

[84] See Rotman, *Byzantine Slavery*, 144–146 and 151 (citing *Novellae Justinian* 5.2, 123.17 and 123.35), but also Morris, "Emancipation in Byzantium: Roman law in a medieval society," 138. The import and duration of Justinian's laws on this point are controverted. A reading of Rotman suggests that Byzantine law allowed slaves to join monasteries without their masters' consent from Justinian until Leo VI (for more than three centuries), whereas Morris interprets the Novels of Justinian differently, taking *Novella Justinian*

Islamic law developed extensive guarantees to protect slaves and further their welfare. These laws varied over time and place, but speaking generally and for the most part:[85] *Shari'a* law prohibited killing, castrating, or otherwise seriously injuring a slave. A master who punished his slave in a way that left lasting scars was to be compelled to free the slave.[86] Slaveholders were required to feed, house, and cloth their slaves "according to established local conventions of humane treatment," including slaves who were sick, debilitated or elderly. Muslim slaves had the right to perform required daily prayers, and a Muslim master was not to compel his non-Muslim slave to convert. Muslim masters also had to allow their *dhimmi* slaves to fulfill their religious obligations. (A *dhimmi* is a member of a conquered non-Muslim group, typically Jews or Christians but sometimes Zoroastrians, Hindus or others, living under Muslim rule and assigned certain rights and duties by Islamic law.) Masters were required to arrange a marriage for a slave who requested it (male or female), and according to three of the four main Sunni schools of law, masters could not force male slaves to marry or divorce. Masters "could not prevent a slave woman who was married from being with her husband at night," and slave mothers and their young children (till about the age of seven) could not be separated.[87] A conditional sentence near the end of Qur'an 24:33 ("compel not your female slaves into prostitution if they desire to be chaste") may have given rise to an unconditional prohibition of the hiring out of slaves as prostitutes. The Qur'an also specifies the freeing of a Muslim slave as the preferred means of expiation for the unintentional or unwitting killing of a Muslim, for the killing of a *dhimmi*, and for men who put away their wives but then wish to take

123 (promulgated 546 AD) to overrule *Novella Justinian* 5 (535 AD), so that consent of the master was required from 546 AD.

[85] The following list of legal protections for slaves is a partial selection from a longer discussion of the rights of slaves in *shari'a* law in Brown, *Slavery & Islam*, 93–98. Quotations are from 98 and 95, respectively.

[86] The command to free abused slaves is attributed to Muhammad: "We were staying in the house of Suwaid b. Muqarrin. There was among us an old man who was hot-tempered. He had a slave-girl with him. He gave a slap on her face. I never saw Suwaid more angry than on that day. He said: there is no alternative for you except to free her. I was the seventh child in order of Muqarrin and we had only a female servant. The youngest of us gave a slap on her face. The prophet (May peace be upon him) commanded us to set her free." [*Sunan Abi Dawud* 5166, translation from: https://sunnah.com/abudawud/43/394.]

[87] The figure of seven years is from Brunschvig, "'Abd," section 3(a).

them back (4:92, 58:3).[88] Freeing a slave is listed as one possible means of expiation for the breaking of a sworn oath (5:89). According to the commentator al-Qurtubi (1214–1272), if the guilty party does not own any slaves, he or she may make expiation by paying for the freeing of another's slave.[89]

A comparison with non-Islamic societies proximate in time and space to the Abode of Islam reveals that some of the *shari'a*'s ameliorating laws were distinctive while others were fairly commonplace. Early Roman law allowed masters to kill their slaves, but by the time of Hadrian (r. 117–138 AD) the power of execution was reserved to the courts.[90] Later Roman law also gave slaves a right to "demand sale out of the possession of an abusive master."[91] Castration of slaves for sale as eunuchs was prohibited by Domitian (r. 81–96 AD); the prohibition was extended by Hadrian to outlaw both voluntary and involuntary castration of slave and free.[92] Islamic law was more favorable to slave marriage than Roman law, which barred slaves from true legal marriages.[93]

Of Islam's ameliorating laws, perhaps the most significant from a broad sociological point of view were those regarding enslaved concubines who gave birth to their master's child. The taking by military victors of women of vanquished groups, for sexual use, has been common throughout recorded history.[94] As noted in the previous chapter, Muslims engaged in this practice; indeed, according to traditional interpretations based on the example of Muhammad, Islamic law specifically authorizes it.[95] But starting from the time of the second Caliph, 'Umar (r. 632–634), Islamic law also imposed a set of requirements on owners of enslaved concubines: If a free man fathered a child with his female slave, the slave attained the status of *umm al-walad* (mother of the child). Once possessed of this status, the woman could not be sold or separated from

[88] According to traditional commentators the killing itself need not be unintentional, the case envisaged is rather one in which a Muslim kills someone intentionally, not knowing that he or she is in fact a Muslim. See *The Study Quran*, commentary on 4:92, 234. Regarding the killing of a *dhimmi*, it is not clear to us whether the killing need be unintentional for the punishment to be compensation to the family and manumission of a believing slave, or whether 4:92 sets this as the punishment for both intentional and unintentional killing of a *dhimmi*.

[89] As cited in *The Study Quran*, commentary on 58:3, 1343.

[90] Westermann, *Slave Systems*, 75–76, 114–115.   [91] Ibid., 108.   [92] Ibid., 114.

[93] Ibid., 81.

[94] To cite just one example, Deut 21:10–14 allows the taking of a captive woman as a wife.

[95] See Section 2.5, and Freamon, *Possessed by the Right Hand*, 136 and 142–143.

her child and she was to be freed upon the death of her owner. The child was free from birth and the legal equal of any other of the man's children. Though there are earlier precedents of this policy in ancient Mesopotamia, the Sasanian (Neo-Persian) Empire and the Mauryan Empire (India), ancient Roman law had it that the child of a male slave-owner and his female slave would be a slave and illegitimate.[96] As historian and legal scholar Bernard Freamon explains:

[Islamic law on this point] had a tremendous impact on the nature of the society and the relations between enslaved and free, especially those who were products of such relationships. It also affected prevailing attitudes toward slavery. The child of such a union might rise to become head of the family, head of the community, or even caliph. It is said that 34 of the 37 caliphs of the Abassid Caliphate were the products of such unions.[97]

The *umm al-walad* regulations had the consequence that the children of enslaved concubines and their masters became incorporated into free society, in stark contrast to the situation, for example, of the children of Black female slaves and White slaveholders in the New World. But while these regulations severed the hereditary transmission of enslaved status for one important category of slaves, they also had a dark side – as did the relatively high rate of manumission in Islamic societies in general. If many slaves were freed but demand for slaves remained high, new slaves would have to found. Demand for slaves did remain high in Islamic societies, and since Islamic law ruled out the enslaving of free Muslims, these new slaves had to come from outside Islamic society. Thus, in the words of historian Robert Brunschvig, "slavery could scarcely continue to exist in Islam without the constantly renewed contribution of peripheral or external elements, either directly captured in war or imported commercially, under the fiction of the Holy War, from foreign territory."[98] Alongside Islam's

---

[96] On precedents in ancient Mesopotamia, see Daniel C. Snell, "Slavery in the ancient Near East," in K. Bradley and P. Cartledge (eds.), *The Cambridge World History of Slavery: Volume 1, The Ancient Mediterranean World* (Cambridge, Cambridge University Press, 2011), 4–21, 10, and Freamon, *Possessed by the Right Hand*, 33, 157–158. According to Sasanian law (at least early Sasanian law), the child of a slave mother and a free father was free. Cf. Freamon, *Possessed by the Right Hand*, 76, citing M. Macuch, "Barda and Bardadari, ii, in the Sasanian period," in E. Yar-shater (ed.), *Encyclopedia Iranica* (London and New York: Routledge & Kegan Paul, 1989), 3:764. On India, see Kautilya, *Kautilya's Arthasastra*, book 3, chap. 13, 207. On Roman law, see Brown, *Slavery & Islam*, 81.
[97] Freamon, *Possessed by the Right Hand*, 157.
[98] Brunschvig, "'Abd," section 3(a). See also Seymour Drescher, *Abolition: A History of Slavery and Antislavery* (Cambridge: Cambridge University Press, 2009), 7.

comparatively extensive collection of ameliorating practices and laws, a vigorous slave trade flowed into many Islamic societies through the nineteenth century.[99]

3.4 EQUALITY BEFORE GOD

Although human beings have a natural inclination to altruistic behavior, we are drawn to helping those within our own social group. In the words of psychologist Paul Bloom, "We are constituted to favor our friends and family over strangers, to care more about members of our own group than people from different, perhaps opposing groups."[100] This preference for "in-group" members seems to be a default state:

Adults who live in small-scale societies respond to strangers with hatred and disgust, and toddlers get highly anxious when they encounter strangers; they experience fear, not fondness. And while we do see all sorts of spontaneous kindness by babies and young children – soothing, sharing, helping, and the like – these are directed toward family and friends.[101]

There is also some evidence that humans are inclined to think of the out-group as deficient in uniquely human emotions (such as envy and regret) and uniquely human attributes (such as rationality, civility, and moral sensibility), and therefore to think of out-group members as less than fully human.[102] But this tendency to "parochial altruism" and a natural capacity for dehumanization need not imply any sort of biological determinism. As Bloom goes on to note, "many adults transcend our initial indifference toward strangers … But this is because of how we were

99 B. W. Higman, "Demographic trends," in David Eltis, Stanley Engerman, Seymour Drescher, and David Richardson (eds), *The Cambridge World History of Slavery: Volume 4, AD 1804–AD 2016* (Cambridge: Cambridge University Press, 2017), 20–48, 34–35; David Northrup, "Overseas movements of slaves and indentured workers," in D. Eltis, S. Engerman, S. Drescher, and D. Richardson (eds.), *The Cambridge World History of Slavery: Volume 4, AD 1804–AD 2016*, 49–70, 50–54.

100 Paul Bloom, *Against Empathy: The Case for Rational Compassion* (New York: Ecco, 2016), 94.

101 Paul Bloom, *Just Babies: The Origins of Good and Evil* (New York: Crown Publishers, 2013), 178–179.

102 Jacque-Philippe Leyens, Paola M. Paladino, Ramon Rodriquez-Torres et al., "The emotional side of prejudice: the attribution of secondary emotions to ingroups and outgroups," *Personality and Social Psychology Review*, 4 (2000), 186–197; Nick Haslam, "Dehumanization: an integrative review," *Personality and Social Psychology Review*, 10 (2006), 252–264; and David Livingstone Smith, *Less Than Human: Why We Demean, Enslave, and Exterminate Others* (New York: Macmillan, 2011).

raised and the societies in which we live; we did not start off that way."[103] It was culture, more than nature, that enabled Jefferson and the other signatories of the Declaration of Independence to consider it self-evident that "all men are created equal." While this conclusion was absurdly underapplied (Jefferson himself was a slaveholder), it was nonetheless a cultural achievement. Ancient Greek and Roman societies, for example, tended to hold that an unequal social hierarchy is reasonable and to be expected, with Greeks/Romans superior to foreigners, men superior to women, and free people superior to slaves. Political philosopher Larry Siedentop finds "the assumption of natural inequality" at "the core of ancient thinking":

Whether in the domestic sphere, in public life or when contemplating the cosmos, Greeks and Romans did not see anything like a level playing field. Rather, they instinctively saw a hierarchy or pyramid. Different levels of social status reflected inherent differences of being. The paterfamilias, priest or citizen did not have to win or justify his status. His superior status reflected his 'nature'.[104]

And the historian Moses Finley reports that it was commonplace "in Roman Republican speeches that Jews, Syrians, Lydians, Medes, indeed all Asiatics, are 'born to slavery'."[105] Similarly, ancient Hindus accepted a divine origin of the four unequal social castes mentioned in the *Rig Veda*, and *The Laws of Manu* explicitly assert that the Creator produced the four castes and assigned them their roles:

[I]n order to protect this universe He, the most resplendent one, assigned separate (duties and) occupations to those who sprang from his mouth, arms, thighs, and feet. To Brahmanas he assigned teaching and studying (the Veda), sacrificing for their own benefit and for others, giving and accepting (of alms). The Kshatriya he commanded to protect the people, to bestow gifts, to offer sacrifices, to study (the Veda), and to abstain from attaching himself to sensual pleasures; The Vaisya to tend cattle, to bestow gifts, to offer sacrifices, to study (the Veda), to trade, to lend money, and to cultivate land. One occupation only the lord prescribed to the Sudra, to serve meekly even these (other) three castes.[106]

The Laws of Manu are clear in their assertion of a natural hierarchy, with Brahmans at the pinnacle, and "Whatever exists in the world is the

---

[103] Bloom, *Just Babies*, 179.
[104] Larry Siedentop, *Inventing the Individual: The Origins of Western Liberalism* (Cambridge, MA: Harvard University Press, 2014), 51.
[105] Moses Finley, *Ancient Slavery and Modern Ideology* (New York: Viking Press, 1980), 119.
[106] *The Laws of Manu*, 1.87–91, 24.

property of the Brahmana; on account of the excellence of his origin the Brahmana is, indeed, entitled to it all."[107]

Social inequality tended to increase with the transition from hunting and gathering to farming. Large proportions of the productive surplus made possible by advanced farming techniques were captured by elites, and, plausibly, various ideologies were developed in order to reinforce social stratification. Sociologists Patrick Nolan and Gerhard Lenski elaborate:

As this gulf widened [between literate, urban, governing elites and illiterate, rural peasants], members of the governing class found it increasingly difficult to recognize the ignorant, downtrodden peasants as fellow human beings. The scribes of ancient Egypt were fond of saying that the lower classes lacked intelligence and had to be driven like cattle, with a stick.[108]

A number of ancient societies, then, were characterized by a background assumption of natural human inequality. Christian doctrine offered a challenge to this assumption, emphasizing the unity of the human race in its origin, predicament, and goal. According to Christian teaching, all human beings alike are made in God's image (Gen 1:26), all are subject to sin and death (Rom 5:12), and all are called by God to relationship and eternal happiness (1 Tim 2:4, Matt 28:19). Moreover, among believers the importance of human divisions is to be overturned by a new shared identity as disciples of Jesus:

For as many of you as were baptized into Christ have put on Christ. There is neither Jew nor Greek, there is neither slave nor free, there is neither male nor female; for you are all one in Christ Jesus. (Gal 3:27–28)

This belief in the fundamental moral and spiritual equality of all Christians was expressed in their religious practice, as David Bentley Hart explains:

One of the reasons why [pagan] slaves had to form their own cultic societies is that they were not allowed to join those of their masters. The Christians, by contrast, admitted men and women, free and bound, to equal membership and obliged them to worship together. This was, in many ways, the most radical novelty of their community: that it transcended and so, in an ultimate sense, annulled "natural" human divisions.[109]

---

[107] *The Laws of Manu*, 1.99–100, 26. Cf. 1.96.

[108] Patrick Nolan and Gerhard Lenski, *Human Societies: An Introduction to Macrosociology*, 11th ed. (Boulder: Paradigm Publishers, 2011), 145–146.

[109] David Bentley Hart, *Atheist Delusions: The Christian Revolution and Its Fashionable Enemies* (New Haven: Yale University Press, 2009), 158. See Westermann, *Slave Systems*, 150–151.

According to Lactantius, writing in the early fourth century, the slaves of Christians were slaves in name only:

Someone will say, "Are there not some amongst you who are poor, and some rich, some slaves and some masters? Is there no distinction between individuals?" No, none; the only reason why we share the name of brother among us is our belief that we are equal. Since we measure all things human spiritually and not physically, even though our physical conditions differ, yet we have no slaves: we both name them and treat them as brothers in spirit and fellow slaves in worship.[110]

We suppose that Lactantius' idealized vision was not a reality for most Christian slaves of Christian masters, but his testimony does provide evidence that the doctrine of spiritual equality ameliorated the condition of Christian slaves in some cases.

Human equality under God was also explicitly referenced as a rationale for social practices and laws that ameliorated slavery. Burchard of Worms (c. 950–1025), a canon lawyer in the Holy Roman Empire, argues that since all have one Father (God) and one Mother (the Church), people of all social conditions should treat each other with kindness and mercy. Similarly, says Burchard, a free woman should be able to marry an enslaved man, since "we all have one father in heaven." According to Gratian and Ivo of Chartres, slave marriages are indissoluble because, as all have one Father, there is one law for all people, slave and free, when it comes to matters relating to God.[111] Centuries later George Fox (1624–1691), a leading personality in the first generation of Quakers, exhorted a group of Christian slaveholders in Barbados to instruct their Black slaves in Christianity and manumit those who had served faithfully after a considerable term of service, on the grounds of their equality before God:

And therefore now you should preach Christ to your Ethyopians that are in your Families, that so they may be free Men indeed, and be tender of and to them, and walk in Love, that ye may answer that of God in their Hearts, being (as the Scripture affirms) all of one Blood & of one Mold … for Christ (I say) shed his Blood for them, as well as for you, and tasted Death for them, as well as for you, and hath enlightened them, as well as he hath enlightened you …[112]

---

[110] Lactantius, *Divine Institutes*, trans. Anthony Bowen and Peter Garnsey (Liverpool: Liverpool University Press, 2003), 5.15.1, 311.

[111] *Decretum Burchardi* 15.32, 9.27; *Decretum* of Ivo, 8.156; *Decretum Gratiani* 29.2.1, in Carlyle and Carlyle, *A History of Mediaeval Political Theory in the West, Volume II*, 118.

[112] George Fox, "Gospel family-order," 14, reprinted in J. William Frost (ed.), *The Quaker Origins of Antislavery* (Norwood, PA: Norwood Editions, 1980), 35–55, 47. For the recommendation of manumission after a term of service, see 49.

Similarly, writing in the 1660s, the Puritan Richard Baxter addressed "those Masters in foraign Plantations who have Negro's and other Slaves," counseling them to

remember that God is their reconciled tender Father ... And therefore you must use the meanest of them no otherwise, than beseemeth the beloved of God to be used; and no otherwise than may stand with the due signification of your Love to God by Loving those that are his.[113]

Judaism, too, was committed to the idea that all human beings are made in the image of God (Gen 1:26). And Islam emphasized the unity of the human race and deemphasized the importance of worldly status and ethnic identity as a measure of one's worth. An important Qur'anic verse insists that the ultimate measure of one's value is the extent of one's reverence for God:

O mankind! Truly We created you from a male and a female, and We made you peoples and tribes that you may come to know one another. Surely the most noble of you before God are the most reverent of you. (49:13, see also 18:32–46)

As compared to slaveholders lacking beliefs in the fundamental spiritual equality of all human beings and their shared eternal destiny, Jewish, Christian, and Muslim slaveholders thus had an additional reason to treat their slaves well – both slaves and masters were of importance to God and each should regard the other as brothers. And compared to slaves lacking such beliefs, Jewish, Christian, and Muslim slaves had an additional reason to recognize their own human dignity and experience hope for a blessed afterlife.

But did such beliefs impact the actual behavior of slaveholders? Did such beliefs impact the lived experience of slaves? It is difficult to know. Old habits die hard, and the powerful, even when well intentioned, are reluctant to cede their privileges. One may also question the extent to which abstract beliefs in dignity and salvation affected the day-to-day subjective experience of slaves. Still, it is likely that the numerous ameliorating exhortations and requirements present in Judaism, Christianity, and Islam and surveyed in this chapter were animated in part by these religions' commitment to the brotherhood and spiritual equality of all human beings.

---

[113] Richard Baxter, *A Christian Directory: Or, a sum of practical theology, and cases of conscience* (London: Thomas Parkhurst, 1673), book 2, chap. 14, tit. 2, 469.

4

Restricting Slavery

It is unclear how rare or extensive slavery was in the distant past. But by the time of the domestication of plants and animals roughly 10,000 years ago and the resulting transition to larger units of social organization, slaveholding had become common practice. Using data on hundreds of preindustrial societies, sociologists Patrick Nolan and Gerhard Lenski estimate that 45 percent of agrarian societies had slavery. For advanced horticultural societies, their figure is 83 percent.[1] Slaves were easy to find in ancient Mesopotamia, Greece, Rome, India, Egypt, and China, in precolonial Africa and Southeast Asia, and in many parts of the Americas prior to the coming of Europeans.[2] Against this backdrop, Western Europe in the High Middle Ages stands out as an anomaly. As historian Jeffrey Fynn-Paul notes, "The absence of any large-scale slave-holding system in high medieval Europe is almost unique in the

[1] Nolan and Lenski, *Human Societies*, 126. A society was classified as "advanced horticultural" if agriculture was the dominant mode of subsistence, metals were present, but the plow was absent. A society was classified as "agrarian" if agriculture was the dominant mode of subsistence, and metals and the plow were present. See also Jack Goody, "Slavery in time and space," in J. Watson (ed.), *Asian and African Systems of Slavery* (Berkeley: University of California Press, 1980), 16–42, especially 25–26. Some historians believe slavery was even more prevalent than Nolan and Lenski's figures suggest. Thus Jeffrey Fynn-Paul: "Slavery was an integral feature of almost every ancient society of Europe, Africa, and Asia" ["Empire, monotheism and slavery," 7].

[2] James L. Watson (ed.), *Asian & African Systems of Slavery* (Berkeley: University of California Press, 1980); Cameron, *Captives: How Stolen People Changed the World*, chap. 1; Richard Hellie, "Slavery," *Encyclopedia Britannica*, Aug. 17, 2020: www.britannica.com/topic/slavery-sociology.

history of civilization."[3] With some exceptions in border regions, Latin Europe was largely slave-free from around 1000 till the second wave of plague in 1363, when the resulting labor shortage spurred a small-scale revival in slaveholding.[4] Yet even this revival was limited to southern Europe, where it "did not move too far beyond the circles of wealthier households in international trading centres."[5] Historian David Eltis goes so far as to suggest that in light of the virtual absence of full chattel slavery in northern and northwestern Europe since the Middle Ages, perhaps the beginnings of abolition should be seen not after 1750 "but in the failure to revive serfdom or even slavery [in those regions] during the late-fourteenth-century labor shortages following the Black Death."[6] Why did slavery fade away in medieval Latin Europe, and remain virtually absent in northwestern Europe thereafter? The Roman Empire was a slave society through and through, and the Celts and Vikings and other early Europeans held slaves. So why did large portions of Europe break with global patterns and their own past? Adam Smith (c. 1723–1790) remarks in *The Wealth of Nations* that the "time and manner ... in which so important a revolution was brought about, is one of the most obscure points in modern history."[7] Scholarship since Smith's time has shed light on what was once obscure, indicating that the religious restriction of slavery was one important factor in medieval Europe's transition away from slavery – as we shall discuss below.

At numerous points in history, religious groups and religiously inspired individuals have attempted to restrict slavery without also aiming for total abolition. We use the phrase "restricting slavery" to mean reducing the scope of slavery by making it more difficult to turn a free person into a

[3] Fynn-Paul, "Empire, monotheism and slavery," 13 and 31–34.

[4] Fynn-Paul, "Empire, monotheism and slavery," 31. The mainstream view among historians appears to be that slavery had died out in northern and northwestern Europe by the eleventh century, but some recent scholars have found evidence of the persistence of slavery into the thirteenth century in what is now southern Germany and Austria. (See Samuel S. Sutherland, "The study of slavery in the early and central Middle Ages: Old problems and new approaches," *History Compass*, 18:11 [2020], 6.) Our arguments relating to the decline of slavery in Europe rely principally on the uncontroversial claim that by the end of the medieval period, slavery in northern and northwestern Europe was very rare.

[5] Fynn-Paul, "Empire, monotheism and slavery," 34. See also Eltis and Engerman, "Dependence, servility, and coerced labor in time and space," 19.

[6] David Eltis, *The Rise of African Slavery in the Americas* (Cambridge: Cambridge University Press, 2000), 6–7.

[7] Adam Smith, *An Inquiry into the Nature and Causes of the Wealth of Nations* (New York: The Modern Library, 1937), book 3, chap. 2, 367.

slave or to designate a newly born person as a slave at birth, or by making it more difficult to sell or trade slaves, or by placing limits on who could hold a slave of a certain category, without at the same time intending to abolish or reject all slavery. Attempts to thus restrict slavery have occurred in at least three forms: (i) attempts to prohibit or limit a particular pathway into slavery or to limit slavetrading, (ii) efforts to remove certain classes of people from the category of the "legitimately enslavable," and (iii) attempts to restrict who may hold slaves. An example of the first category is the Christian theologian John Duns Scotus' (1266–1308) rejection of the traditional position that capture of the defeated in war provides the victor with just title to slavery. An example of the second is the Muslim prohibition of enslaving another Muslim (i.e. making a formerly free Muslim into a slave), which does not merely involve closing off this or that particular route into slavery or limit slavetrading in some way, but altogether removes free people of a certain category from being "legitimately" reduced to slavery at all. Examples of the third are the Byzantine law of Justinian that Jews and pagans could not hold Christians as slaves and the similar Islamic law that non-Muslims could not hold Muslims as slaves.

In what follows we examine Jewish, Christian, and Muslim restrictions on slavery, and tell the story of how Muslim and Christian restrictions on enslaving members of their own religion conjoined with economic factors to lead to the absence of large-scale slaveholding in high medieval Europe.[8] We then turn to religiously informed criticism of enslavement

---

[8] We have found only a few examples of the religious restriction of slavery in Buddhism and Confucianism (though this may be due to our limitations as scholars): (1) In the *Anguttara Nikaya*, a discourse probably first committed to writing in the first century BC. but passed down orally long before, the Buddha includes slavetrading in a list of five types of forbidden work: "Mendicants, a lay follower should not engage in these five trades. What five? Trade in weapons, living creatures, meat, intoxicants, and poisons. A lay follower should not engage in these five trades." [*Numbered Discourses: A sensible translation of the Anguttara Nikaya*, v. 3, trans. Bhikkhu Sujato (Eastwood, Australia: SuttaCentral, 2018), 5.177, p. 201.] As for monks themselves, they were discouraged or perhaps forbidden from holding slaves as personal property, but communities of monks could and did accept gifts of slaves to contribute to the maintenance of the community. (See Gregory Schopen, "The monastic ownership of servants or slaves: local and legal factors in the redactional history of two *Vinayas*," *Journal of the International Association of Buddhist Studies*, 17:2 (1994), 145–74; and Kim, "Perception of monastic slaves by scholar-officials and monks in the Late Koryo and early Choson periods.") (2) It is sometimes said that the slave trade was prohibited by Ashoka, the devout Buddhist ruler of the Mauryan Empire (third century BC), but this appears to be an error. The assertion is made by Clarence-Smith, *Islam and the Abolition of Slavery*, 230. But neither the sources cited by Clarence-Smith nor the Rock Edicts of Ashoka, nor an important monograph on

in the New World through the close of the seventeenth century. Discussion of eighteenth- and nineteenth-century Anglo American attacks on the slave trade by Christian abolitionists is deferred until the next chapter, since such attacks were typically part of a larger strategy to reject slavery as such.

4.1 JUDAISM AND THE RELIGIOUS RESTRICTION OF SLAVERY

All three major monotheisms have, in at least some periods, discouraged the enslavement of their own. With respect to slavery, the Torah makes a firm distinction between Jews and Gentiles. Jews were permitted to buy "slaves from among the nations that are round about you" and hold them and their offspring as slaves in perpetuity (Lev 25:44–46), but the indefinite enslavement of Jews by Jews was largely prohibited by biblical law. In the case of a Jew being sold to another Jew, the term of servitude was limited to six years:

If your brother, a Hebrew man, or a Hebrew woman, is sold to you, he shall serve you six years, and in the seventh year you shall let him go free from you. And when you let him go free from you, you shall not let him go empty-handed; you shall furnish him liberally out of your flock, out of your threshing floor, and out of your wine press; as the Lord your God has blessed you, you shall give to him. You shall remember that you were a slave in the land of Egypt, and the Lord your God redeemed you; therefore I command you this today. (Deut 15:12–15. See also Exod 21:1–2)

The case envisioned in the text above appears to be one of involuntary slavery ("If your brother ... is sold to you"), whereas a separate passage envisions the case of voluntary self-sale on account of destitution:

And if your brother becomes poor beside you, and sells himself to you, you shall not make him serve as a slave: he shall be with you as a hired servant and as a sojourner. He shall serve with you until the year of the jubilee; then he shall go out from you, he and his children with him, and go back to his family, and return to

---

Ashoka, reveal any such claim, so far as we can determine. Cf. *The Edicts of Asoka* and Romila Thapar, *Asoka and the Decline of the Mauryas* (London: Oxford University Press, 1961). (3) In his examination of slavery in Korea, James Palais notes that while "the moral message of neither Buddhism nor Confucianism served to eliminate slavery," there are nonetheless examples of Confucian scholars criticizing slavery. In the seventeenth century, Yu Hwongwon argued against Korea's system of hereditary slavery, praising instead the policy that only those guilty of serious crimes should be enslaved (a view he attributed to certain ancient Chinese sage kings). See Palais, *Confucian Statecraft and Korean Institutions*, 210, 217–219, and 232–237.

the possession of his fathers. For they are my servants, whom I brought forth out of the land of Egypt; they shall not be sold as slaves. You shall not rule over them with harshness, but shall fear your God. (Lev 25:39–43)

While the term of service is limited to six years in the case of involuntary slavery, no six-year limit is mentioned in the case of voluntary self-sale. Instead, release is to be granted in the year of the jubilee (every fiftieth year). Despite the longer possible duration of voluntary servitude, we still see an overarching concern that Jews not be held as slaves by Jews in the stipulation that the one who has sold himself be worked "as a hired servant" rather than "as a slave." It should also be noted that debt slavery among fellow Jews was discouraged by Lev 25:35–37, which directs the Israelites to maintain those Israelites among them who cannot maintain themselves due to poverty, and to refrain from attempting to profit at their expense via usury or inflated food prices. The passage allowing voluntary self-sale in cases of destitution thus appears to be intended to address an undesirable situation which was meant to have been avoided in the first place via charitable care for the poor.

The Torah did allow for a Jewish slave sold involuntarily to later opt for perpetual slavery to a Jewish master, a transition which was marked by a ceremonial ear-piercing:

But if he says to you, "I will not go out from you," because he loves you and your household, since he fares well with you, then you shall take an awl, and thrust it through his ear into the door, and he shall be your bondman forever. And to your bondwoman you shall do likewise. (Deut 15:16–17)

But as far as relations within Judaism were concerned, a Jew was never to be an involuntary slave for more than six years.

Although the Hebrew Bible attempted to restrict involuntary slavery for Jews, it is an open question how much this attempt affected actual practice. Jer 34:8–22 records a set of instances in which the command to free Hebrew servants after six years was widely ignored. In an examination of Jewish slavery in the Greco-Roman context between 500 BC and 500 AD, Catherine Hezser argues that "the seventh and Jubilee year rules were not commonly practiced."[9] Nonetheless, it should be noted that the Hebrew Bible *attempted* to restrict the enslavement of Jews by Jews, by attempting to limit the duration of involuntary slavery, by enjoining a less

---

[9] Catherine Hezser, "Slavery and the Jews," in K. Bradley and P. Cartledge (eds.), *The Cambridge World History of Slavery: Volume 1, The Ancient Mediterranean World* (Cambridge: Cambridge University Press, 2011), 438–455, 443.

severe type of servitude for voluntary slaves, and by prohibiting some pathways into slavery and restricting others. Study of the ancient world reveals at least eight pathways into slavery: capture in war, capture in slaveraiding or by kidnapping/manstealing, birth to a slave parent (typically a slave mother), enslavement as a judicial penalty for a crime, enslavement of self or family members for nonpayment of a debt, self-sale to avoid destitution, the sale of one's children or wife, and the raising of foundlings (often exposed infants) as slaves.[10] Of these, the Hebrew Bible clearly censures the practice of Jews enslaving fellow Jews captured in war (2 Chr 28:8–15) and punishes manstealing with death (Exod 21:16 and Deut 24:7). It also appears to limit the circumstances in which birth to a slave parent results in enslavement of the child (Exod 21:3–6 and Lev 25:41) and to limit enslavement as a judicial penalty to the case of thieves unable to make restitution (Exod 22:3). Regulations regarding the sale of daughters are given (Exod 21:7–11); the sale of sons is not mentioned.

The biblical laws discussed above are obscure on various points which subsequent generations attempted to clarify. In his influential compilation of Jewish law, Moses Maimonides fills in some detail: A Jewish court could sell a Jew into slavery to another Jew as punishment for theft (but only for that crime), and a Jew who was severely impoverished (owning nothing, not even clothing) could sell himself into slavery to another Jew.[11] The term of service for a Jew sold by a court was six years, but in cases of self-sale the term could be longer.[12] A Jewish court could not sell a Jew to a Gentile, nor could a Jew sell himself to a Gentile.[13] And as noted in the previous chapter, Jews were obliged to attempt to redeem Jewish slaves owned by Gentiles.[14] A father could not sell his daughter unless he owned nothing, and could not sell her after she reached twelve years of age and showed signs of physical maturity. She was to gain her freedom after six years of service or at the jubilee year, or when she showed signs of physical maturity, or at the death of her master, which-ever was sooner, unless she was designated as a wife for the master or his son, in which case she was released only through the death of her husband or a bill of divorce.[15]

[10] See Westermann, *Slave Systems*, 70, 84, 86, 135; Freamon, *Possessed by the Right Hand*, 155–156; Gardner, "Slavery and Roman law," 415.

[11] Maimonides, *Mishneh Torah*, book 12 (The Law of Slaves), 1.1 and 1.3.

[12] Ibid., 2.2 and 2.3.   [13] Ibid., 1.3 and 8.1, but see 3.12.   [14] Ibid., 1.4 and 2.6–7.

[15] Ibid., 4.1–7.

4.2 ISLAM AND THE RELIGIOUS RESTRICTION OF SLAVERY

From its beginnings, Islam attempted to restrict slavery – by removing free Muslims from the category of the legitimately enslaveable, by prohibiting non-Muslims from owning Muslim slaves, and by prohibiting or limiting certain common pathways into slavery. Unlike Christianity and Judaism, which for much of their histories did not prohibit a free Christian or free Jew from being made a slave by fellow coreligionists, the evidence indicates that Islam has, from very early on, deemed it unacceptable for a free Muslim to be reduced to slavery by another Muslim (or a Muslim state). Despite no clear source for this restriction in either the Qur'an or the Hadith, rulings dating to "within 15 years of the death of the Prophet" have led the *shari'a* to hold "that no Muslim could be lawfully enslaved."[16] This is not to say that Islamic law prohibited Muslims from holding other Muslims as slaves – a slave who converted to Islam could continue to be held as a slave, a Muslim could be born a slave at birth, and a Muslim slave could be purchased by a Muslim. But if free, a Muslim was in theory secure from any future enslavement by Muslims. This prohibition was sometimes thought not to apply to heretical Muslims deemed outside the fold of Islam (as, for example, some Shiite Muslims were viewed by some Sunnis), and warring Muslim sects would accordingly sometimes enslave each other.[17] Free Black African Muslims were also sometimes made slaves by Muslim states or captured in slave raids and sold as slaves in northern Africa, the Middle East or elsewhere.[18] But in the main, the content of Islamic law was clear, and was reiterated by Islamic jurists in contexts where it was often disregarded in practice.

Muslims enjoyed another immunity according to Islamic law: No Muslim could legitimately be held as a slave by a non-Muslim master. In the case of a Muslim slave held by a non-Muslim, the non-Muslim was to either free the slave or transfer him to a Muslim master.[19]

Consistently with the rule that free Muslims are unenslaveable, Islamic law restricted most pathways into slavery. By the ninth century the *shari'a*

---

[16] Freamon, *Possessed by the Right Hand*, 156; Brown, *Slavery & Islam*, 84 with n. 86 (364).

[17] Brown, *Slavery & Islam*, 304–307.

[18] Brunschvig, "'Abd"; Hunwick, "Islamic law and polemics over race and slavery."

[19] Brunschvig, "'Abd," section 3.b. There appears to have been a precedent in the Sasanian Empire: A slave who converted to Zoroastrianism and was owned by a non-Zoroastrian could become free after compensating the owner (cf. Freamon, *Possessed by the Right Hand*, 76).

did not allow Muslims to be made slaves as punishment for crime or for nonpayment of debt and prohibited Muslims from selling themselves or their children into slavery. Kidnapping, of course, was also prohibited.[20] Historian Robert Brunschvig reports that "on the whole" Muslim jurists "have come down on the side of regarding as free the foundling (*laḳiṭ*) whose origin remains unknown."[21] These restrictions stand in contrast to much historical precedent in many regions where Islam later became the dominant religion. Enslavement for crime was allowed in the legal codes of Sumer, Babylonia, the Achaemenid (First Persian) Empire, Israel (for theft), and Rome.[22] Enslavement for debt was allowed by the Sumerians, Babylonians, Aryans, Achaemenids, early Romans, and Sasanians (Neo-Persians).[23] Self-sale was legal among the Babylonians,[24] Romans,[25] early Byzantines,[26] and Jews.[27] Sale of children by parents or the seizure of children for nonpayment of debt was allowed in Babylonia (though the Code of Hammurabi places a limit of three years of service),[28] ancient

[20] Brown, *Slavery & Islam*, 82–83; Freamon, *Possessed by the Right Hand*, 155–156.

[21] Brunschvig, "'Abd," Encyclopedia of Islam, section 3a.

[22] Freamon, *Possessed by the Right Hand*, 32, 35, 36, 48, 66, citing Muhammad Dandamaev, "Slavery: Ancient Near East," in D. N. Freedman (ed.), *Anchor Bible Dictionary* (New York: Doubleday, 1992), 6:59; William E. Dunstan, *The Ancient Near East* (Fort Worth, TX: Harcourt Brace, 1998), 71 and 85; Muhammed Dandamaev and Vladimir G. Lukonin, *The Culture and Social Institutions of Ancient Iran* (Cambridge: Cambridge University Press, 1989), 156. For the Roman Republic and Roman Empire, see Westermann, *Slave Systems*, 81, 84, 94. For Israel, see Exodus 22. Regarding the Byzantine Empire, Freamon cites Rotman, *Byzantine Slavery*, 25 as evidence that the Byzantines allowed enslavement for crime. And indeed Rotman does seem to say this on 25–26, but Rotman also writes that "slavery as a penalty was abolished by Justinian" in 536, and implies that enslavement for crime was replaced by penal mutilation among the Byzantines (172–173). *Novella Justinian* 22.8 appears to abolish penal enslavement.

[23] Freamon, *Possessed by the Right Hand*, 32, 35, 36, 38, 48, 75 citing Dandamaev, "Slavery: Ancient Near East," 6:59; Dunstan, *Ancient Near East*, 71 and 85; Chanana, *Slavery in Ancient India*, 19; Dandamaev and Lukonin, *Ancient Iran*, 156; Macuch, "Barda and Bardadari." For the Roman Republic, see Westermann, *Slaves Systems of Greek and Roman Antiquity*, 70, 81. Westermann notes Livy's statement that debt slavery was abandoned in Rome in 326 BC. But it still occurred, apparently legally, in the Eastern provinces of the Roman Empire – cf Westermann, *Slave Systems*, 123.

[24] Freamon, *Possessed by the Right Hand*, 35.

[25] Maxwell, *Slavery and the Catholic Church*, 46 n.69.

[26] Self-sale was legal in Byzantium until the Novella of Leo VI (r. 886–912), which outlawed the practice [Rotman, *Byzantine Slavery*, 25 and 173–175].

[27] Lev 25:39 and 25:47.

[28] Freamon, *Possessed by the Right Hand*, 33, 35, 36, citing Isaac Mendelsohn, *Slavery in the Ancient Near East: A Comparative Study of Slavery in Babylonia, Assyria, Syria and Palestine from the Middle of the Third millennium to the End of the First Millennium*

Israel (daughters),[29] the Achaemenid Empire,[30] the Roman Empire at some times,[31] and the Sasanian Empire.[32] In the early Roman Empire the enslavement of foundlings was permitted absent proof of free status of the child, but by 529 AD Justinian decreed that all abandoned male children were to have free status.[33] Islamic law's ban on enslavement (of Muslims) for crime, debt, by self-sale, and by the sale of one's minor children also stands in contrast to the laws of many contemporaneous societies, including early medieval Western Europe, in which it appears to have been legal for Christians to enslave other Christians in each of these four ways.[34]

Islamic law's restrictions regarding penal slavery, debt slavery, self-sale and sale of children were thus importantly different than many preexisting and contemporaneous legal approaches. But perhaps no restriction imposed by the *shari'a* was more significant than the rule that a child born to a female slave and her free male Muslim owner was free. As mentioned in the previous chapter, from the time of the second Caliph, 'Umar, Islamic law imposed a set of requirements on owners of enslaved concubines: If a free man fathered a child with his female slave, the slave attained the status of *umm al-walad* (mother of the child). Having attained this status, the woman could not be sold or separated from her child and she was to be freed upon the death of her owner. The child was free from birth and the legal equal of any other of the man's children. Muslims may have been influenced on this point by the Sasanians, who controlled much of the Middle East in pre-Islamic times (224–651 AD). According to early Sasanian law, the child of an enslaved mother and a free father was free.[35] But Islamic law and practice contrasted with that of ancient Greece, Rome, and Byzantium, where any child born to a slave

---

(New York: Oxford University Press, 1949), 74, who in turn is citing para 117 of the Hammurabic Code; and Dunstan, *Ancient Near East*, 85.

[29] Exod 21:7–11.

[30] Freamon, *Possessed by the Right Hand*, 48, citing Dandamaev and Lukonin, *Ancient Iran*, 156.

[31] See Westermann, *Slave Systems*, 115.

[32] Freamon, *Possessed by the Right Hand*, 75, citing Macuch, "Barda and Bardadari."

[33] Westermann, *Slave Systems*, 86 and 147.

[34] Regarding early medieval Europe, see Pierre Bonnassie, *From Slavery to Feudalism in South-Western Europe* (Cambridge: Cambridge University Press, 1991), 34–36. It should be noted that there was likely some variation within early medieval Europe on this point.

[35] Freamon, *Possessed by the Right Hand*, 76, citing Macuch, "Barda and Bardadari." The policy that the child of a slave mother and a free father inherits the father's free status has deep historical roots in the Near East, being evidenced much earlier in the Code of Hammurabi. See Snell, "Slavery in the ancient Near East," 10.

mother was a slave from birth.[36] Jewish rabbis writing within the ambit of the Roman Empire also typically held that children born to free men and female slaves inherited their mother's slave status.[37]

We are not clear about the extent to which the restrictions of *shari'a* law on pathways into slavery applied to non-Muslims living under Muslim rule. While free *dhimmis* (members of a conquered non-Muslim group who had accepted Muslim rule and taxes) were generally protected from enslavement, they could be enslaved for not paying the poll tax (*jizya*) required of non-Muslims.[38] The *devshirme* system of the Ottomans involved a regular culling of free male youth from *dhimmi* Christian populations, in order to train them to serve as slaves in administrative posts or the military.[39] Muslims also frequently bought slaves from non-Muslims, and in those cases the route into slavery could have been of any sort.

There were three historically common pathways into slavery that Muslims certainly did not shut down: birth to two slave parents, capture of defeated enemies (including noncombatants) in war, and smaller-scale slaveraiding. The enslavement of captured non-Muslims was a major source of slaves imported into some Islamic societies well into the nineteenth century. It is estimated that in the nineteenth century some 1.9 million Africans were taken into Islamic lands as slaves.[40] Many of these would have been initially captured in slave raids, sometimes by Muslim raiders, sometimes not. Within Africa, the Sokoto Caliphate in northern Nigeria (1804–1901 AD) enslaved a huge number of prisoners of war, possibly more than 1 million.[41] Naval raids in and around the Mediterranean were also a significant source. Robert C. Davis tentatively estimates that between 1500 and 1800, maritime slaveraiders from Muslim polities captured 2 million Christians.[42] (Davis also reckons that during the same period maritime slaveraiders from Christian polities captured approximately 1 million Muslims.) Although there are

---

[36] On Greece, see Freamon, *Possessed by the Right Hand*, 53, citing Jean Andreau and Raymond Descat, *The Slave in Greece and Rome*, trans. Marion Leopold (Madison, WI: University of Wisconsin Press, 2011), 58. On Rome, see Westermann, *Slave Systems*, 81. On Byzantium, see Rotman, *Byzantine Slavery*, 25.

[37] Hezser, "Slavery and the Jews," 446.

[38] "Dhimmi," *New World Encyclopedia*: www.newworldencyclopedia.org/entry/Dhimmi; Fynn-Paul, "Empire, monotheism, and slavery," 12 n.19.

[39] Brown, *Slavery & Islam*, 138–139.

[40] Northrup, "Overseas movements of slaves and indentured workers," 52.

[41] Higman, "Demographic trends," 28.   [42] Davis, *Holy War and Human Bondage*, 64.

considerable resources within Islamic law to object to many of these captures (as we'll discuss in Chapter 5), Islamic jurists before the twentieth century rarely availed themselves of those resources. Indeed, as late as 1987, Saudi Arabia's Permanent Council for Academic Research and Fatwa argued in print that, "if there were legitimate wars today, then non-Muslim prisoners could be taken as slaves if the Muslim ruler judged it appropriate" (Jonathan Brown's paraphrase).[43] Still, it should be noted that the *shari'a* lays down restrictions on the enslavement of captives, and at various junctures some Islamic jurists have discouraged the purchase of captives whose mode of acquisition was illicit or questionable. The key questions regarding slaves captured in war or raiding have been (a) whether the conflict was considered legitimate in the first place and (b) whether the acquisition and distribution of prisoners was carried out in the prescribed manner. These attempts to discourage the purchase of slaves whose capture was illicit or questionable extended to cases involving non-Muslim captives as well as cases involving Muslim captives. Brown describes the position of the Persian jurist Abu Muhammad Juwayni (d. 1047), who in a book on pious caution "stated that it was best to avoid buying slave girls who had been taken via raiding into non-Muslim territory since the proper procedures for taking in and distributing spoils were regularly ignored."[44] Centuries later, the Egyptian jurist Taqi al-Din Subki (1284–1355) argued for the same view.[45]

4.3 CHRISTIANITY AND THE RELIGIOUS RESTRICTION OF SLAVERY (TO THE FOURTEENTH CENTURY)

From late antiquity through the Middle Ages, many Christian thinkers and leaders in Europe attempted to restrict slavery in a number of ways. Early on, their efforts evince only a concern that Christians not be held as slaves by non-Christians, but as time passes the historical record reveals a growing and increasingly successful attempt to restrict the enslavement and sale of Christians by Christians as well.

In the fourth through sixth centuries numerous Roman emperors prohibited or limited the right of Jews to hold Christian slaves, apparently

---

[43] Brown, *Slavery & Islam*, 255, citing Ahmad 'Abd al-Razzaq al-Dawish (ed.), *Fatawa al-Lanja al-da'ima li'l-buhuth al-'ilmiyya wa'l-ifta*. 5th ed. vol. 16. (Riyadh: Dar al-Mu'ayyad, 2004), 573. The quoted words are Brown's description.

[44] Brown, *Slavery & Islam*, 89. (Brown's words.)

[45] Brown, *Slavery & Islam*, 89. See also 211.

motivated by a desire to prevent conversions from Christianity to Judaism. Circa 530 AD, Justinian decreed that Jews and pagans were not permitted to own Christian slaves; the law was later extended so that Christian heretics were also prohibited from keeping Christian slaves.[46] The Council of Clichy (626–627) in the Frankish kingdom prohibited the sale of Christians to Jews or pagans, and in the eighth century such bans were common in Latin Europe. Muslim expansion in the seventh and eighth centuries provided a military motivation for restriction of the sale of Christian slaves to Muslims, evidenced in Charlemagne's prohibition of the sale of slaves, stallions, and weapons outside his kingdom. But a religiously motivated concern for the spiritual welfare of Christians sold to Muslims (as well as other non-Christians) seems also to have been operative, as in a letter to Charlemagne by one Cathwulf, who urged the King never never to allow the selling of a Christian to a pagan people, lest he face divine judgment before "the throne of Christ." Both the state and the Church made efforts to enforce this restriction. Historian Michael McCormick relates that the Benedictine monk Regino of Prum (840–915), in a work on Church governance, counsels that "bishops visiting their dioceses should ask whether there have been any kidnappings and sales into foreign slavery, or [whether] anyone has sold Christian slaves to Jews or pagans, or whether Jews have sold any Christian slaves there" (McCormick's words).[47]

These examples all relate to Christians owned by or sold to non-Christians, but the enslavement of Christians by Christians and the sale of Christians to Christians was also restricted in medieval Latin Europe. The warring kingdoms that emerged after the fall of the Western Roman Empire continued the traditional practice of enslaving war captives (including noncombatants), but by the ninth century we see religiously framed attempts to prohibit the enslavement of Christian war captives.[48] A prime example is provided by the Benedictine monk Smaragdus

---

[46] Ramelli, *Social Justice and the Legitimacy of Slavery*, 98–99; Rotman, *Byzantine Slavery*, 43, citing *Novellae Justiniani* 37.7, 144.2, *Novellae et Aureae Bullae imperatorum post Justinianum* coll. 1, nov. 7, and *Appendix Eclogae* 8.1–3.

[47] Michael McCormick, *Origins of the European Economy: Communications and Commerce, A. D. 300-900* (Cambridge: Cambridge University Press, 2001), 740–749, especially 740 n.57 and 748 n.79. For an example from eleventh-century England similar to that of Cathwulf, see A. G. Kennedy, "Cnut's law code of 1018," *Anglo-Saxon England*, 11 (1983), 57–81, 74.

[48] See McCormick, *Origins of the European Economy*, 741–752 and Fynn-Paul, "Empire, monotheism and slavery," 17–18.

(c. 770–c. 840), abbot of a monastery in Saxony, who in the early ninth century addressed a treatise on kingship to Louis the Pious, King of the Franks and the son of Charlemagne (or possibly to Charlemagne himself – historians are uncertain).[49] Among many other topics, Smaragdus addresses slavery. After marshaling several Old Testament texts prohibiting the manstealing of Israelites (Deut 24:7), condemning the sale of fellow Israelites (Amos 2:6), urging that the oppressed by freed (Isaiah 58:6), and exhorting good treatment of slaves (Sirach 33:31), he draws two countercultural conclusions. First, he urges the king to "forbid captivity in your kingdom."[50] Second, he urges every man in the kingdom, including the King, to free his slaves:

Truly, man ought to obey God and his precepts, to the extent that God grants the possibility to obey. And among other salutary precepts and righteous works, for the sake of the exceedingly great love of God, every man ought to release his slaves as free men, considering that not nature but sin subjected them to him. (For we were created in an equal condition, but some were conquered by others because of sin.) And at the same time considering that if you forgive, you will be forgiven. For with this conditional [regarding forgiveness], the yoke of the Lord presses down upon even you. Therefore, most just and pious king, give honor to the Lord your God before all, since, as was written above, he has given honor to you before all. Whether with regard to slaves subjected to you or with regard to riches granted to you, do not cease to obey His precepts, making free men of your slaves and giving alms from your riches.[51]

From this passage alone it is not clear whether Smaragdus was arguing, more restrictively, for an end to the practice of taking Christian war captives and for the manumission of the many Christian war captives held by the King and others in consequence of recent Frankish military victories, or whether he was arguing, more expansively, for an end to all slavery and the manumission of all slaves. But the former is much more plausible, given the acceptance of slavery in Christian tradition preceding Smaragdus. Noting that the Abbot quotes the Old Testament prohibition

---

[49] McCormick, *Origins of the European Economy*, 750–751.

[50] "Prohibe ergo, clementissime rex, ne in regno tuo captivitas fiat." Smaragdus, *Via regia*, in J. P. Migne (ed.), *Patrologia cursus completes, series Latina*, vol. 102 (Paris, 1851), 102.967B. Translation is Rota's.

[51] This passage from the *Via regia* is located in chap. 30 in Migne's *Patrologia Latina*, 102.968B, whereas it is placed in chap. 31 in a recent critical Latin text: Smaragdus of Saint-Mihiel, *Via Regia*, ed. Matthew Ponesse, trans. James F. LePree (Leuven: Peeters, 2023). We have used the Latin text from Ponesse (graciously shared with the authors in advance of publication, Oct. 29, 2020); translation is Rota's, with assistance from Andrew Rosato.

against kidnapping and enslaving fellow Israelites, historian Michael McCormick contends that "Smaragdus was not worried about enslaving Arab infidels, but about Christians."[52] The same position is explicit in a ruling of a local Church council in Narbonne in 1054, which made those making "booty out of any Christian man or woman" liable to excommunication; and again in the legislation of King Alphonso X of Castile (r. 1252–1284), which makes clear that "those taken captive in war" are enslaved only when they are "enemies of the faith."[53] In the fourteenth century the influential Italian jurist Bartolus of Saxoferrato (1313–1357), after mentioning the ancient Roman laws allowing enslavement of war captives, explains that "according to the mores of modern times and the customs of old observed by Christians, we do not keep the laws of captivity ... Captives are not sold nor held as slaves."[54]

There is additional evidence from Latin Europe of the condemnation of the selling of Christians, even to other Christians. St. Bathilde, a former slave from Saxony who from 657 AD ruled in Burgundy after the death of her husband King Clovis II, "forbade the sale of Christians within her kingdom and forbade the transportation of Christian slaves beyond it."[55] According to his eighth-century biographer, St. Bonitus of Clermont (in the seventh century) attempted to restrict the slave trade in Marseilles:

[A]s it was customary in that place that men were sold and condemned by the punishment of exile and enslavement, he commanded by his decree that it should never occur; rather, those whom he could find who had been sold, he redeemed and brought home, as was his habit.[56]

[52] McCormick, *Origins of the European Economy*, 751.

[53] The quotation from the Council of Narbonne is from Noonan, *A Church That Can and Cannot Change*, 53, citing G. D. Mansi (ed.) *Sacrorum conciliorum nova et amplissima collectio* (Florence, 1759–1767; Venice, 1769–1798), 16, 831–832; *Las Siete Partidas*, 4th partida, title XXI, law 1, 977

[54] Quoted by Noonan, *A Church That Can and Cannot Change*, 54, citing Bartolus de Saxoferrato, *Commentaria: cum additionibus Thomae Diplovatatii aliorumque excellentissimorum doctorum, una cum amplissimo repertorio noviter elucubrato per dictum calrissimum doctorem dominum Thomam Diplovatatium*, ed. G. Polari (Venice, 1526; facsimile Rome 1996), 49.15.24.1.

[55] Noonan, *A Church That Can and Cannot Change*, 43, citing *Vita Sanctae Balthildis, Scriptores Rerum Merovingicarum* (Hannover, 1888), 2, 494.

[56] Quoted in McCormick, *Origins of the European Economy*, 735, citing *Vita Boniti Arverni* (*Bibliotheca hagiographica latina* 1418), 3, 121.3–6. As McCormick notes, it is ambiguous whether Bonitus was objecting to penal enslavement only, or the slave trade in general.

The *Life of Anskar* records an instance in which St. Anskar (801–865), Bishop of Hamburg and missionary among the Scandinavians, learned of a group of Christians who had been taken captive by pagans to the north, then had escaped, but thereafter had been reduced to slavery by Christians in the area to which they had fled (north of Hamburg). Anskar, says his ninth-century biographer, "was greatly distressed that so great a crime had been perpetrated in his diocese, but he could not devise how he might mend matters because there were many involved who were esteemed to be powerful and noble." After a dream or vision of Jesus convinced Anskar that he would have divine help in the endeavor, he traveled to the region in question and managed to secure the liberty of the slaves, attempting also to prevent reoccurrences of such an event there in the future.[57] Minimally, we can interpret this as a case of a Christian bishop striving to restrict the enslavement of captured Christians by other Christians. Similarly, when in the late ninth century Pope John VIII (r. 872–882) learned of Sardinians buying Christian slaves who had been captured by Muslims and then sold to the Greeks, he wrote to a group of Sardinian rulers, exhorting them to free "your own" lest they "incur a great sin."[58]

The sale of children is condemned as sinful in an Old English penitential, a manual for confessors dating from between the ninth and eleventh centuries, which specifies that:

If any Christian man sells his own child for any price, or his nearest kin, he is to have no communion with Christian men until he has released him (the sold one) from that servitude. If he is not able to obtain it, he is to distribute as great a stipend on his behalf as he previously received for him, and he is to release another from servitude and to manumit him, and he is to fast 7 weeks on bread and water.[59]

Slaveraiding, the enslavement of war captives, and slavetrading were not uncommon in tenth- and eleventh-century England, with many English

---

[57] Rimbert, *Life of Anskar*, chap. 38. Translation from Charles H. Robinson, *Anskar: The Apostle of the North, 801–895* (London: 1921), available online at Fordham University's Internet Medieval Sourcebook: sourcebooks.fordham.edu/basis/anskar.asp#lifeans.

[58] Quoted in Noonan, *A Church That Can and Cannot Change*, 53, citing Heinrich Denzinger and A. Schonmetzer (eds.), *Enchiridion Symbolorum Definitionem Et Declarationum De Rebus Fidei et Morum*, 35th ed. (Friburg in Br.: Herder, 1965), n.668.

[59] Text from Oxford Bodleian Library MS Laud Misc. 482 (Y) 16b, translation from Allen J. Frantzen (ed.), *Anglo-Saxon Penitentials: A Cultural Database:* www.anglo-saxon.net/penance/index.php?p=TOEP482_16b. Accessed Dec. 17, 2020.

slaves being sold abroad to Ireland. But in the century following the Norman Conquest this changed. William the Conqueror (r. 1066–1087), urged on by the Archbishop of Canterbury, Lanfranc, prohibited "the sale of any man by another outside the country."[60] In 1102 the subsequent Archbishop of Canterbury, St. Anselm, presided over a council of the whole English Church which included in its decrees a prohibition of the slave trade: "No one is henceforth to presume to carry on that shameful trading whereby heretofore men used in England to be sold like brute beasts." This council was held with the approval of the English King, and "the leading men of the Kingdom" were present at it, "in order that whatever was decreed on the authority of that Council should be observed as having been ratified by the approval … of each of these estates of the realm."[61] In 1335 the King of Sweden and Norway Magnus Eriksson went considerably further, not merely restricting the slave trade but "declaring that no child of a Christian parent was henceforth to be a slave."[62] As historian Jeffrey Fynn-Paul summarizes, "the Latin Church in conjunction with secular rulers developed and gradually enforced a prohibition against reducing fellow Christians to slavery, especially by capture."[63]

The attempts by medieval Christians to restrict slavery which we have thus far examined have focused on the plight of formerly free Christians. But in the case of one important medieval theologian, the focus of concern seems to have been more universal. The Scottish Franciscan Blessed John Duns Scotus rejects several of the traditionally accepted "just titles" to slavery, on grounds that apply equally to all human beings. By Scotus' time, the Latin "servus" could be used variously to refer to serfs, servants or slaves, depending on the context.[64] But Scotus makes it clear that he is discussing full chattel slavery: "The servitude about which we are speaking, according to which the master can sell his slave like an animal, is that

---

[60] Marc Morris, *The Norman Conquest: The Battle of Hastings and the Fall of Anglo-Saxon England* (New York: Pegasus Books, 2013), 294–296, quotation from William's Laws at 296.

[61] Eadmer, *Eadmer's History of Recent Events in England: Historia Novorum in Anglia*, trans. Geoffrey Bosanquet (London: The Cresset Press, 1964), 149–152.

[62] Joan Dyste Lind, "The ending of slavery in Sweden: social structure and decision making," *Scandinavian Studies*, 50:1 (Winter 1978), 57–71, 68. Quoted words are Lind's.

[63] Fynn-Paul, "Empire, monotheism and slavery," 24.

[64] See Allan B. Wolter, O. F. M., "Introduction," in John Duns Scotus, *Duns Scotus on the Will and Morality* (Washington, DC: Catholic University of America Press, 1986), 115.

spoken of by Aristotle in Book I of the *Politics* ..."[65] Scotus goes on to ask how slavery of this sort can ever be just:

I say that this vile form of servitude can be just only in two cases: the first is when a person voluntarily subjects himself to such; but such subjection is foolish. Indeed, it may even be against the law of nature that a man abdicate his freedom in this fashion. Nevertheless, once he has done so, he must carry out his part of the bargain, because this is only just. The other way servitude can originate is if one who is justly charged with the government of the community, seeing that some criminals are so vicious that their liberty would harm both themselves and the public, can justly punish them with slavery, just as he could execute them in certain cases for the welfare of the state.

And if you insist that there is also a third legitimate reason for servitude, for instance, that if one captured in war is preserved unharmed, and thus spared from death, he may become a slave destined to serve. I doubt this – unless [playing on words] you mean by "servus" here one who is "pre*served*." Neither is such enslavement a clear case of justice, even if the captor, perhaps, might have otherwise killed his captive (assuming the war was a just one of self-defense and not one of invasion, and that the captive persisted in his obstinacy against the person fighting defensively). Nevertheless, given that the captive could cease to be obstinate, since he has it in his power to change his mind, it seems inhuman to inflict on him a punishment that is against the law of nature.[66]

We shouldn't overlook the importance of Scotus' position here. In early medieval Europe no less than six mechanisms of enslavement had been recognized as legitimate.[67] Slavery could and was imposed for (i) the failure to pay a debt and (ii) as a punishment for certain crimes. The destitute could and did sometimes sell (iii) their children or (iv) themselves into slavery. (v) Birth to a slave mother was a common route into slavery. Finally, as discussed above, (vi) captives in war (Christian and non-Christian) were often enslaved in early medieval Europe, though by Scotus' time the practice of enslaving Christian war captives had long since been suppressed. Scotus asserts that slavery can only be just in cases of (iv) voluntary self-sale and (ii) judicial punishment of vicious criminals. Furthermore, the reasons he gives for questioning the permissibility of enslaving war captives have nothing to do with the captive's religion. This means that Scotus' position was a significant deviation from the common

---

[65] Scotus, *Ordinatio* IV.36.1, Latin text from Scotus, *Duns Scotus on the Will and Morality*, 522. Translation is Rota's.

[66] Scotus, *Ordinatio* IV.36.1, translation from Scotus, *Duns Scotus on the Will and Morality*, 525.

[67] See Maxwell, *Slavery and the Catholic Church*, 44–45; Bonnassie, *From Slavery to Feudalism in South-Western Europe*, 32–7.

medieval view in Europe, for at least one and likely two reasons. First, Scotus does not accept the idea that the child born to a slave mother was *ipso facto* legitimately a slave – a major deviation from earlier medievals.[68] Second, Scotus' reasoning suggests that he would reject the enslavement of any war captives, Christian or otherwise. If these two positions had been heeded by Scotus' fellow Christians, the large-scale enslavement of Africans and Native Americans by Europeans (from the fifteenth through the nineteenth centuries) would have been widely recognized in Europe for the grave injustice that it was.

4.4 RELIGION AND THE WANING OF SLAVERY IN EUROPE

Given the prevalence of slavery since the development of agriculture, medieval Latin Europe stands out as an anomaly. From around 1,000 on, there was no large-scale system of slavery within Latin Europe, and in north and northwestern Europe slavery had essentially disappeared from view by the late Middle Ages. What explains this important shift? Historian Jeffrey Fynn-Paul has leveraged the concept of a "no-slaving zone" to provide an intriguing and plausible answer. A no-slaving zone, for a given society, is "the area considered off limits for slaveraiding by that society."[69] Fynn-Paul contends that:

the creation of the Christian and Islamic monotheistic blocs was a major turning point in the history of the Greater Mediterranean slave system, since these empires came to adopt a religio-ethical taboo against the enslavement of the majority of their inhabitants. In the process, they created what might be called the world's first 'perfect' no-slaving zones.[70]

And again:

it was Christianity itself, rather than any political force, which began to maintain most of western Europe as a no-slaving zone akin to what had existed under the [Roman] empire. Thus, through the spread of Christianity, the majority of western Europeans were spared the resumption of pre-Roman slaving norms despite the empire's fall. This is remarkable in so far as it was the first time in history that a philosophical system, rather than political force, maintained the integrity of a large-scale no-slaving zone.[71]

---

[68] See, for example, Aquinas' defense of the traditional rule that the child of a slave mother and a free father was legitimately a slave, at Thomas Aquinas, *Commentary on the Sentences of Peter Lombard*, IV.36.1.1 et seq.; *Summa theologiae* III *Supplementum* q. 52, a. 4. It is curious that Scotus does not explicitly discuss this view.

[69] Fynn-Paul, "Empire, monotheism and slavery," 4.   [70] Ibid., 4–5.   [71] Ibid., 17–18.

Religious restrictions combined with political interests and economic factors to render it increasingly difficult for Christians to reduce other Christians to slavery within medieval Latin Europe.[72] Within the medieval Muslim world, similarly, religious beliefs about the impermissibility of enslaving free Muslims meant that new slaves had to be sought principally from outside the Abode of Islam. As the kingdoms of Europe became powerful enough to maintain their borders and control their merchants, Europeans sold fewer slaves abroad, and the conversion to Christianity of formerly pagan peoples in Britain, Germany, central Europe, Scandinavia, and Russia increased the size of the European no-slaving zone. But within Latin Christendom, on the one hand, and the Islamic world, on the other, the fate of slavery diverged. Whereas slavery continued to play a central role within Islamic society, slavery waned in Latin Europe, with Europeans largely ceasing to hold even non-Christian slaves. Why? Here, economics appears to be key. The economies of the early medieval Muslim world were considerably more developed than those of Western Europe, and this together with a high demand for slaves within Islamic polities led to a huge disparity in the price of slaves between the two areas: "Between the eighth and tenth centuries, the price of slaves in North Africa was three to five times higher than the price of slaves in Europe."[73] During these centuries slave merchants who acquired slaves in the British Isles, northern Europe, or Russia (at or beyond the northern and northeastern boundaries of the Latin European no-slavery zone) had every incentive to sell those slaves into the Muslim world. Within Europe slaves were not easily acquired, and labor – prior to the Black Death in the latter half of the fourteenth century – was cheap. By "the time the European economy had developed to the extent that it could compete with North African demand, the Europeans had learned how to do almost entirely without slaves."[74]

All this suggests that Christian strictures on the enslavement of fellow Christians had an important, though unforeseen, long-range consequence. Religiously motivated restrictions on slavery within Latin Christendom, together with political and economic factors, led to a

---

[72] Fynn-Paul does not discuss the Byzantine Empire in any detail but does note in passing that Latin Europe and Byzantium developed somewhat distinct no-slaving zones, with some slaveraiding occurring between the two. Cf. Fynn-Paul, "Empire, monotheism and slavery," 13, 22, and 25 n.58.

[73] Fynn-Paul, "Empire, monotheism and slavery," 29, drawing on McCormick, *Origins of the European Economy*.

[74] Fynn-Paul, "Empire, monotheism and slavery," 30.

largely slave-free Europe in the later Middle Ages and the modern era. While Europeans then become slavers on a massive scale in their New World colonies, slavery remained rare within Europe itself, particularly in northern Europe. This in turn provided a fertile ground for the growth of the abolitionist movement. As historian Seymour Drescher has observed, the "eighteenth-century sources of Old World abolitionism [arose] chiefly in areas that were distinguished by not being centers of an otherwise ubiquitous institution."[75] Similarly, sociologist Rodney Stark notes that:

[I]n every case [of abolition], a powerful nonslave area imposed abolition on a weaker slave-owning region. That is, the American abolitionists mobilized the North to free the slaves of the South; abolitionists in slave-free Britain convinced the government to outlaw slavery in its far-flung colonies; it was in metropolitan France that the fate of slavery in the French West Indies was decided; it was in Madrid, not in Havana or San Juan, that emancipation of Spain's Caribbean slaves was accomplished; and it was in Rio that Brazilian slaves were emancipated.[76]

In any society in which the class holding political power owns slaves, perceived economic self-interest together with the human proclivity to engage in rationalization will make it difficult for those with political power to perceive accurately the injustice of slavery. But in a society where many with political power do not own slaves, and thus have less to lose by recognizing the injustice of slavery, abolitionist sentiment is much more likely to take root, spread, and find success.[77] Thus it may well be that a crucial facilitating condition for the emergence of the abolitionist movement in eighteenth-century Europe and North America was the comparative absence of slavery in Europe in the preceding centuries. And this absence itself appears to have had among its principal causes the religiously motivated restriction of the enslavement of coreligionists.

4.5 CHRISTIANITY AND THE RESTRICTION OF SLAVERY: THE NEW WORLD

If Christopher Columbus was the discoverer of the New World, he was also its first transatlantic human trafficker. On October 12, 1492, he

---

[75] Drescher, *Abolition: A History of Slavery and Antislavery*, 7.
[76] Stark, *For the Glory of God*, 359.
[77] For elaboration and defense of these claims, see Rota, "Moral psychology and social change: the case of abolition."

made landfall on an island somewhere in the Turks or Bahamas. After a day or two of peaceful interactions with the natives, he kidnapped seven with the intention of carrying them off to Spain "in order to learn our language and return, unless your Highnesses [King Ferdinand and Queen Isabella of Castile] should choose to have them all transported to Castile, or held captive in the island."[78] Two of the seven successfully escaped by jumping ship near a neighboring island, but Columbus took the others to Spain, along with several more from other islands. In the first letter he penned upon his return, Columbus says that if the King and Queen give him assistance for a second voyage, he "shall give them all the gold they require ... spices also, and cotton ... and mastic, [and] slaves, as many of these idolators as their Highnesses shall command to be shipped."[79] During his second expedition (1493–1496) he engaged in military action on Hispaniola (the island now divided between Haiti and the Dominican Republic), capturing more than 1,000 natives and shipping 500 back to Spain to be sold as slaves.[80]

Despite the officially stated rationale of evangelization, Columbus' actions throughout his four journeys to the New World suggest that economic goals were foremost in his mind, as evidenced by his dogged quest for gold and other valuable commodities. When sufficient quantities of gold proved hard to obtain, his thoughts turned to slaves as a source of revenue.[81] This would have been natural for any Genoese merchant of the time – while in the late Middle Ages slavery waned in northern and northwestern Europe, maritime cities in proximity to the Muslim world, notably Venice and Genoa, had continued to trade in slaves, especially Slavs from beyond the borders of Latin Christendom. And by Columbus' lifetime both Portuguese and Spanish mariners were regularly capturing, buying, and trading in slaves from both North and West Africa. When European exploration of the Atlantic Islands and the west coast of Africa quickened pace in the fifteenth century, the Portuguese and Spanish used

---

[78] The quotation is from the Oct. 14, 1492, entry in Las Casas' abstract of Columbus' logbook from his first voyage, published as Christopher Columbus, *Journal of First Voyage to America* (New York: Albert & Charles Boni, 1924), 29. See also 31.

[79] Columbus, *Letter to Luis de Santangel, Chancellor of the Exchequer*, Feb. 15, 1493, translation from Christopher Columbus, *Select Letters of Christopher Columbus, with Other Original Documents, relating to his Four Voyages to the New World*, trans. and ed. by R. H. Major (London: Hakluyt Society, 1870), 15.

[80] See Gustavo Gutierrez, *Las Casas: In Search of the Poor of Jesus Christ*, trans. Robert R. Barr (Maryknoll, NY: Orbis Books, 1993), 23, and Felipe Fernandez-Armesto, *Columbus* (Oxford: Oxford University Press, 1991), 101, 107, 111, 138.

[81] Fernandez-Armesto, *Columbus*, 107, 138, and Gutierrez, *Las Casas*, 22–23.

slave labor on sugar plantations in the Madeiras and Canaries. The slaves included natives of those islands and then increasingly Africans, both Muslim and non-Muslim. Genoese traders took an active role in these ventures.[82]

To her credit, Isabella had serious qualms about the legitimacy of Columbus' enslavement of the Native Americans. In 1495 she arranged for a commission of scholars, theologians, and canon lawyers to consider the question of whether Columbus' 500 captives could be sold as slaves lawfully. To Isabella, the morality of enslaving non-Christian war captives was an open question in the context, largely depending on whether the war was considered just. The enslavement of conquered peoples had already been condemned by the Church earlier in the century: In 1435 Pope Eugene IV had denounced the enslavement of the natives of the Canaries and ordered their emancipation. More generally, since Pope Innocent IV (r. 1243–1254), the law of the Church was that Christians did *not* have the right to conquer and enslave non-Christians simply because they were infidels. But canon law also held that under certain conditions the Pope could authorize Christian rulers to wage war on newly encountered peoples and allow them to enslave the defeated, the principal conditions being that the non-Christians refused to allow Christian missionaries to peacefully evangelize or that they regularly violated the natural moral law in some serious way. In 1500 the King and Queen suspended the traffic in Native American slaves (which had continued) and ordered that the natives already in Spain be freed and returned to the "Indies."[83]

Yet this was not the end of slavery for the Native Americans in territory conquered by Spain. Far from it. To understand the subsequent history of slavery in Spanish America it is helpful to go back to the mid fifteenth century, when Pope Nicholas V (r. 1447–1455) granted a right of conquest to King Alfonso V of Portugal. Portuguese explorers and

---

[82] Fernandez-Armesto, *Columbus*, 11; Joseph C. Miller, *The Problem of Slaving as History: A Global Approach* (New Haven: Yale University Press, 2012), 65; William D. Phillips, Jr., "Slavery in the Atlantic islands and the early modern Spanish Atlantic World," in D. Eltis and S. Engerman (eds.), *The Cambridge World History of Slavery: Volume 3, AD 1420–AD 1804* (Cambridge: Cambridge University Press, 2011), 325–349.

[83] Gutierrez, *Las Casas*, 23–24 and 473 nn.14–15; Lesley Byrd Simpson, *The Encomienda in New Spain: The Beginning of Spanish Mexico* (Berkeley: University of California Press, 1966), 3–5. On Eugene IV, see Joel S. Panzer, *The Popes and Slavery* (New York: Alba House, 1996), 8. On canon law regarding conquest and enslavement, see James Muldoon, *Popes, Lawyers, and Infidels* (Philadelphia: University of Pennsylvania Press, 1996).

merchants had begun trading in slaves on the West African coast, and apparently had led the Pope to believe that this region was inhabited in part by Muslims.[84] Given the frequent maritime slaveraiding between Muslims and Christians, Ottoman expansion in the fifteenth century, and the long history of conflict between Muslims and Christians from the Iberian peninsula to the Middle East, European Christians could easily see themselves as participants in an ongoing struggle against the Abode of Islam. Against this backdrop, Pope Nicholas V in 1452 granted to Alfonso and his successors:

full and free permission to invade, search out, capture and subjugate the Saracens [i.e. Muslims] and pagans and any other unbelievers and enemies of Christ wherever they may be, as well as their kingdoms, duchies, counties, principalities, and other property ... and to reduce their persons into perpetual slavery ...[85]

After the fall of Constantinople to the Ottoman Turks in 1453, Nicholas explicitly confirmed this grant in the Papal Bull *Romanus Pontifex* (Jan. 8, 1454), citing the ultimate goal of evangelization and the proximate goal of bestowing "suitable favors"

on those Catholic kings and princes, who, like athletes and intrepid champions of the Christian faith ... not only restrain the savage excesses of the Saracens and of other infidels ... but also for the defense and increase of the faith vanquish them and their kingdoms and habitations ...[86]

The political and economic advantage Portugal had gained by this Papal grant (which included a monopoly on trade) was not lost on the Spanish Monarchy. Upon the return of Columbus from his first voyage, King Ferdinand and Queen Isabella promptly petitioned the Pope for his sanction of their present and future conquests in the Americas. In May 1493 Pope Alexander VI obliged, granting to the Spanish Crown the right to take possession of hitherto undiscovered islands and mainlands lying south of the Azores and to the west of a north/south line 100 leagues to the west of the Azores, and granting to the Portuguese

---

[84] Maxwell, *Slavery and the Catholic Church*, 53; Noonan, *A Church That Can and Cannot Change*, 62–67.

[85] Nicholas V, *Dum Diversas*, Jun. 16, 1452, quoted and translated in Maxwell, *Slavery and the Catholic Church*, 53.

[86] Nicholas V, *Romanus Pontifex*, Jan. 8, 1454; translation from Frances Gardiner Davenport (ed.), *European Treaties bearing on the History of the United States and Its Dependencies to 1648* (Washington, D. C.: Carnegie Institution of Washington, 1917), 20–26, reproduced at: www.papalencyclicals.net/nicholo5/romanus-pontifex.htm.

Crown the same right for lands lying to the East of said line.[87] Enslavement of the natives was not mentioned by Alexander VI, nor was it the policy preference of Isabella and Ferdinand, who seem to have wanted the Native Americans to be their free subjects.[88] But the desire to extract wealth from the Americas, on the part of both colonists and Crown, led to the use of both *de jure* chattel slavery and forced labor on a large scale. In 1503 Isabella issued an order that the prohibition on enslavement of the natives did not apply to cannibals who resisted evangelization, and it appears that, as far as Spanish law was concerned, colonists could enslave those natives forcefully resisting Spanish authority and could also buy natives already held as slaves by other natives.[89] After the death of Isabella, King Ferdinand was even less scrupulous, allowing the colonists to supply labor in Hispaniola by enslaving formerly free (and peaceable) natives from other islands.[90]

More prevalent than *de jure* chattel slavery, however, was the forced labor extracted from natives via the *encomienda* system, described by a twentieth-century historian as being in its early years "a thin disguise for slavery."[91] The first governors of Hispaniola entrusted large groups of natives to particular colonists, who then had rights to their service. The *encomienda* (entrustment) system was authorized in 1503 by an order from Ferdinand and Isabella that borders on the contradictory. The order commands the governor of Hispaniola to "impel and pressure" the natives to labor for the Spaniards in such work as construction, farming, and the mining of gold, and yet also includes the injunction that the natives were to "do and perform [these services] as the free persons that they are, and not as bondservants."[92] A native thus given "in trust" to a Spaniard (the *encomendero*) was technically a vassal of the Crown, but

---

[87] See Pope Alexander VI, *Inter caetera*, May 4, 1493, available at: www.papalencyclicals .net/alex06/alex06inter.htm, and also Maxwell, *Slavery and the Catholic Church*, 55–56, and Noonan, *A Church That Can and Cannot Change*, 65–66. Panzer interprets a subsequent letter of Alexander VI as making explicit a condition: The Europeans have a right to possess the newly encountered lands in question *only if* the natives are willing to accept their rule [Panzer, *The Popes and Slavery*, 13]. But see Hector Avalos, "Pope Alexander VI, slavery and voluntary subjection: 'Ineffabilis et Summi Patris' in context," *Journal of Ecclesiastical History*, 65:4 (2014), 738–760 for a convincing rebuttal of Panzer's interpretation. *Contra* Panzer, no such condition appears to have been implicitly intended by Alexander in 1493.

[88] Fernandez-Armesto, *Columbus*, 111, 136–39.

[89] Simpson, *The Encomienda in New Spain*, 6.

[90] See Simpson, *The Encomienda in New Spain*, 16–28.

[91] Simpson, *The Encomienda in New Spain*, 37.   [92] Gutierrez, *Las Casas*, 26.

owed labor to the *encomendero*. Legislation in 1513 called for natives to work for their *encomendero* for nine months of the year and use the remaining three months to work on their own farms or for wages – and this was reforming legislation meant to soften the burden on the native population.[93] Under the onslaught of armed invasion, European diseases to which the natives lacked immunity, slavery, and forced labor, the population of Hispaniola plummeted from several hundred thousand or more in 1492 to 29,000 in 1514.[94] Historian Andrés Reséndez underlines the important role played by slavery and forced labor in Hispaniola's depopulation: "Left to their own devices, the Native peoples of the Caribbean would have limited their exposure to illness," but they were not left to their own devices: "In the wake of the epidemics, slavers appeared on the horizon."[95]

One witness to the decimation was a young man from Seville, Bartolomé de Las Casas. Las Casas' father had served on Columbus' second voyage, and on his return in 1498 had given the young Bartolomé a Native American slave, one of the very captives later freed by order of the Crown in 1500. Las Casas himself came to Hispaniola in 1502. He received an *encomienda* there and subsequently, after having been ordained a Catholic priest, accompanied the Spaniards in the role of chaplain during their brutal conquest of Cuba in 1513. For this service he was granted a second *encomienda*, in Cuba. With the labor of the natives "entrusted" to him, Las Casas and a partner ran a successful farming and goldmining operation until he experienced a crisis of conscience in 1514. His conscience had already been pricked a few years earlier by a group of Dominican friars recently arrived in Hispaniola.[96] Las Casas had not then

---

[93] Simpson, *The Encomienda in New Spain*, 35. See also Andrés Reséndez, *The Other Slavery: The Uncovered Story of Indian Enslavement in America* (Boston: Houghton Mifflin Harcourt, 2016), 34–39.

[94] Simpson, *The Encomienda in New Spain*, 30, 48.

[95] Reséndez, *The Other Slavery*, 45.

[96] The Dominicans seem to have been early critics of European aggression in the New World. Writing in the early sixteenth century, Cardinal Cajetan, the master-general of the Dominican order, asserted that in lands in which Christianity had never been established, pagan rulers were lawful rulers: "Against them no king, no emperor, nor the Roman Church can wage war to occupy their lands or bring them under temporal subjection. Because no reason for a just war exists. For Jesus Christ, the king of kings, to whom is given all power in heaven and on earth, sent to take possession of the world not soldiers of an armed military but holy preachers as sheep among wolves ... Hence we would sin most gravely if we were to attempt to enlarge the faith of Jesus Christ in this way, and we would not be their legitimate rulers, but we would commit great robberies and be bound to restitution as unjust conquerors or occupiers." Without naming names, Cajetan was

been convinced, but in spring 1514 he had a dramatic change of heart, while meditating on Sirach 34:18–20: "If one sacrifices from what has been wrongfully obtained, the offering is blemished ... Like one who kills a son before his father's eyes is the man who offers a sacrifice from the property of the poor." Las Casas concluded that "everything perpetrated upon the Indians in these Indies was unjust and tyrannical," and realized that on the ground in the Americas, the notion that Spain was bringing salvation to the Native peoples was a mere rationalization that concealed Spanish greed, exploitation, and cruelty. He resigned from his role as an *encomendero* and began a lifelong struggle to expose and combat the Spaniard's mistreatment of Native Americans.[97]

Las Casas was one of many Spaniards, mostly clerics, who advocated on behalf of the Native Americans in the sixteenth century. To our knowledge their efforts comprise the first coordinated action that could be called an antislavery "campaign" or "movement," in that it included a wide range of actors – in the law, government, and the religious hierarchy – seeking to severely restrict or abolish the institution of slavery in the Spanish New World. If this First Antislavery Movement is less known than those that followed, this is due in large part to the fact that it was the least like a modern popular or social movement, and more the work of a small group of activists focused on influencing the political and religious elite. At times, support was forthcoming from the very top of the Spanish Empire. Yet royal sponsorship was both a blessing and a curse. It opened doors and forcefully required that public bodies must listen to, even if they rejected, arguments for universal freedom. But, crucially, royal support could be capricious, and it expired with the life of the royal sponsor – for these reasons the derivative royal power held by antislavery activists was ephemeral. It was also the case that while Spanish law extended across continents in the sixteenth century, royal power decreased with distance. The elderly royals in Madrid might announce imperial edicts, but the (often self-appointed) leaders in Peru or northern Mexico could

denouncing the policy of the conquistadores. (Thomas de Vio Cajetan, *Commentary on the* Summa theologiae *of Thomas Aquinas*, II-II.66.8. Translation is Rota's; Latin text from the Leonine edition, Thomas Aquinas, *Opera omnia sancti Thomae Aquinatis*, tome 9 [Rome: Typographia Polyglotta, 1897].) For further discussion, see Noonan, *A Church That Can and Cannot Change*, 71–72.

[97] We rely here on Gutierrez, *Las Casas*, 27–53, and George Sanderlin, "Introduction," in George Sanderlin (ed.), *Witness: Writings of Bartolome de Las Casas* (Maryknoll, NY: Orbis Books, 1992), 1–19. The quotation from Las Casas is from his *History of the Indies*, book 3, chap. 79, quoted in Gutierrez, *Las Casas*, 48.

simply put these orders on the shelf and continue with business as usual. Local power was insulated by distance from the meddling royals, and local powers were decidedly proslavery. Indigenous slaves were needed to fuel the labor-intensive extraction of silver and gold, and to convert land into fiefdoms to be held by individuals and institutions.

The efforts of Las Casas and others to restrict slavery and forced labor met with tantalizing short-term successes but never achieved their ultimate goals. Important remedies obtained from the Spanish Crown were often reversed: In 1523 the Spanish King Charles V ordered the conquistador Hernán Cortés to allow the natives of Mexico to have their liberty and not to institute the *encomienda* system there, only for the order to be disobeyed by Cortés. In 1530 the Queen halted all slavetrading in New Spain, but in 1534 Charles V reinstituted the legality of the enslavement of prisoners of war, which in practice gave colonists an incentive to engage in slaveraiding. In 1542 Charles V declared the *encomiendas* noninheritable, only to backpedal in 1545 after noncompliance and opposition by colonists in the New World (opposition that included rebellion by the colonists and the killing of the King's viceroy in Peru).[98]

European opponents of the exploitation of Native Americans also went directly to the Pope. The bishops of Mexico and other religious leaders, including Las Casas, met in Mexico in 1536 and sent the Dominican friar Bernardino de Minaya (1485–1565) to Pope Paul III (r. 1534–1549). Paul III responded with three important documents, including the Papal Bull *Sublimis Deus* (Jun. 2, 1537), on the enslavement of Native Americans. The Pope notes that some:

desiring to satisfy their own avarice, are presuming to assert far and wide that the Indians of the West and the South … be reduced to our service like brute animals, under the pretext that they are lacking the Catholic Faith. And they reduce them to slavery, treating them with afflictions they would scarcely use with brute animals.[99]

He then forbids this practice, in strong terms:

The aforementioned Indians and all other people who in the future come to the knowledge of Christians, although they be outside the faith of Christ, neither are nor ought to be deprived of their freedom or dominion over their goods. Indeed,

---

[98] Simpson, *The Encomienda of New Spain*, 56–72, 88, 107; Gutierrez, *Las Casas*, 289 and 305, and Geoffrey Parker, *Emperor: A New Life of Charles V* (New Haven: Yale University Press, 2019), 359–367.

[99] Latin text and translation from Panzer, *The Popes and Slavery*, 79–81.

they may freely and licitly use, possess, and enjoy freedom and such dominion and must not be reduced to slavery.[100]

Emperor Charles V reacted by prohibiting the Bull's publication in Spain, urging the Pope for a revocation, and putting Minaya in prison or under house arrest for two years.[101] But later popes applied and underscored the condemnation of the enslavement of Native Americans and other newly encountered peoples. Thus, for example, Urban VIII, writing in 1639:

We ourselves, following the footsteps of Paul our Predecessor and wishing to repress the efforts of impious men ... severely prohibit anyone from reducing to slavery, selling, buying, exchanging, giving away, separating from wives and children, despoiling of their property, taking away to other places, depriving of liberty in any way and keeping in servitude said Indians ...[102]

These papal teachings were not abolitionist in the strict sense – the Catholic Church did not object to slavery under certain "just titles," which in practice included capture in war with Muslims, the purchase in or from a non-Christian land of individuals already deemed slaves according to the laws of that land, or birth to slave parents (whether Christian or not).[103] Yet from the sixteenth century we do see a stream of criticism, among Catholic theologians and jurists, of a naïve acceptance of claims of just title. Las Casas himself had actually lobbied for the importation to the New World of both Black and white slaves in order to secure the freedom of enslaved Native Americans. But by the end of his life, he realized that "the captivity of the Blacks was as unjust as that of the Indians," and deeply regretted his previous position.[104] The Dominican Tomás de Mercado (1525–1575), in a sixteenth-century treatise on contracts, argued that titles to slaves derived from capture in war were unjust in "many or almost all" cases and criticized the slave trade on moral

---

[100] Translation from Gutierrez, *Las Casas*, 305.

[101] Paul III did not in fact revoke *Sublimis Deus*, though he did revoke a related brief that had placed a sentence of excommunication on those opposing efforts to defend Native Americans from slavery. For details, see Gutierrez, *Las Casas*, 302–310, with n.4 on 561, and Parker, *Emperor*, 359.

[102] Pope Urban VIII, *Commissum Nobis*, Apr. 22, 1639, quoted and translated in Panzer, *The Popes and Slavery*, 33–34. See also Panzer's discussion of the antislavery teachings of Gregory XIV (1591), Benedict XIV (1741), and others at 29ff.

[103] Noonan, *A Church That Can and Cannot Change*, 78–80, 247–248. See also Panzer, *The Popes and Slavery*, 27–28.

[104] The quotation from Las Casas is from his *Historia de las Indias*, III, 129, translated and quoted in Noonan, *A Church That Can and Cannot Change*, 76. On Las Casas and Black slavery, see Gutierrez, *Las Casas*, 324–330.

grounds. In the late sixteenth century, the Jesuit Luis de Molina (1535–1600) blasted European involvement in the African slave trade, arguing that the vast majority of wars yielding slaves in Africa were unjust and that Portuguese merchants did little or nothing to verify just title; he called for Portuguese rulers and bishops to outlaw the trade, describing it as a sin against justice. In the early seventeenth century Jesuit Tomás Sánchez (1550–1610), discussing the African slave trade to the New World, argued that it was a mortal sin for a person to buy slaves *en masse* in cases where the buyer was in doubt about whether the seller had just title to the slaves being offered, and furthermore that restitution must be made when slaves had been bought in such a circumstance.[105] In 1686 the Holy Office, an ecclesiastical body at the Vatican charged with clarifying matters of doctrine, taught that "buyers of Blacks and other natives" are obliged "to inquire about their title of servitude, viz. whether they have justly or unjustly been enslaved," and that the "possessors of Blacks and other natives who have harmed no one and been captured by force or deceit" are obliged "to set them free."[106] In a book published posthumously in 1758, Portuguese priest Manoel Ribeiro Rocha (1687–1745) denounced the African slave trade as piracy and presented a scheme for gradual emancipation.[107] But such strictures did little to restrict the African slave trade or promote emancipation. Effective opposition to slavery as such would have to arise from other quarters, perhaps the most important being the Religious Society of Friends, a small religious community also known as the Quakers.

---

[105] On Molina, see Henrique Joner, "Impressions of Luis de Molina about the trade of African slaves," *Patristica et Mediaevalia*, 36 (2015), 39–50. On Mercado and Sanchez, see Noonan, *A Church That Can and Cannot Change*, 80–83.

[106] *Response of the Congregation of the Holy Office*, No. 230, Mar. 20, 1686, selections translated and quoted in Panzer, *The Popes and Slavery*, 35–37.

[107] Celia M. Azevedo, "Rocha's 'The Ethiopian Redeemed' and the circulation of anti-slavery ideas," *Slavery & Abolition*, 24:1 (2003), 101–126.

5

Rejecting Slavery

In summer 1785, a tall, red-haired young man on his way to London halted his horse and sat down by the side of the road. The man was Thomas Clarkson (1760–1846), an ambitious and energetic Deacon in the Church of England. While a student at the University of Cambridge in 1784, Clarkson had won a coveted Latin essay prize, and in 1785, his final year of studies, he prepared an entry to the University's most prestigious Latin essay competition. No student had ever won both. After two months of research and writing, Clarkson submitted his essay and won first place. He had completed his studies with great distinction and was en route to a successful career in the Church. But as he rode to London, he was not thinking about his successes or his career. The topic of the essay competition had been sobering: Is it lawful to make slaves of others against their will? Although he had entered the competition "wholly ignorant" of the African slave trade, and with no motive other than to advance his reputation, the process of research and writing had left him deeply disturbed: "It was but one gloomy subject from morning to night. In the day-time I was uneasy. In the night I had little rest. I sometimes never closed my eye-lids for grief."[1] In the course of his reading Clarkson

---

[1] Thomas Clarkson, *The History of the Rise, Progress, and Accomplishment of the Abolition of the African Slave-Trade by the British Parliament* (New York: J. S. Taylor, 1836), vol. 1, 159 and 160–161. For our discussion of Clarkson and the London Abolition Committee we are indebted to: Adam Hochschild, *Bury the Chains: Prophets and Rebels in the Fight to Free an Empire's Slaves* (Boston: Houghton Mifflin, 2005), esp. 85–97; Ellen Gibson Wilson, *Thomas Clarkson: A Biography* (New York: St. Martin's Press, 1990); Judith Jennings, *The Business of Abolishing the British Slave Trade, 1783–1807* (London: Frank Cass, 1997); J. R. Oldfield, *Popular Politics and British Anti-Slavery: The*

came across passages including this, drawn from an eyewitness on the coast of West Africa:

[T]he Negroes are so loathe to leave their own country that they often leap out of the canoe, boat, or ship, into the sea, and keep under water till they are drowned to avoid being taken up and saved by the boats which pursue them. ... They had about twelve Negroes who willingly drowned themselves; others starved themselves to death. ... [the Captain of the ship] Phillips was advised to cut off the legs and arms of some to terrify the rest (as other captains had done) but this he refused to do.[2]

And from a former slavetrader, describing the purchase of slaves from West Africa:

We found about two hundred [slaves] confined in one place. But here how shall I relate the affecting sight I there beheld! How can I sufficiently describe the silent sorrow which appeared in the countenance of the afflicted father, and the painful anguish of the tender mother, expecting to be forever separated from their tender offspring...[3]

On his ride to London, Clarkson's mind was "almost wholly engrossed" with the ugly realities of slavery:

I became at times very seriously affected while upon the road. I stopped my horse occasionally, and dismounted and walked. I frequently tried to persuade myself in these intervals that the contents of my Essay could not be true. The more however I reflected upon them, or rather upon the authorities on which they were founded, the more I gave them credit.

Finally, he continues, sitting by the road, "a thought came into my mind, that if the contents of the Essay were true, it was time some person should see these calamities to their end."[4] Feeling a call to action, Clarkson hesitated at the enormity of the task. As he well knew, humans had made slaves of each other for millennia. Before writing, before the wheel, before money, there were slaves. And while slavery had waned in Western Europe in the Middle Ages, the massive incorporation of slave labor in

---

Mobilisation of Public Opinion against the Slave Trade, 1787–1807 (London: Frank Cass, 1998); Roger Anstey, *The Atlantic Slave Trade and British Abolition, 1760–1810* (London: MacMillan, 1975); Davis, *The Problem of Slavery in the Age of Revolution*; and Leo d'Anjou, *Social Movements and Cultural Change: The First Abolition Campaign Revisited* (New York: Aldine de Gruyter, 1996).

[2] Anthony Benezet, *Some Historical Account of Guinea*, in Benezet, *The Complete Antislavery Writings of Anthony Benezet, 1754–1783*, ed. David L. Crosby (Baton Rouge, LA: Louisiana State University Press, 2013), 173.

[3] Ibid., 174.

[4] Clarkson, *The History of the Rise, Progress, and Accomplishment*, vol. 1, 161–162.

the economies of the New World meant that by the eighteenth century, slavery was as present as ever as a global reality. Powerful interests in Britain had much to lose by any attack on the slave trade. Conventional wisdom agreed with Adam Smith, who had argued some twenty years earlier that slavery "has hardly any possibility of being abolished … [it] has been universall in the beginnings of society, and the love of dominion and authority over others will probably make it perpetuall."[5] Common, too, would have been the view of a Londoner in 1764: "The impossibility of doing without slaves will always prevent this traffic being dropped. The necessity, the absolute necessity, then, of carrying it on, must, since there is no other, be its excuse."[6] For Clarkson this was unacceptable. After numerous walks in the woods spent pondering the matter, he resolved as a first step to translate his Latin essay into English, find a publisher, and wait to "see how the public received it."[7]

When Clarkson went in search of a publisher in January 1786, a chance meeting with a family friend led him to the shop of the printer James Phillips, a Quaker. Unbeknownst to Clarkson, Quakers had been quietly working against slavery for decades. American Quakers had encouraged their British counterparts to agitate against the slave trade, and in 1783 British Quakers had formed a twenty-three-member committee on the issue, of which Phillips was a member. Phillips, moreover, had printed most of the antislavery writings that had appeared in London to that point and had heard of Clarkson's prize essay. He agreed to publish it on the spot and connected the young Deacon to an antislavery network of a breadth, depth, and influence beyond Clarkson's hopes. As Clarkson saw it, he "had been providentially directed" and thrown suddenly among his future coworkers "as into a new world of friends."[8] These included William Dillwyn (1743–1824), an American Quaker living in London who together with five fellow Quakers had formed an informal committee of their own in 1784 for the purpose of influencing public opinion against slavery; Granville Sharp, an Anglican who had led the charge in a number of legal cases in Britain seeking rights for slaves under English law; James Ramsay (1733–1789), an Anglican priest who had served in the West Indies and whose eyewitness account of the sufferings

---

[5] Adam Smith, *Lectures on Jurisprudence*, ed. R. L. Meek, D. D. Raphael, and P. G. Stein (Oxford: Clarendon Press, 1978), 187, quoted in Hochschild, *Bury the Chains*, 86–87.

[6] Quoted in d'Anjou, *Social Movements and Cultural Change*, 70.

[7] Clarkson, *The History of the Rise, Progress, and Accomplishment*, vol. 1, 163.

[8] Clarkson, *The History of the Rise, Progress, and Accomplishment*, vol. 1, 166 and 168.

of slaves there provoked one of the first noteworthy public controversies over the issue in the British press; and William Wilberforce (1759–1833), an evangelical Anglican who would become the cause's champion in Parliament. Clarkson and his Quaker coworkers judged the time ripe for more deliberate action, and on May 22, 1787, twelve men met at Phillips' shop and formed what came to be known as the London Abolition Committee. They included five of the six members of Dillwyn's informal committee, James Phillips and three other Quakers, and Sharp, Clarkson, and one other Anglican. Working closely with Wilberforce and other allies, the Committee launched a campaign to bring about an abolition of the African slave trade by the British Parliament. In the years to come they gathered reams of evidence regarding the slave trade, published and distributed pamphlets and books (beginning with Clarkson's essay), distributed visual material (including a famous diagram of slaves packed into a slave ship), organized lectures, secured notices in the press, and managed several massive petition campaigns to Parliament.

What was not possible in the time of Las Casas was the use of community organizing to build and activate an antislavery movement – which we call the Second Antislavery Movement. In the eighteenth century it was possible to mobilize three "convening" forces – faith, commerce, and place – to draw individuals together. Such forces played a core role in stimulating changes to existing social and cultural norms and underpinned the developing consensus on the human right to be free from slavery. A second key ingredient that facilitated a *popular* antislavery movement has been described as "moral redefinition"[9] – the process that privileges, and ultimately codifies the *victim's* definition of evil across a wider population of nonvictims. Unlike Spain in the time of Las Casas, Britain in the 1780s held large numbers of people who were open to trying to see the world from the perspective of an enslaved person. Indeed, this redefining of slavery, from business activity or legal possession to an immoral act of evil exploitation, was a key first step in the formation of human rights as we know them today. Such processes of "moral redefinition" start with individuals but are sustained and given momentum by groups – leading by example, suggesting, sharing, and working together to express moral choices through considered action. Faith groups, commerce, and place (the communities where people live and act) became the

---

[9] Kevin Bales, "Slavery and the human right to evil," *Journal of Human Rights*, 3:1 (2004), 55–65, 63.

centres of antislavery organizing. The mechanism of social change built upon a new moral interpretation illustrates the idea that:

social change is actually the physical manifestation of a spreading idea. Through that lens we see that it is the family, the church, the school, the club, the sports-team, the workmates, the friends, the people who inhabit one's immediate social world, and only occasionally outside influences, that carry the 'infection' of viral ideas [such as abolitionism].[10]

In his first seven years working for the Abolition Committee, Clarkson traveled 35,000 miles, mostly by horseback, as he canvassed England to gather evidence, distribute antislavery literature, give lectures, and work with local abolition committees. And of course he was not alone in such work. The former slave Olaudah Equiano (c. 1745–1797) published his autobiography in 1789 and it soon became a bestseller. Equiano followed it with a lecture tour throughout the British Isles that lasted over five years.[11] Wilberforce and other Evangelical Anglicans in his circle worked strenuously to garner support among Britain's legislators. Also important was the use of graphic imagery, for example the drawing of the slaves packed within the slave ship *Brookes*, plastered on walls and reproduced in many, often very large-scale, formats. (See Figure 5.1.) To the eighteenth-century viewer, well aware of the risks involved in transatlantic travel, the horror would be immediately apparent: people chained and stacked like cordwood in a four-foot high ship's hold would be lying in their own excrement and filth for weeks, often chained to corpses as people died around them.

On the grass-roots level, hundreds of thousands of Britons, women and men, boycotted West Indian sugar in the early 1790s, and almost 400,000 signed petitions opposing the slave trade, the highest number of petitions Parliament "had ever received on any subject."[12] The abolitionists' attempts to rouse public opinion against the slave trade could scarcely have gone better.

And yet victory proved elusive. In the House of Commons, Wilberforce's 1792 motion to abolish the slave trade was watered down

---

[10] Kevin Bales and Alison Gardner, "Free soil, free produce, free communities," in G. LeBaron, J. Pliley, and D. Blight (eds.), *Fighting Modern Slavery and Human Trafficking: History and Contemporary Policy* (Cambridge: Cambridge University Press, 2020), 73–96, 79.

[11] On Equiano, see Hochschild, *Bury the Chains*, 167–180.

[12] Hochschild, *Bury the Chains*, 213, with 193–194, and d'Anjou, *Social Movements and Cultural Change*, 166.

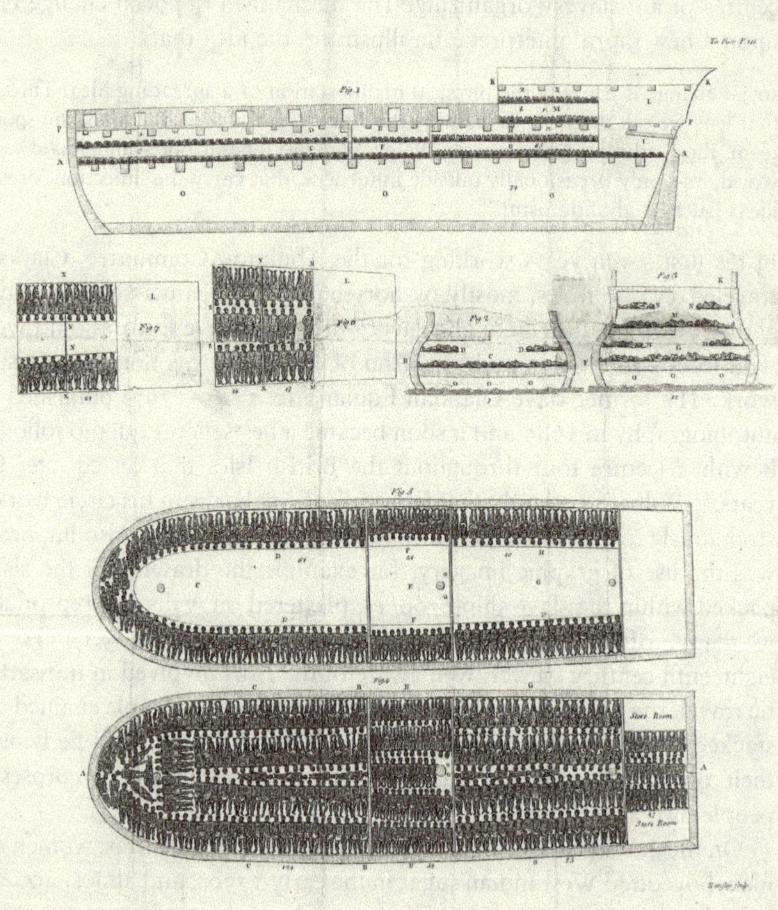

FIGURE 5.1 Drawing of the slave ship *Brookes*. Image courtesy of the David Rumsey Map Collection, David Rumsey Map Center, Stanford Libraries.

with a hostile amendment to insert "gradually" into the language of the bill, and then the bill stalled altogether in the House of Lords. A massive and ultimately successful revolt by slaves in Haiti (then the French colony St. Domingue) followed by the French Revolution itself cast the abolitionist cause in a radical and unpatriotic light in the eyes of many Britons. Further attempts by the abolitionists in 1793 and 1794 in both the House of Commons and the House of Lords met with failure. Clarkson had spent himself in the struggle. Exhausted, in ill-health and demoralized after the defeat in Parliament, he retired to private life as a gentleman farmer.

In the disappointment of the moment, it must have been easy to miss what is apparent in hindsight: The work of the London Abolition Committee and its many allies had not in fact been a failure. In less than a decade, that work had raised the slave trade from fringe concern to major public issue in Great Britain. Popular support had been mobilized. But what were the sources of that earlier "fringe concern"? How was it that the network of antislavery figures whom Clarkson chanced to find in 1786 was there to be found at all?

Central to any answer to this question is the opposition to slavery among Quakers starting in the late seventeenth century, even as the history of antislavery thought and activism is a large one and includes many actors. In previous chapters we have examined the ways in which religious groups and religiously motivated individuals of the past have variously attempted to justify, ameliorate, or restrict slavery. We turn now to the religious rejection of slavery. Under the label "rejecting slavery" we include both the intention to cease holding or using slaves oneself and the intention to stop others from doing so.

5.1 EARLY VOICES

The earliest identifiable persons or groups to unambiguously reject slavery are the Essenes, a rigorous religious society of Jews who flourished in Palestine from the second century BC through the first century AD, and the Therapeutae, a Jewish community living in Alexandria (Egypt) in the early years of the Common Era.[13] Josephus, writing in 93 or 94 AD, reports:

> The Essenes like to teach that in all things one should rely on God ... Compared to all others adept in virtue, their practice of righteousness is admirable ... They put their property into a common stock, and the rich man enjoys no more of his fortune than does the man with absolutely nothing ... In addition, they take no wives and acquire no slaves; in fact, they consider slavery an injustice, and marriage as leading to discord.[14]

---

[13] Our discussion of the Essenes and Therapeutae relies on Joan E. Taylor, *The Essenes, the Scrolls, and the Dead Sea* (Oxford: Oxford University Press, 2012), Geza Vermes and Martin Goodman (eds.), *The Essenes according to the Classical Sources* (Sheffield: JSOT Press, 1989), and Maren E. Niehoff, *Philo of Alexandria: An Intellectual Biography* (New Haven: Yale University Press, 2018).

[14] Josephus, *Antiquities of the Jews*, 18.18–21, translated in Vermes and Goodman (eds.), *The Essenes according to the Classical Sources*, 55.

According to Philo of Alexandria, writing between 40 and 49 AD, the Essenes:

are men utterly dedicated to the service of God ... Almost alone among all mankind, they live without goods and without property ... There are no slaves among them, not a single one, but being all free they help one another. And they condemn slave-owners, not only as unjust in that they offend against equality, but still more as ungodly, in that they transgress the law of nature which, having given birth to all men equally and nourished them like a mother, makes of them true brothers, not in name but in reality.[15]

In another work, Philo says of the Therapeutae that:

they are not waited on by slaves, because they deem any possession of servants whatever to be contrary to nature. For she hath begotten all men alike free; but the injustice and greedy oppression of some who were zealous for the inequality that is the source of all evil, laid a yoke on the weaker ones and gave the control into the hands of the stronger.[16]

Three details of these short texts indicate that slavery was rejected by the Essenes and Therapeutae for religious as well as moral reasons. First, Philo makes a point of asserting that the Essenes reject slavery as both "unjust" and "ungodly." Second, the use of the concept of nature suggests the presence of Stoic ideas, and traditional Stoic teaching identified "God's will" and "nature,"[17] so that what is "contrary to nature" or what transgresses "the law of nature" would have been thought to be contrary to God's will. Finally, for devout Jews the pursuit of moral excellence would have been seen as part of their service to God, and so any moral motivation to reject slavery as unjust would have carried in its wake a religious reason to reject slavery.

In the Christian tradition, the first strong condemnation of slaveholding *per se* is due to St. Gregory of Nyssa. Nyssa had read Philo and it is possible he was influenced by the position of the Essenes and Therapeutae on slavery.[18] In a remarkable homily, commenting on Ecclesiastes 2:7

[15] Philo, *Quod omnis probus liber sit*, 75–79, translated in Vermes and Goodman (eds.), *The Essenes according to the Classical Sources*, 21.

[16] Philo, *On the Contemplative Life*, 70, translation due to F. C. Conybeare (1895), emended slightly and presented in Vermes and Goodman (eds.), *The Essenes according to the Classical Sources*, 93.

[17] See Susanne Bobzien, *Determinism and Freedom in Stoic Philosophy* (Oxford: Oxford University Press, 1999), 45–46.

[18] On Gregory's familiarity with the works of Philo, see Ramelli, *Social Justice and the Legitimacy of Slavery*, 88.

("I bought male and female slaves ..."), Nyssa asserts that slaveholding is a sin of pride and a contravention of God's will:

[W]hat is such a gross example of arrogance ... as for a human being to think himself the master of his own kind? ... "I bought male and female slaves." What do you mean? You condemn man to slavery, when his nature is free and possesses free will, and you legislate in competition with God, overturning his law for the human species. The one [man] made on the specific terms that he should be the owner of the earth, and appointed to government by the Creator – him you bring under the yoke of slavery, as though defying and fighting against the divine decree.

You have forgotten the limits of your authority, and that your rule is confined to control over things without reason ... Why do you go beyond what is subject to you and raise yourself up against the very species which is free, counting your own kind on a level with four-footed things and even footless things? ...

"I bought male and female slaves." For what price, tell me? What did you find in existence worth as much as this human nature? What price did you put on rationality? How many obols did you reckon the equivalent of the likeness of God? How many staters did you get for selling the being shaped by God? God said, let us make man in our image, after our likeness [Gen. 1:26]. If he is in the likeness of God, and rules the whole earth, and has been granted authority over everything on earth from God, who is his buyer, tell me? Who is his seller? To God alone belongs this power; or rather, not even to God himself. For his gracious gifts, it says, are irrevocable [Rom. 11:29]. God would not therefore reduce the human race to slavery, since he himself, when we had been enslaved to sin, spontaneously recalled us to freedom. But if God does not enslave what is free, who is he that sets his own power above God's?[19]

According to Gregory, God has made human beings in his own image, with the ability to be the master of their own actions, and God intends humans to be able to exercise this ability, so that anyone who takes away another's freedom by enslaving him acts against God's will. This carefully reasoned rejection of slavery is unique among all premodern sources. The most similar attitude of which we are aware is Scotus' rejection of slavery, except in the case of dangerous criminals and self-sale, which did not appear until the fourteenth century.[20] And it is not until the eighteenth century that the critique of slavery as such begins to gain momentum.

A final set of early abolitionist voices should be mentioned, though the details are obscure: From its beginnings in the eleventh century, the Muslim sect known as the Druzes prohibited concubinage and slavery

---

[19] *Ecclesiasten Homiliae IV (et al.)*, Homily IV on Eccl 2:7, in Gregory of Nyssa, *Opera*, vol. 5, ed. J. McDonough and P. Alexander (Leiden, 1962), translated in Garnsey, *Ideas of Slavery from Aristotle to Augustine*, 81–82.

[20] On Scotus' views on slavery, see Section 4.3.

within their largely isolated and self-contained community in the mountains of Syria.[21] We encourage scholars to uncover the story of this earliest Muslim rejection of slavery.

5.2 THE REJECTION OF SLAVERY IN THE SEVENTEENTH AND EARLY EIGHTEENTH CENTURIES

Several Protestant thinkers in the seventeenth century advanced arguments for the amelioration of slavery – but not its outright rejection – based on general principles of Christian ethics. Thus while Richard Baxter, an English Puritan writing in the 1660s, accepts voluntary self-sale and the enslavement of criminals and enemies captured in a lawful war, he argues forcefully for good treatment of slaves (since they are "beloved of God") and denounces the kidnapping that was a regular part of the African slave trade, holding that slavetraders were "fitter to be called incarnate Devils than Christians."[22] Preaching in Barbados in 1671, the prominent early Quaker George Fox went a step further, recommending to his listeners that they follow the example of the Old Testament (Hebrew slaves were to be released after seven years), and "let them go free after a considerable Term of Years," providing them with some financial provision with which to begin their life as freedmen.[23] In his argument Fox relies on the Golden Rule and on Luke 6:36 ("Be merciful, even as your Father is merciful."). The Quaker William Edmundson (1627–1712) makes a similar case in 1675, in a letter to Quakers in the American colonies.

All of these texts contain arguments based on general Christian principles for the conclusion that the life of slaves should be improved, whether through gentler treatment, invitation to inclusion in the religious community, or manumission, but they do not contain arguments for the more significant conclusion that Christians should not buy, sell, or hold slaves, full stop. Yet just a few decades on, some Christians began to employ the very same principles to reject slavery itself. The first clear

---

[21] See Clarence-Smith, *Islam and the Abolition of Slavery*, 59–60.

[22] Baxter, *A Christian Directory*, book 2, chap. 14, tit. 2, 468. In the same work, Baxter tells Masters to "remember that even a slave may be one of those neighbors that you are bound to love as yourselves, and to do as you would be done by, if your case were his" (469). Baxter's tentative use of "may" here is interesting, and is dropped by later thinkers who invoke the Golden Rule and the command to love one's neighbor in the service of arguments for a vigorous rejection of slavery.

[23] Fox, "Gospel family-order," 16, 49.

instance is a letter written by four Quakers in Germantown, Pennsylvania in 1688, addressed to their local monthly meeting of Quakers, at a time when many Quakers bought, sold, and kept slaves. The authors give six distinct arguments in this concise and densely reasoned letter. Their first can be reduced to three steps:

(1) "There is a saying, that we shall doe to all men like as we will be done ourselves; making no difference of what generation, descent or colour they are."

(2) No one of us "would be done or handled at this manner … viz., to be sold or made a slave for all the time of his life."

(3) Thus We should not make someone a perpetual slave, or sell such slaves.

Observing that the majority of the Blacks in the colonies were brought to the New World against their will, and that many were stolen (as opposed to being purchased with just title), the authors go on to argue that it is equally wrong "to steal or robb men" and to "buy or purchase" those who are stolen, indicating that their target is not just (3) but the wider prohibition:

(3)*We should not make someone a perpetual slave, or buy or sell such slaves.

Continuing, they offer additional considerations: Slavery as practiced in the colonies is wrong because it results in wives being separated from husbands, and children from parents – the former leading to adultery and both the former and the latter contradicting the Golden Rule. Next, the practice of slavery by the Quakers is bad press for many in Europe, who might otherwise wish to immigrate to Pennsylvania. Finally, purchasing many slaves will risk violent revolt, which would lead many Quaker masters to "take the sword at hand and war against these poor slaves," which would violate the Quakers' pacifism.[24] After having been passed up the hierarchy, the letter's call for a rejection of slavery by the Quaker community as a whole was deemed a Pandora's box and set aside.

---

[24] The text of the Germantown letter is reproduced in Bruns (ed.), *Am I Not a Man and a Brother*, 3–4. Helpful background on the Germantown Quakers is provided in Katharine Gerbner, "Antislavery in print: The Germantown protest, the 'Exhortation,' and the seventeenth-century Quaker debate on slavery," *Early American Studies*, 9:3 (Fall 2011), 552–575.

Many of the Quakers of Germantown, including one of the authors of the Germantown protest, later broke off from the main Quaker community and formed a short-lived splinter group, the Christian Quakers, led by George Keith (1638/1639–1716). In 1693 this group published a second attack on slavery, printed as "An Exhortation and Caution to Friends concerning buying or keeping of Negroes." In it we find arguments against the buying and holding of slaves based on the Golden Rule, various passages from Scripture (e.g. against man-stealing, Exod 21:16), and the general notion that Christians should imitate Christ's love and goodness:

Therefore we judge it necessary that all faithful Friends should discover themselves to be true *Christians* by having the Fruits of the Spirit of Christ, which are *Love, Mercy, Goodness, and Compassion* towards all in Misery, and that suffer Oppression and severe Usage, so far as in them is possible to ease and relieve them, and set them free of their hard Bondage ... in true *Christian Love*, we earnestly recommend it to all our Friends and Brethren, Not to buy any Negroes, unless it were on purpose to set them free, and that such who have bought any, and have them at present, after some reasonable time of moderate Service ... may set them at Liberty ...[25]

The rejection of slavery in these early years was not limited to Quakers. Judge Samuel Sewall of the Massachusetts Superior Court, a Puritan, published a tract in 1700 in which he argued against the African slave trade and the practice of slaveholding on several grounds, including: (a) the purchase of African slaves promotes much evil, separating wives from husbands and children from parents, causing the death of many slaves during the journey across the ocean, and promoting war in Africa; (b) it is unknown (to potential buyers in New England) whether the slaves for sale were captured in lawful wars, and an application of the Golden Rule implies that New Englanders should not buy slaves while lacking such knowledge; and (c) since the Israelites were forbidden from holding one another as slaves, and the New Testament calls Christians to a higher standard, so Christians should not hold others in perpetual servitude. Citing Jesus' command to love one's enemies (Matt 5:43–44) and to "love one another, even as I have loved you" (John 13:34), Sewall observes:

Our Blessed Saviour has altered the Measures of the ancient Love Song, and set it to a most Excellent New Tune, which all ought to be ambitious of Learning ...

[25] George Keith and the members of the Christian Quaker Monthly Meeting in Philadelphia, "An Exhortation and Caution to Friends concerning buying or keeping of Negroes," from Bruns (ed.), *Am I Not a Man and a Brother*, 6–8. For context on the document, see Gerbner, "Antislavery in print." Italics in original.

These Ethiopians, as black as they are, seeing they are Sons and Daughters of the First Adam, the Brethren and Sisters of the Last Adam, and the Offspring of God; They ought to be treated with a Respect agreeable.[26]

The prevalence of antislavery viewpoints increased dramatically in the eighteenth century. The American Quakers John Hepburn, Ralph Sandiford, Elihu Coleman and Benjamin Lay published strenuous attacks on slaveholding in 1715, 1729, 1733, and 1737, respectively, and there were others as well. Reading these writings along with the texts of the Germantown Quakers, the Christian Quakers, and Sewall, we find a lengthy catalogue of separate considerations advanced against slavery, as well as a number of replies to common proslavery objections. Their case against slavery refers both to the concrete harms associated with slaveholding and to various moral principles violated by slaveholding. To buy and keep slaves is to participate in a practice that promotes war in Africa and that involves extreme physical violence to the enslaved, high mortality for Africans in the transatlantic journey, rape of female slaves, and the separation of wives from husbands and children from parents. The circumstances of slaves result in their being tempted to steal (to supplement meager rations), lie (to escape punishment), fornicate (when not allowed to marry) or commit adultery (when spouses are separated), and even commit suicide or murder to escape their plight. What is more, when Christians keep slaves nonbelievers are given a reason to reject Christianity. In addition to an enumeration of the evils caused by slavery, these writers invoke a number of Christian moral principles and specific biblical passages to construct their arguments, of which six are summarized here. First, as we have already seen, there are arguments against slavery from the Golden Rule. Second, there are what we might call Arguments from the Spirit of Christianity, as in Hepburn:

It is not in singularity or Ostentation that I appear in Print, but my Christian Duty ... in the Detection of the Anti-christian Practice in *making Slaves* of them who bear the Image of God ... A Practice so *cruel* and *inhumane*, that the more it is thought upon by judicious men, the more they do abhor it; It being so vile a contradiction to the Gospel of the blessed Messiah.[27]

---

[26] Sewall, *The Selling of Joseph a Memorial*, in Bruns (ed.), *Am I Not a Man and a Brother*, 13.

[27] Hepburn, *The American Defense of the Christian Golden Rule*, in Bruns (ed.), *Am I Not a Man and a Brother*, 16.

Third, there is an Argument from God's Gift of Free Will (already suggested by Nyssa). In Coleman's formulation:

we may observe, when God had created man, that he gave him a free will, and would not compel the will of man, no not to that which was good, much less to that which was evil; therefore we ought not to compel our fellow creatures.[28]

Fourth, these writers sometimes criticized slavery by arguing that the motive for slaveholding was a sinful desire for wealth and idleness.[29] Next, the early eighteenth-century critics of slavery seem to have been aware of the circumstances under which Africans were captured and sold to European traders, and so without having to challenge the traditional doctrine that capture in a lawful war provides just title, they could attack slavery as it was practiced in the New World by invoking the biblical prohibition of man-stealing (Exod 21:16 and 1 Tim 1:10). Finally, given the outsider status of Black slaves in the American colonies, they occasionally invoked God's command that the Israelites "not oppress a stranger" (Exod 22:21 and 23:9).

5.3 THE QUAKERS' INSTITUTIONAL RESPONSE TO SLAVERY

The Quakers slowly united in their opposition to slavekeeping as the eighteenth century unfolded. A description of this process requires some reference to organizational structure and decision-making practices within the Society of Friends. From the late 1600s Friends organized their meetings for worship and Church governance in a hierarchical structure. Particular Meetings were gatherings of the Quakers in a given locale, similar to local congregations. A number of Particular Meetings would report to a Monthly Meeting, a number of Monthly Meetings to a Quarterly Meeting, and a number of Quarterly Meetings to a Yearly

---

[28] Coleman, *Testimony against Making Slaves of Men*, in Bruns (ed.), *Am I Not a Man and a Brother*, 41.

[29] See Coleman, *Testimony against Making Slaves of Men*, in Bruns (ed.), *Am I Not a Man and a Brother*, 42; Hepburn, *The American Defense of the Christian Golden Rule*, in Bruns (ed.), *Am I Not a Man and a Brother*, 18–19; and Benjamin Lay, *All Slave-keepers That keep the Innocents in Bondage, Apostates...*, in Bruns (ed.), *Am I Not a Man and a Brother*, 56, 60. Criticism of slavery based on its connection to greed was a theme common to the Therapeutae and Nyssa (and possibly the Essenes), whose rejection of slavery was situated within a wider effort to reject avarice and the injustice to which it leads, adopting instead a lifestyle of holy simplicity. On the connection between asceticism, the rejection of social injustice, and antislavery, see Ramelli, *Social Justice and the Legitimacy of Slavery*.

Meeting. Any Friend in good standing could attend the Monthly Meeting to which his or her Particular Meeting reported, as could traveling Friends from elsewhere if they carried a letter of endorsement from their own Monthly Meeting. Quarterly Meetings were attended by representatives from subsidiary Monthly Meetings, and Yearly Meetings were attended by representatives from subsidiary Quarterly Meetings.[30]

The Quakers were one of several nonconforming Protestant groups that formed amid the political and religious turmoil of the English Civil Wars (1642–1651). Unlike most of these sects, they had managed to survive and thrive as time passed, in part by learning to coexist with established powers without losing their distinctive identity. Maintaining unity, even uniformity, was important for their survival. By the late 1600s the London Yearly Meeting was sending out "Queries" and "Advices" relating to many aspects of behavior, and leaders exercised oversight and control over any publications authored by Friends. By the 1700s Yearly Meetings began to issue formal Books of Discipline that laid out rules of individual conduct and rules relating to Church governance. Friends were expected, for example, to dress and speak plainly, attend Meetings regularly, and conduct their business affairs with honesty and moderation. They were expected not to use liquor or tobacco immoderately, not to marry outside the Society of Friends, and, as early as 1704 in Philadelphia, not to buy or sell Native American slaves. Continued unrepentant violation of rules led to expulsion from the community (disownment).

While enforcement of such rules came from the top down (or the middle down – Monthly Meetings could disown), the rules' initial introduction seems in some cases (perhaps many) to have come from the bottom up. Friends believed that the pursuit of moral and spiritual perfection was their duty, and they also believed that God could enlighten

---

[30] Our discussion of the Quakers and their fight against slavery relies on Robynne Rogers Healey, "History of Quaker faith and practice: 1650–1808," in S. W. Angell and P. Dandelion (eds.), *The Cambridge Companion to Quakerism* (Cambridge: Cambridge University Press, 2018), 13–30; Thomas E. Drake, *Quakers and Slavery in America* (New Haven: Yale University Press, 1950); J. William Frost (ed.), *The Quaker Origins of Antislavery* (Norwood, PA: Norwood Editions, 1980); Rayner W. Kelsey, "Early Books of Discipline of the Philadelphia yearly meeting," *Bulletin of Friends Historical Association*, 24:1 (1935), 12–23; Brycchan Carey, *From Peace to Freedom: Quaker Rhetoric and the Birth of American Antislavery, 1657–1761* (New Haven: Yale University Press, 2012); and Elizabeth Cazden, "Quakers, slavery, anti-slavery, and race," in S. W. Angell and B. P. Dandelion (eds.), *The Oxford Handbook of Quaker Studies* (Oxford: Oxford University Press, 2013), 347–362.

every person directly about His will. These beliefs were reflected in the distinctive customs of Quaker Business Meetings,[31] at which Friends would sit in silence until moved to speak:

First, an individual ... purified his own mind of earthly thoughts so that God could direct him. He then could communicate by speaking that truth to others in a meeting ... After an item had been considered for a period of time which could be in silence or after hearing several Friends speak, the clerk summarized what the members thought God had directed and individuals orally expressed their concurrence. Decisions were made by the clerk's ascertaining the "sense of the meeting," or the "weight of the meeting."[32]

Clearly, the priority given to individual insight into God's will could pose obstacles to the unity of the Society. At a time when many Quakers in the colonies owned slaves, criticism of slaveholding within meetings by Friends such as Sandiford and Lay often provoked a defensive reaction. When Meetings turned a deaf ear to their insight into the injustice of slavery, Sandiford and Lay raised the volume to eleven. On one occasion Lay kidnapped the young son of a slaveowning couple to help them appreciate the seriousness of the separation of children from parents that the African slave trade involved.[33] On another, he went to a Philadelphia Yearly Meeting wearing a large overcoat to conceal a military uniform, a sword, and a hollowed-out book in which he had placed an animal bladder filled with red pokeberry juice. At the right moment in the meeting, he stood up and denounced slavekeeping as the greatest sin in the world.

He then threw off his great coat, revealing the military garb, the blade, and the book to his astonished [and pacifist] co-religionists ... In a rising crescendo of emotion, the prophet thundered his judgment: "Thus shall God shed the blood of those persons who enslave their fellow creatures." He pulled out the sword, raised the book above his head, and plunged the sword through it. The people in the room gasped as the red liquid gushed down his arm; several women swooned at the sight. To the shock of all, he spattered "blood" on the heads and bodies of the slave keepers.[34]

---

[31] Termed a "Meeting for Worship for the Conduct of Business."

[32] J. William Frost, Introduction, in Frost (ed.), *The Quaker Origins of Antislavery*, 6–7.

[33] Marcus Rediker, *The Fearless Benjamin Lay: The Quaker Dwarf Who Became the First Revolutionary Abolitionist* (Boston: Beacon Press, 2017), 146. Lay came upon the six-year-old boy wandering some distance from his parents' farm and invited him to visit his cave for the day, so that the kidnapping was done without force. (Yes, Lay lived in a cave.)

[34] Rediker, *The Fearless Benjamin Lay*, 2.

The slavekeeper targets were easy to find: At least two-thirds of Philadelphia Quaker leaders held slaves at the time.[35] In reaction to their persistence in criticizing slavery, the most vocal of the Quaker critics were disowned by their Monthly Meetings (including Sandiford, and Lay) or left the mainstream Quaker body of their own accord (as did at least some of the authors of the Germantown Protest). Hepburn's pamphlet seems mainly to have been ignored. But the antislavery cause did gain ground in some circles: Coleman's 1733 pamphlet was officially endorsed by the Nantucket Monthly Meeting of Quakers, who in 1716 had already resolved "that it is not agreeable to truth for Friends to purchase slaves and hold them term of life."[36] By 1729 the Chester, Gloucester, Salem, and Shrewsbury Quarterly Meetings took the position that Friends should be restrained from buying slaves. Many within the Society of Friends were clearly troubled by slavery.

The record of institutional action against slavery by Quaker Meetings displays a slowly building momentum: In 1696 the Philadelphia Yearly Meeting counseled Friends not to encourage further importation of African slaves. In 1712, in response to the moral concerns about slave-keeping voiced by some of its members, the Philadelphia Yearly Meeting wrote to the London Yearly Meeting to request a policy on Quaker involvement with slavery. In 1715, 1720, and 1727 the London Yearly Meeting responded to the Philadelphia Yearly Meeting by criticizing the African slave trade, taking the position that Quakers should not take part in the trafficking of slaves from Africa to the New World, though no disciplinary action was attached to this decision, and it seems not to have been promulgated among Quakers in Britain.[37] But by 1729 it was a rule of discipline among Quakers under the Philadelphia Yearly Meeting that they not be involved in importing African slaves as a business. And given that fact, some members also asked "whether it is not as reasonable we should be restricted from buying of them when imported."[38] In 1730 the Philadelphia Yearly Meeting concluded that "Friends ought to be very cautious of making such purchases [of Negroes as may be hereafter Imported] for the future, it being disagreeable to the sense of this

---

[35] Carey, *From Peace to Freedom*, 179, relying on research by Jean Soderlund.

[36] Bruns (ed.), *Am I Not a Man and a Brother*, 39.

[37] See David Brion Davis, *The Problem of Slavery in Western Culture* (Ithaca: Cornell University Press, 1966), 315 n.43.

[38] Inquiry of the Chester Friends to the Philadelphia Yearly Meeting, 1729, quoted in Drake, *Quakers and Slavery in America*, 41.

Meeting."[39] Throughout the 1730s the Philadelphia Yearly Meeting reiterated the caution both against importing and buying slaves, and in 1743 began formally inquiring of the local meetings whether they were following this policy: "Do Friends observe the former advice of our Yearly Meeting, not to Encourage the Importation of Negroes or to buy them after Imported?"[40] In 1754 the Overseers of the Press of the Philadelphia Yearly Meeting published and distributed, at its own expense, a powerful antislavery essay by the Quaker tailor and traveling minister John Woolman (1720–1772). Thanks to the distribution efforts of Quaker leadership, it became the most widely circulated antislavery text ever distributed, in any language, up to that date.[41] In 1758 the Philadelphia Yearly Meeting then made a pivotal judgment: The Golden Rule "appears to this Meeting" to "induce such Friends who have any Slaves to sett them at Liberty," and accompanied it with a pivotal action – all Friends who imported, sold, or purchased slaves were prohibited from exercising any leadership or authority within the Society.[42] In 1776 the Philadelphia Yearly Meeting instructed its Quarterly and Monthly Meetings to disown any Friend who refused to manumit his or her slaves. In the 1770s and early 1780s Friends manumitted hundreds (probably thousands) of slaves, typically providing monetary compensation for having extracted forced labor.[43] And by 1784, every Yearly Meeting in North America had disallowed its members from keeping slaves.

The most prolific antislavery writer of the mid eighteenth century was the American Quaker schoolmaster Anthony Benezet (1713–1784). His *Some Historical Account of Guinea* (1771) was the very book that opened the young Thomas Clarkson's eyes to the ugly realities of the slave trade. And Benezet's protégé William Dillwyn was an influential member of the group of Quakers Clarkson encountered in 1786. The antislavery network that Clarkson happily discovered owed its existence to decades of prayerful reflection and social action by the Quakers, the only religious body of the era to unite in rejecting slavery.

It is natural that the enslaved saw the injustice in slavery, but what enabled the Quakers – who were not slaves, and many of whom kept slaves – to reject slavery in a world that accepted it? Historians have noted the relevance of war on the Pennsylvania frontiers in the 1750s, which led

---

[39] Text from Frost (ed.), *The Quaker Origins of Antislavery*, 132.

[40] Quoted in Frost (ed.), *The Quaker Origins of Antislavery*, 133.

[41] According to Drake, *Quakers and Slavery in America*, 56.

[42] Philadelphia Yearly Meeting Minutes, 1758, in Frost (ed.), *The Quaker Origins of Antislavery*, 170.

[43] See Drake, *Quakers and Slavery in America*, 76–82.

American Quakers into an intense period of soul-searching and a renewed quest for spiritual purity. More generally, the Quaker disavowal of violence and war may have inclined them to distrust slavery in the New World, insofar as it relied on war in Africa, and insofar as all slavery ultimately relies on violence. But most importantly, two distinctive features intrinsic to Quaker spirituality put Friends in a strong position to perceive that slavery was evil. First, they held that freedom from sin was possible and prioritized the pursuit of spiritual perfection. Second, they believed that something of God's Spirit was present in every human person, and that by attending to this Inner Light, one could discern between good and evil. Their mode of worship was adapted to this core belief: Quakers waited in silence for God to reveal himself inwardly. As a consequence, in their pursuit of holiness Quakers emphasized the importance of listening to the inner call of the Spirit and deemphasized reliance on tradition and traditional Christian theology. This meant that they were at the same time well-disposed to attend to the quiet voice of conscience condemning slavery, and less likely than other Christians to reason that slavery must be acceptable given the fact that Christian churches had accepted it for ages past, or given Scriptural passages which suggested its permissibility.[44]

5.4 ABOLITION OF THE SLAVE TRADE AND EMANCIPATION

His health restored, Thomas Clarkson returned to the fray in 1805, traveling throughout England to rally support for yet another petition campaign. Abolitionists in Parliament secured a partial victory with the passage of the Foreign Slave Trade Act in 1806, which prohibited British subjects from importing slaves to the colonies of foreign powers. This was swiftly followed by the Slave Trade Abolition Act of 1807, which made illegal all British participation in the African slave trade.[45] In 1823,

---

[44] We rely here on Frost, *The Quaker Origins of Antislavery*, 1–8; d'Anjou, *Social Movements and Cultural Change*, 86, and Davis, *Problem of Slavery in Western Culture*, 306 and 330–332.

[45] Significantly, the Act authorized the Royal Navy to intercept and capture slave ships, freeing their enslaved cargos, prosecuting the ship captains, and confiscating the ships. Between 1807 and 1860, some 1,600 slave ships were captured and 150,000 slaves freed – though this freedom was circumscribed by colonial administrators and was often achieved in locations thousands of miles from the original homes of the freed slaves. (See Maeve Ryan, *Humanitarian Governance and the British Antislavery World System* [New Haven: Yale University Press, 2022].) This more than fifty-year military action is often neglected by historians, with much more attention given to public and political campaigns, yet by our reckoning it stands as the most costly antislavery program in human history.

Wilberforce and a group of Quakers and Evangelicals formed an Anti-Slavery Society aimed at emancipation, and one of their number introduced a motion in the House of Commons that "the state of slavery is repugnant to the principles of the British Constitution and of the Christian Religion; and that it ought to be gradually abolished throughout the British Colonies ..."[46] In 1824 the Quaker Elizabeth Heyrick (1769–1831) urged immediate emancipation in an influential pamphlet, and by 1831 the Anti-Slavery Society had come round to the same target.[47] Pressed on by a successful public opinion campaign, the British Parliament passed the Emancipation Act in 1833, and the slaves of the British West Indies were fully emancipated by 1838.

Antislavery activism in North America (which we might consider a third antislavery movement) was fairly vigorous during and immediately after the American Revolution. In the midst of war, Congregationalist minister Samuel Hopkins contended that slavery was a national sin calling down God's vengeance and made a careful case for emancipation. In *Slavery Inconsistent with Justice and Good Policy* (1792), the Presbyterian David Rice argued against slavery based on the natural right to liberty, the inconsistency between divine law which makes every human being a free and responsible agent and human laws allowing slavery, and the political danger posed by an enslaved population. Some popular biblical commentaries in the early nineteenth-century United States also took strong antislavery stances.[48] Among those influenced by such commentaries was George Bourne, an English-born Presbyterian minister in Virginia who in 1816 published *The Book and Slavery Irreconcilable*, in which he denounces slavery as man-stealing, invokes the Old Testament prohibition against returning escaped slaves to their masters, and warns of the possibility of divine judgment on the nation if slavery is not rejected.[49] Bourne's work proved

---

[46] Quoted in Roger Anstey, "The pattern of British abolitionism in the eighteenth and nineteenth centuries," in C. Bolt and S. Drescher (eds.), *Anti-Slavery, Religion, and Reform: Essays in Memory of Roger Anstey* (Folkestone, Kent: Wm Dawson & Sons, 1980), 19–42, 24.

[47] On Heyrick, see David Brion Davis, "The emergence of immediatism in British and American antislavery thought," *The Mississippi Valley Historical Review*, 49:2 (1962), 209–230, 220.

[48] For example, Thomas Scott, *The Holy Bible Containing the Old and New Testaments with Original Notes, Practical Observations and Copious Marginal References* (Philadelphia, 1805) and Brown, *A Dictionary of the Holy Bible*.

[49] Bourne, *The Book and Slavery Irreconcilable*, reproduced in John W. Christie and Dwight L. Dumond (eds.), *George Bourne and The Book and Slavery Irreconcilable* (Wilmington, DE: The Historical Society of Delaware, 1969).

to be important through its effect on William Lloyd Garrison (1805–1879), who credited Bourne with "enabling me to apprehend, with irresistible clearness, the inherent sinfulness of slavery under all circumstances, and its utter incompatibility with the spirit and precepts of Christianity."[50]

Despite such pleas by Bourne and many others, the abolitionist cause in the United States lost momentum after the Revolution. It was reenergized as a consequence of the Second Great Awakening, a series of religious revivals culminating in the early 1830s. The "New School Theology" associated with the movement shifted emphasis away from human depravity and predestination and toward the idea that human beings could, with God's help, freely turn away from sin and reform their lives and society. A number of societal reform movements, abolitionism among them, were accordingly vivified in the wake of religious revival. The cause of immediate emancipation was championed by Congregationalists (Lewis and Arthur Tappan, Theodore Dwight Weld, Gerrit Smith and Eilzur Wright Jr.), Baptists (William Lloyd Garrison) and Quakers (Lucretia Mott, Arnold Buffum, and John Greenleaf Whittier). Most Black abolitionist leaders were Methodist or Baptist ministers, and Black churches played an important role in the protection of fugitive slaves.[51] Reform Jews such as Michael Heilprin and David Einhorn also contributed to the abolitionist cause.[52]

Religious argumentation was an important arrow in the abolitionists' quiver. In *The Bible against Slavery* (1838) Theodore Dwight Weld attempted to answer proslavery interpretations of the Old Testament, while in *The Chattel Principle* (1839) Beriah Green focused on the New Testament.[53] Weld argues – ingeniously but in the end implausibly – that the Jews did not in fact hold involuntary slaves (Jew or Gentile).

[50] Garrison to Theodore Bourne, Nov. 18, 1858, quoted in Christie and Dumond (eds.), *George Bourne and The Book and Slavery Irreconcilable*, v.

[51] Auping, *Religion and Social Justice*, 41–68; James Brewer Stewart, *Holy Warriors: The Abolitionists and American Slavery* (New York: Hill and Wang, 1976), 33–44 and 135; James Brewer Stewart, "Antislavery and abolitionism in the United States, 1776–1870," in D. Eltis, S. Engerman, S. Drescher, and D. Richardson (eds.), *The Cambridge World History of Slavery: Volume 4, AD 1804—AD 2016* (Cambridge: Cambridge University Press, 2017), 399–421, 405–407.

[52] See Jayme A. Sokolow, "Revolution and reform: the antebellum Jewish abolitionists," *Journal of Ethnic Studies*, 9 (1981), 27–43.

[53] Theodore Dwight Weld, *The Bible against Slavery: An Inquiry into the Patriarchal and Mosaic Systems on the Subject of Human Rights* (New York: American Anti-Slavery Society, 1838); Beriah Green, *The Chattel Principle: The Abhorrence of Jesus Christ and the Apostles; Or, No Refuge for American Slavery in the New Testament* (New York: American Anti-Slavery Society, 1839).

More convincing are his discussions of the ameliorating aspects of Jewish law and of slavery as man-stealing. Green builds a stronger overall case, noteworthy because of his attention to rival pro- and antislavery interpretations of Scripture. He argues, first, that since one needs to use reason to judge the Bible as having divine authority, one should not interpret it in such a way that it speaks against a first principle of reason, viz. the principle that all have a natural right to liberty. And second, he argues that the Golden Rule and the second great commandment ("Thou shalt love thy neighbor as thyself") imply the sinfulness of slavery and that *given* this, nothing in the Bible can imply the permissibility of slavery, since God does not lay down inconsistent legislation. We should therefore interpret apparently proslavery passages, like Paul's "slaves, obey your masters," as consistent with the sinfulness of slavery (Green argues at length for the plausibility of such antislavery interpretations).[54]

Frederick Douglass (1818–1895), a former slave and one of the nation's most influential abolitionists, responded forcefully to those who used Christianity to justify slavery:

I love the religion of our blessed Saviour, I love that religion that comes from above, in the "wisdom of God, which is first pure, then peaceable, gentle, and easy to be entreated, full of mercy and good fruits, without partiality and without hypocrisy." [Jas 1:27] And it is because I love the pure and hallowed Christian religion that I hate this slave-holding, this woman-whipping, this mind-darkening, this soul-destroying religion that exists in the Southern States of America.[55]

And in another speech Douglass argued that slavery hinders man's journey to God:

It cuts him off from his Maker, it hides from him the laws of God, and leaves him to grope his way from time to eternity in the dark, under the arbitrary and despotic control of a frail, depraved, and sinful fellow-man.[56]

---

54 See Green, *The Chattel Principle*, 4, 13, 19–26, 41–42. On such interpretations of Paul, see Section 2.6.

55 Frederick Douglass, "England should lead the cause of emancipation: an address delivered in Leeds, England, on December 23, 1846," *Leeds Times*, Dec. 26, 1846, reproduced in Frederick Douglass, *The Frederick Douglass Papers: Series One – Speeches, Debates, and Interviews*, eds. John Blassingame et al. (New Haven: Yale University Press, 1979), vol. 1, 474.

56 Frederick Douglass, from a Lecture on Slavery at Rochester, Dec. 1, 1850, in Frederick Douglass, *My Bondage and My Freedom*, ed. John Stauffer (New York: The Modern Library, 2003), 264.

5.5 THE ROLE OF CHRISTIANITY IN THE REJECTION OF SLAVERY

How important was Christianity in the popular antislavery movements of the eighteenth and nineteenth centuries? In the words of historian David Brion Davis, "It would be difficult to exaggerate the central role Quakers played in initiating and sustaining the first antislavery movements."[57] Quaker antislavery thought and writing from the late seventeenth century led to the creation of a committed network of Quaker antislavery activists by the late eighteenth century. The work of this network then became successful in moving public opinion when, with the help of Clarkson, the Quakers joined forces with Evangelicals such as Wilberforce and Sharp.[58] Approached by the Quaker Anthony Benezet, John Wesley (1703–1791, founder of Methodism) was the first major religious leader in England to denounce slavery, and Methodists as well as Baptists played a large role in the drive to British emancipation in the early nineteenth century.[59] An overwhelming majority of the first abolitionists were serious Christians, and their antislavery work was animated by moral and religious motivation. When as a young man John Woolman first spoke up against slavery, it was because he "believed slavekeeping to be a practice inconsistent with the Christian religion."[60] Wilberforce saw his antislavery work as a divine calling: "God Almighty has set before me two great objects, the suppression of the slave trade and the reformation of manners [public morality]."[61] And as Clarkson struggled over whether to forsake a prestigious ecclesiastical career to instead devote his life to the cause of antislavery, he was pulled between "thirst for worldly interest and honors" and recognition of the duties of benevolence and "Christian charity."[62] As Roger Anstey argues, "it was mainly religious conviction,

---

[57] Davis, *The Problem of Slavery in the Age of Revolution*, 215.

[58] d'Anjou, *Social Movements and Cultural Change*, 157.

[59] Anstey, "The pattern of British abolitionism," 26–30; Anstey, *The Atlantic Slave Trade and British Abolition*, 240–241; Seymour Drescher, *Capitalism and Slavery: British Mobilization in Comparative Perspective* (Oxford: Oxford University Press, 1987), 126–128; Drescher, *Abolition: A History of Slavery and Antislavery*, 252–253.

[60] From John Woolman, *The Journal of John Woolman*, in John Woolman, *The Journal and Major Essays of John Woolman*, ed. P. P. Moulton (Oxford: Oxford University Press, 1971), 33.

[61] From Wilberforce's diary, quoted in James Walvin, "The rise of British popular sentiment for abolition, 1787–1832," in Bolt and Drescher (eds.), *Anti-Slavery, Religion, and Reform*, 149–162, 149.

[62] Clarkson, *History of the Rise, Progress, and Accomplishment*, vol. 1, 175–6.

insight and zeal, which made it possible for anti-slavery feeling to be subsumed in a crusade against the slave trade and slavery."[63]

In the American context, the Second Great Awakening rekindled the abolitionist movement after it had stalled for several decades. Clergy were heavily overrepresented in the surge of abolitionist activity: in the 1830s they constituted 29 percent of the officers in major national antislavery societies and 52 percent of the traveling agents of the American Anti-Slavery Society. Instructions to the traveling agents indicate both (a) the abolitionists' recognition of the importance of religious motivation: "Insist principally on the SIN OF SLAVERY, because our main hope is in the conscience of men"; and (b) their recognition of the importance of churches for their success in affecting public opinion: "Ministers are the hinges of the community and ought to be moved." The travelling agents had some success in this second task: 77 percent of the local agents of the American Anti-Slavery Society were clergy. These local agents were leaders in the formation and work of local abolition societies, which counted between 165,000 and 200,000 members in the North by 1840.[64] Although none of the major Christian denominations in the United States united in condemning slavery (most split on the slavery issue), it was nevertheless the case that the abolitionists themselves were "primarily religious in outlook, whether conservative or liberal in theology and whether part of the organized church or not."[65]

We have here claimed that Christian doctrine, individuals inspired by their Christian faith, and Christian groups played a central causal role in promoting early antislavery movements. Yet when one considers the long history of Christians justifying slavery, it is natural to conclude *a priori* that Christianity could not have been an important factor facilitating abolition and emancipation. If it were, why did it take 1,800 years for that factor to have an impact? And if the Christianity of Protestants in England and the Northern United States was inclining them against

---

[63] Anstey, "The pattern of British abolitionism in the eighteenth and nineteenth centuries," 20. See also Anstey, *The Atlantic Slave-Trade and British Abolition*, 153.

[64] Auping, *Religion and Social Justice*, 65 and 77–81. Quotations are from Auping, 77, citing Theodore Dwight Weld, *Letters of Theodore Dwight Weld, Angelina Grimke and Sarah Grimke 1822–1844*, eds. G. H. Barnes and D. L. Dumond (New York: Da Capo Press, 1970), vol. 1, 125–129.

[65] Carleton Mabee, *Black Freedom: The Nonviolent Abolitionists from 1830 through the Civil War* (London: Collier-Macmillan Limited, 1970), 242–243. See also Bertram Wyatt-Brown, *Yankee Saints and Southern Sinners* (Baton Rouge, LA: Louisiana State University Press, 1985), chap. 2.

slavery, why wasn't the Christianity of Protestants in the American South and in British West Indian colonies doing the same?[66]

These questions reveal the need for a nuanced theory of the causes promoting abolition and emancipation. There were indeed many such causes: slave resistance and revolt, numerous instances in which war or revolution promoted manumission, and the free labor and free soil movements, in addition to widespread popular opposition to slavery in Britain and the United States fueled in large part by religious considerations and basic moral intuition.[67] To elucidate the explanatory role of Christianity in the origin and success of the early antislavery movements, we suggest relying on an idea from philosophical reflection on causation: in some cases A has a natural tendency to cause B, but is prevented from doing so by an obstacle C. Suppose, for example, that a globe has stood for years on a ceramic pedestal, but then one day the pedestal is shattered. The gravitational mass of the Earth (A) has a natural tendency to cause the downward motion of the globe (B), but had been prevented from doing so by the pedestal (C). With the removal of the pedestal, the globe falls, and we are right to say both that the globe fell because of gravity and because the pedestal was destroyed. Both gravity and the removal of an obstacle to gravity's influence were necessary for the effect to occur, but gravity has a certain priority as a cause: It is what actually inclines the globe to fall downward.

So why did the world of slavery come crashing down? Not because of one cause, but because of many. Yet among those many causes, and certainly no less important than any other, was a religious ideal of love, tugging at the hearts and eliciting a response from so many early abolitionists. The Judeao-Christian ideal of love of neighbor had been appreciated for centuries, but its tendency to result in the rejection of slavery had been blocked by an obstacle: motivated cognition. Motivated cognition (or motivated reasoning) refers to the fact that the conclusions

[66] See Robin Blackburn, *The American Crucible: Slavery, Emancipation and Human Rights* (London: Verso, 2011), 26 and Drescher, *Capitalism and Antislavery*, chap. 6.

[67] For an excellent entry into the literature on the causes of antislavery, see Joel Quirk, *The Anti-Slavery Project: From the Slave Trade to Human Trafficking* (Philadelphia: University of Pennsylvania Press, 2011), 23–112 and Christopher Leslie Brown, *Moral Capital: The Foundations of British Abolitionism* (Chapel Hill, NC: The University of North Carolina Press, 2006), 3–22. On free labor and free soil, see Eric Foner, *Free Soil, Free Labor, Free Men: The Ideology of the Republican Party before the Civil War* (Oxford: Oxford University Press, 1995). On the importance of slave resistance and slave revolt, and on social crises relating to war and revolution, see Blackburn, *The American Crucible*.

"people reach are shaped not only by the evidence the world provides to them but also by motivations, goals, needs, and desires internal to the reasoner."[68] Experiments indicate that human beings are subject to several specific biases which push us in the direction of favorable conclusions. First, we want to think well of ourselves. (The power of this desire is well-illustrated by the fact that most people believe they are above average on a vast array of characteristics.) Second, we want our beliefs to match our behavior. As research on cognitive dissonance has shown, this sometimes means that we change our beliefs so that they match our behavior, rather than adjusting our beliefs in response to evidence and changing our behavior accordingly. Third, the mere fact that those with whom we interact believe something creates some inclination in us to believe it, too. Given these psychological tendencies, anyone who was himself a slaveholder – or anyone personally connected with a slaveholder – was bound to face powerful internal pressures to avoid the conclusion that enslaving human beings is wrong. Such a person's thinking about the morality of slavery would have been strongly influenced by the desire to think well of oneself and the desire to avoid the cognitive dissonance caused by believing both "I'm a decent person" and "I'm engaged in a seriously evil practice." Add to this the powerful effect of group membership on a person's beliefs, and we can begin to see how a culture in which the powerful had "always" held slaves would be a culture in which the truth was hard to see.[69]

The relevance of bias to debates about slavery was explicitly noted by several participants in the debate over American slavery. Thus in the eighteenth century Woolman observed, "Customs generally approved and opinions received by youth from their superiors become like the natural produce of a soil, especially when they are suited to favourite inclinations."[70] And in the early nineteenth century, Black abolitionist George Lawrence (1802–1869) called the Southern states "so biased by

---

[68] David Dunning, "Motivated cognition in self and social thought," in M. Mikulincer and P. R. Shaver (eds.) *APA Handbook of Personality and Social Psychology. I. Attitudes and Social Cognition* (Washington, DC: American Psychological Association, 2015), 777–803, 778.

[69] For a fuller exposition of the argument that motivated cognition was an obstacle to recognition of the injustice of slavery, see Rota, "Moral psychology and social change: the case of abolition."

[70] John Woolman, *Some Considerations on the Keeping of Negroes*, in Woolman, *The Journal and Major Essays of John Woolman*, 198. See also 202: "When self-love presides in our minds our opinions are biased in our own favour." Compare Elihu Coleman, an American Quaker writing in 1733: "I do believe many would see [how great a sin is

interest, that they have become callous to the voice of reason and justice."[71]

Because of the antiquity, near ubiquity and economic advantage conferred by slavekeeping, for the first millennium and a half of Christianity's existence a number of psychological pressures would have been major obstacles (for the nonenslaved especially) to the recognition that enslavement was incompatible with love of neighbor and the Golden Rule. But by the eighteenth and nineteenth centuries many of these obstacles were removed. Slavery and even serfdom had essentially vanished from England by the close of the sixteenth century.[72] Although a few African slaves were brought in to Great Britain in the seventeenth and eighteenth centuries, the numbers were low enough that slavery there continued to be extremely rare.[73] By the late eighteenth century the percentage of slaves was also very low in the Northern United States. US Census data from 1790 indicate that the percentage of slaves (out of the total population) in New York at the time was 6.3 percent; for New Jersey the figure was 6.2 percent; for Connecticut, 1.2 percent; for Pennsylvania, 0.9 percent; for New Hampshire, 0.1 percent; and in Maine and Massachusetts there were no slaves.[74] From a global perspective, this was a remarkable anomaly. As compared to those in past ages and the vast majority of other regions, residents of Britain and the North American colonies (later states) were less affected by motives relating to self-interest and cognitive dissonance which promoted acceptance of slavery. This made it easier for them to perceive the antagonism between Christian ethical principles and slavery. And in a virtuous cycle, the inclination to accept slavery simply because one's peers did grew weaker and weaker as more and more people criticized it. Finally, those Christians who felt less bound by the traditions of the ancient and medieval Church (such as the Quakers and eighteenth-century Protestants holding a notion of progressive revelation) would

slaveholding], were they not blinded by self-interest." From his *Testimony against Making Slaves of Men*, in Bruns (ed.), *Am I Not a Man and a Brother*, 45.

[71] George Lawrence, *An Oration on the Abolition of the Slave Trade* (New York: Hardcastle and Van Pelt, 1813), 11, available via The New York Public Library Digital Collections: digitalcollections.nypl.org/items/510d47e3-fd48-a3d9-e040-e00a18064a99.

[72] See the extended discussion in Michael Guasco, *Slaves and Englishmen: Human Bondage in the Early Modern Atlantic World* (Philadelphia: University of Pennsylvania Press, 2014), chap. 1, esp. 27–33. Also helpful is Eltis, *The Rise of African Slavery in the Americas*, 1–7; and Drescher, *Abolition*, 4–25.

[73] James Walvin, *England, Slaves, and Freedom, 1776–1838* (London: MacMillan Press, 1986), 26–45.

[74] Data cited in Stark, *For the Glory of God*, 321.

have lacked an additional obstacle blocking a wholehearted rejection of slavery based on Christian principles.

It is not controversial that the efforts of religious groups and networks were pivotal in the carrying out of the antislavery campaigns of the eighteenth and nineteenth centuries, and in the final analysis it is hard to deny that religious ideas, motivations, and arguments against slavery were central factors leading to the widespread popular rejection of slavery in the Anglo-American world, and thence to abolition and emancipation. Yet it could still be objected that Christians only came to reject slavery because of nonreligious influences. Thus one historian of religion writes that Christians accepted slavery as "part of God's plan" until "a more secular ethics began to challenge it at the dawn of the modern age."[75] And a historian of the Enlightenment asserts that "[I]t was Enlighteners who made the case against slavery … It was the humanitarianism diffused by the Enlightenment that helped to motivate Wilberforce and other abolitionists."[76] What of the objection that secular Enlightenment values of liberty and benevolence, rather than Christian moral principles, were the real motivators for Christian abolitionists?

In reply: Religious arguments that slavery should be rejected were advanced a half-century before Enlightenment philosophers began to articulate philosophical arguments for the same conclusion. The antislavery writings of the Germantown Quakers (1688), Sewall (1700), and Hepburn (1715) long preceded those of Montesquieu (1748), Francis Hutcheson (1755), George Wallace (1760), the Abbé Raynal (1770), and others. The earliest Christian antislavery advocates therefore cannot have been influenced by Enlightenment critiques of slavery.[77]

On the other hand, the newfound appreciation of personal liberty and benevolence characteristic of the eighteenth century did contribute to the

---

[75] Stephen J. Patterson, *The Forgotten Creed: Christianity's Original Struggle against Bigotry, Slavery, & Sexism* (New York: Oxford University Press, 2018), 102.

[76] Ritchie Robertson, *The Enlightenment: The Pursuit of Happiness, 1680–1790* (New York: Harper Collins, 2021), 766.

[77] It is true that the French lawyer and political theorist Jean Bodin (c. 1530–1596) published a work in 1576 in which he criticized slavery on humanitarian and pragmatic grounds *(Les Six livres de la Republique)*. Yet this was before the Enlightenment and classifying Bodin as a secular rather than a religious thinker is not entirely accurate. He was certainly a theist (and possibly a believing Catholic – historians are unsure) and his treatment of slavery closes with a plea for the general adoption of the Old Testament law limiting servitude to a seven-year term. More importantly for the present argument, there is no evidence of which we are aware that Bodin was a significant influence on the early Christian abolitionists.

positive reception of the first Christian abolitionists' message among later abolitionists and the general public, as is gestured at in the first sentence of Benezet's most important work (1771):

[S]everal tracts have been published setting forth its [Negro slavery's] inconsistency with every Christian and moral virtue, which it is hoped will have weight with the judicious, especially at a time when the liberties of mankind are become so much the subject of general attention.[78]

Yet it should be noted that the "secular" Enlightenment values of liberty and benevolence were not secular in the modern sense of having no religious or spiritual basis. The Enlightenment era's focus on benevolence was as much the product of Christianity as of philosophy, and critiques of slavery based on natural rights were often articulated within a theistic natural philosophy and sometimes coupled with religious considerations.[79] Hutcheson, holding with almost all Enlightenment thinkers that God is the Author of nature, sees all his conclusions in moral philosophy, which stem largely from his reflection on human nature, "as so many indications to us of the will of God concerning our conduct."[80] In defending the right to freedom for those born to slaves, he notes that they are "the workmanship of the same God in their bodies and souls," and criticizing slavery more generally he references the Old Testament limitations on the enslavement of fellow Jews, proceeding to argue that "under Christianity, whatever lenity [leniency] was due from an Hebrew toward his countryman, must be due toward all, since the distinction of nations are removed as to the point of humanity and mercy, as well as natural right."[81] Further cases in point are provided by John Foster, James Beattie, and William Paley.[82] Even Montesquieu (1689–1755)

---

[78] Benezet, *Some Historical Account of Guinea*, in Benezet, *The Complete Antislavery Writings of Anthony Benezet*, 117–118.

[79] As Anstey argues in *The Atlantic Slave Trade and British Abolition*, "the springs of the idea of benevolence are found at least as much in theology as in moral philosophy; and because theology, as mediated by works of piety and devotion, and by even the eighteenth-century pulpit, was more widely influential upon attitudes than philosophy with its more rarified quality, the distinction has some importance" (139). See also 123–127.

[80] Francis Hutcheson, *A System of Moral Philosophy, In Three Books* (London: A. Millar, 1755), vol. 1, book 2, chap. 3. See also xiv.

[81] Hutcheson, *A System of Moral Philosophy*, vol. 2, book 3, chap. 3

[82] John Foster, *Discourses on All the Principal Branches of Natural Religion and Social Virtue*, vol. 2 (London, 1752) says that slavery amounts to "defiance" against God and spurns "all the principles, both of natural and revealed religion" (158). Cf. William Paley, *The Principles of Moral and Political Philosophy* (London, 1785), book 3, pt. 2, chap. 3,

(among the least religious of the early philosophical critics of slavery) credits Christianity with the disappearance of slavery in northern Europe and gives voice to the tension between Christianity and slavery, writing with irony that "It is impossible for us to suppose these creatures [Negroes] to be men; because allowing them to be men, a suspicion would follow that we ourselves are not Christians."[83]

5.6 THE REJECTION OF SLAVERY IN ISLAM

According to Jonathan Brown, a well-known scholar of slavery and Islam, "Moral revulsion over slavery *qua* slavery seems only to have arisen in Muslim societies after prolonged and intensive exposure to European abolitionism."[84] And as Bernard Freamon documents in his thorough analysis of slavery in Islamic law and Muslim cultures, a widespread rejection of slavery and forced labor has yet to fully mature in some parts of the Muslim world.[85] At the same time, many Muslim thinkers from the nineteenth century on have articulated abolitionist arguments based on Islamic principles. Here we summarize three distinct lines of argument: (1) slavery should be prohibited because the actual circumstances in which slavery is practiced involves violations of the *shari'a*; (2) slavery should be abolished because doing so promotes the common good of the Muslim community; and (3) the *shari'a*'s permission of slavery in the past was a concession to conditions that no longer exist, and given that, both Islam's own emancipatory ethic and developed human reflection on the realities of slavery mandate abolition.

The first two of these considerations appear in the earliest abolition decree by an Islamic state. In 1846 Ahmad Bey, the Ottoman governor of Tunis (r. 1837–1855), abolished slavery in his territory, beating the

and James Beattie, *Elements of Moral Science* (Edinburgh: T. Cadell and William Creech, 1793) vol. 2, pt. 2.

[83] M. De Secondat, Baron de Montesquieu, *The Spirit of Laws* (Dublin: G. and A. Ewing, 1751), vol. 1, book 15, chap. 7 and chap. 5. Montesquieu's criticism of slavery was somewhat ambiguous: He argues forcefully against the traditional philosophical justifications of slavery, and contends that in monarchies, democracies, and aristocracies it has no proper place, but then goes on to defend the legitimacy of voluntary slavery by self-sale in despotic countries, and involuntary slavery in "countries where the excess of heat enervates the body, and renders men so slothful and dispirited, that nothing but the fear of chastisement can oblige them to perform any laborious duty" (book 15, chap. 7, but see chap. 8 for some hesitation on this last point).

[84] Brown, *Slavery & Islam*, 245. See also 204.

[85] Freamon, *Possessed by the Right Hand*, chaps. 9–10.

United States' emancipation proclamation to the punch by almost twenty years. The decree lays out a careful argument starting with the premise that, for most Black African slaves in Tunis, it could not be clearly established that the original imposition of slave status had occurred according to the restrictions specified in Islamic law (it was known that many slaves brought from sub-Saharan Africa had been kidnapped and that some were formerly free Muslims). Thus most slaveowners in Tunis were not in compliance with *shari'a* restrictions on slaveholding, and consequently their slaveholding constituted both a harm to their slaves and a spiritual danger to themselves. But "avoiding what is permitted out of fear of falling into the realm of the forbidden is part of the Sacred Law." And, furthermore, the common good would be promoted by abolition, because of the nature of the then-current international political situation.[86] In view of the common good and "out of our worry that [the slaveholders] might fall into something agreed upon by consensus and study as forbidden, namely their harming their brothers whom God put in their care," Bey concludes that the state must prohibit slavery in Tunis despite the fact that it is permissible in principle under Islamic law.[87]

Bey here relies on a concept in Islamic jurisprudence known as "restricting the permissible." Traditionally, Muslim exegetes have held that the early Muslim sources place limits on what Islamic law and Islamic political rulers can rightfully prohibit. Thus the Imam Ja'far Sadiq (c. 702–765): "The permissible of Muhammad is permissible forever …"[88] Yet by the 1300s Islamic jurists had developed the concept of restricting the permissible: "a Muslim ruler (or state) could restrict what was otherwise permissible if this had some basis in the objectives of the Shariah, such as promoting some common good."[89] Bey's decree is an application of this venerable principle to the case of slavery.

Bey's first line of argument (the notion that slavery should be abolished because in practice it involved widespread violations of Islamic law) was reiterated by several Islamic thinkers in the decades that followed, including Major General Heussein of Tunisia in 1864, Muhammad Bayram Khamis (d. 1889), Ahmad Nasiri (1835–1897), and Muhammad 'Abduh

---

86 Here the text refers explicitly to slaves fleeing to European consulates; implicitly Bey may have had in mind the political advantages of greater harmony with Western views on slavery.

87 Translations from Bey's decree are from Brown, *Slavery & Islam*, 229.

88 Quoted and translated in Brown, *Slavery & Islam*, 224.

89 Brown, *Slavery & Islam*, 226.

(1849–1905). And when Saudi Arabia's King Faysal prohibited slavery in 1962 he cited the same principle.[90]

Bey's second line of argument (that slavery should be abolished because doing so promotes the common good of the Muslim community) was taken up by later thinkers as well. Rashid Rida (1865–1935) argued in 1910 that since Islamic slavery derived primarily from the practice of enslaving prisoners of war and defeated populations, and since Muslim political rulers had the authority to forego that practice (as had long been acknowledged in Islamic law), it followed that Muslim rulers could and should prohibit slavery when it was in the best interests of Muslims. And as various writers in the twentieth century suggested and Yusuf Qaradawi (1926–2022) argued forcefully more recently, it is certainly in the best interests of Muslims to abide by international agreements prohibiting the taking of slaves in warfare.[91]

A third line of argument begins by interpreting the early Muslim permission of slavery as a response to conditions that no longer obtain. Rida's teacher Shaykh Husayn Jisr (1845–1909) contended that Islam had allowed slavery out of necessity given the military conventions of the time, and Rida reiterated this view, noting that enslavement of one's enemies was then the norm and also arguing that slavery was too widespread to be abolished at the time of the Qur'an.[92] Next, consider that the Qur'an does not require Muslims to take or hold slaves. Thus, Freamon: "Even though there is considerable regulation of the relation between the free and the enslaved [in the Qur'an], there are no verses suggesting that the practice of slavery ought to continue ..."[93] Traditionally, Islamic law allowed rulers to choose among four options for dealing with prisoners of war: release, ransom, enslavement, or execution. But Qur'an 47:4 mentions only release and ransom: "When you meet those who disbelieve, strike at their necks; then, when you have overwhelmed them, tighten the bonds. Then free them graciously or hold them for ransom, till war lays down its burdens." The options of enslavement and execution were added based on Muhammed's example, but, some contemporary scholars have

---

[90] See Brown, *Slavery & Islam*, 230–234. Nasiri brought another Islamic legal principle, blocking the means, to bear in favor of abolition. According to this principle "otherwise permissible acts that most probably led to prohibited results should themselves be prohibited" [Brown's words, in *Slavery & Islam*, 234].

[91] Brown, *Slavery & Islam*, 234–236. See also Freamon's discussion of common good arguments for abolition at *Possessed by the Right Hand*, 508 and 511–515.

[92] Brown, *Slavery & Islam*, 234–235 and 249.

[93] Freamon, *Possessed by the Right Hand*, 493.

argued, Muhammed's practice in this regard was plausibly a response to the special circumstances of the early Muslim community and by no means need be followed by Muslims in modern times.[94] Two verses in the Qur'an, taken together, might appear to positively promote slavery: Qur'an 8:41 mandates that one-fifth of war booty be "for God and the Messenger," and Qur'an 33:50 mentions enslaved female captives as war booty. Yet, Freamon argues, 8:41 "does not define war booty but instead leaves [its definition] to custom." Since those customs have changed, and since "[e]liminating a practice because it is no longer customary among the people is perfectly permissible in Islamic jurisprudence," Muslims need not interpret 8:41 as a requirement to take slaves as part of the spoils of war today.[95]

If, then, nothing in the Qur'an or Sunnah (the example of Muhammed) requires Muslims to continue the practice of slavery, and if it is plausible to interpret the acceptance by Muhammed and early Muslims of slave-holding and the enslavement of prisoners of war as appropriate for special circumstances that no longer hold, then it follows that Muslims should look to broader principles in the Qur'an and other sources to form a judgment on slavery in the modern era. When we look for these broader principles, Freamon and others argue, we find that Islam promotes an ethics of emancipation which speaks clearly in favor of abolition. Qur'an 2:177 states that giving wealth to ransom slaves is among the essential components of piety. 4:92, 5:89, and 58:3 specify the freeing of a slave as a means of reparation for various sins, and 24:33 counsels slaveowners to grant contracts of manumission to worthy slaves. Chapter 90 distinguishes the two highways (of good and evil), and lists emancipating slaves as an action of one who has fully embarked on the highway of good: "And what will apprise thee of the steep pass? [It is] the freeing of a slave, or giving food at a time of famine to an orphan near of kin, or an indigent, clinging to the dust ..." [90:12–16]. Taken in totality, the Qur'an holds up emancipation as an act of compassion and an expression of obedience to God.[96] And this is confirmed by the example of Muhammed, who eventually freed all fifteen of his male slaves.[97]

---

[94] Sayyed Qutb, *In the Shade of the Qur'an*, vol. 15 (Malaysia: Muslim Welfare House, 1992), 394. Also see Freamon, *Possessed by the Right Hand*, 136–137 on the early Caliph Umar ibn al-Khattab's strong preference against enslavement of prisoners of war.

[95] Freamon, *Possessed by the Right Hand*, 499.

[96] See Freamon, *Possessed by the Right Hand*, 494–495 and 122–125.

[97] Brown, *Slavery & Islam*, 163.

While the Qur'an itself can thus provide a motive for abolition, it is also the case that natural human reason, reflecting on the lived realities of the enslaved, provides another such motive. Ayatollah Mohsen Kadivar (b. 1959) argues that since humans can grow in our understanding of morality, and since slavery is now "condemned by reasonable people," Muslims should interpret the earlier Islamic permission of slavery as "a temporary and seasonal ruling of *shari'a*" that is no longer credible.[98] How is a Muslim jurist to know which traditional rulings of *shari'a* are temporary and which permanent? Turning a traditional Islamic argument on its head, Kadivar contends that it can be known that the permission of slavery was temporary because allowing slavery now would be unjust, and so if the earlier permission was founded in a permanent ruling, then the *shari'a* would license something unjust, which is not possible.[99] In sum, the conditions that necessitated Islam's permission of slavery in the past have ceased, and now Islam's own internal ethics and natural human reason both call for abolition.

Yet slavery remains a serious problem, globally. After noting the continued presence of slavery in some Islamic societies today, Freamon calls his fellow Muslims to action: "We will begin to see an end to slavery in the Muslim world when the Islamic principles I have discussed in this book begin to be implemented by Muslims in a robust and internally oriented fashion …"[100] Religion has been used to justify slavery in the past, but core religious principles are a powerful antislavery force. David Brion Davis, perhaps the pre-eminent twentieth-century scholar of slavery, reminds us: "the abolitionists' deep faith that all human beings are created in the image of God, and that we therefore have a compelling duty to overcome institutions that dehumanize groups of people by treating them as exploitable animals" can "continue to encourage new efforts to achieve social justice, whereas cynicism and relativism can easily lead to apathy, resignation and the sanction of egoism and individual self-interest as the only ends of life."[101]

---

[98] Mohsen Kadivar, *Human Rights and Reformist Islam* (Edinburgh: Edinburgh University Press, 2021), 371–374.

[99] Kadivar, *Human Rights and Reformist Islam*, 373: "Any time that the insightful jurist finds with certainty that one of the rulings of *shari'a* is no longer just or reasonable, he or she will discover that such a ruling was one of the temporary and seasonal ones, and that its credibility (*i'tibar*) has expired, and is no longer legitimate."

[100] Freamon, *Possessed by the Right Hand*, 515.

[101] David Brion Davis, *Inhuman Bondage: The Rise and Fall of Slavery in the New World* (Oxford: Oxford University Press, 2006), 239.

PART II

RELIGION AND CONTEMPORARY SLAVERY

6

Slavery in the Modern World

Having reviewed the main responses to slavery by religious groups historically, we now turn to the connections between religion and slavery in the modern world. In Chapter 7 we reveal the many ways in which religion is still being exploited to support slavery today, and in Chapter 8 we describe how religious groups and religiously inspired individuals are doing crucial work in the fight against contemporary slavery. In the present chapter we aim to set the stage for these discussions by briefly sketching the evolution of slavery, and antislavery efforts, from the mid nineteenth century to the present.

The story of the antislavery movements in Britain, the United States, and across faiths, continents and nations took a specific and profound turning in the mid nineteenth century. The earlier endeavours of religious and political actors, especially in Europe and North America, pressed for new abolitionist laws, for religious bodies to move toward a denunciation of slavery, and especially for a recognition that national wealth and prestige should not come from the toil and suffering of slaves. But it was the unique nature of the new United States, and its Constitution, that exacerbated and hastened a move toward a deadly reckoning over slavery. While the Constitution itself did not include the words "slave" or "slavery," many of the delegates to the Constitutional Convention were deeply invested in the preservation of slavery within the new Republic, even as others were staunchly opposed to its continuation. In 1789 the significant differences in the economies and cultures of the new states led to controversy, even as pressure was building to find compromises that would allow the new national government to establish itself. While many of the proposals touching on the form and

147

organization of government were accepted, compromises had especially to be found to resolve the issues of slavery and proportional representation. Delegates from the Southern states, where slavery was most common, pressed for the continued legality of slavery within their borders and for allowing the importation of slaves from abroad to continue for twenty more years. Slavery was thus locked into eight of the new states and prohibited in five states. By 1800, with territorial expansion, there were nine slave states and eight free states.

The second crucial compromise concerned proportional representation – how state populations were to be counted in voting on national issues. The slave states, being less populous, lobbied for and achieved a compromise, written into the Constitution, that their slaves were to be counted as three-fifths of a person within the census of their state's population. The larger the counted population in a state, the more Representatives it could send to Congress. The result of this compromise was to increase the voting power of slave states in Congress and set a pattern of extensive control exercised by slave states in the overall governing of the country. These compromises created extreme tensions between free and slave states, which increased as free state populations grew rapidly while slave states maintained a disproportionate control over national governance. From the beginning of the nineteenth century the tensions around slavery continued to increase. Much of this was due to a growing abolitionist movement in the North and a hardening of proslavery views in the South.

Religious groups and denominations within the United States began to rupture over the issue of slavery, as the revivalist fervour of the Second Great Awakening tended to pull churches in the North toward an anti-slavery position. Some religious groups, such as the Quakers and Mennonites, were already strongly against slavery and found their congregations in the South being harassed and driven from their communities. While the Roman Catholic Church remained intact, five of the largest American denominations – Presbyterians, Baptists, Methodists, Episcopalians, and Lutherans – split into northern and southern wings over the question of slavery.

In parallel, as the British antislavery movement slowed and the American movement grew rapidly, a World Anti-Slavery Convention in London in 1840 was organized by the British and Foreign Anti-Slavery Society,[1] on the

---

[1] By 1840, the Society for Effecting the Abolition of the Slave Trade, founded in 1787, had evolved into the British and Foreign Anti-Slavery Society, which continues operations today as Anti-Slavery International: www.antislavery.org.

initiative of the Quaker Joseph Sturge. The proceedings of the Convention consisted largely of speeches that reported the situation of slavery in other countries, as well as reports that condemned religious leaders and groups that failed to denounce the practice. The extent of slavery, and the high mortality of slaves in Dutch colonies, was exposed, and the English Quaker Joseph Pease accused the British government of being complicit in extensive slavery in India. The Convention was also controversial in that its circular invitation to other antislavery groups made clear that only men would be seated as participating delegates. American antislavery groups included large numbers of female members, and the American Anti-Slavery Society (led by William Lloyd Garrison) made it a point to include women in its delegation – women who were ultimately forced to sit in the balcony of the hall and refused the right of participation.

If there was a key outcome to the 1840 Anti-Slavery Convention, it was to build and cement relationships between these women abolitionists. Two of these, Lucretia Mott[2] and Elizabeth Cady Stanton,[3] met and became fast friends at the Convention. In 1848 they would organize the Seneca Falls Convention, the first women's rights convention, and one that led to the beginning of campaigns for women's rights and votes.[4] Like most of the factions of the antislavery movement, this growing movement for women's rights was based soundly on religious ideas. Most of the women attending Seneca Falls were Quakers or members of the evangelical branch of Methodism, often using biblical references and claims to support their arguments.

Operating in parallel to the fundamentally faith-based groups that opposed slavery was the militant leader and activist John Brown. While most abolitionists were active and often ready to campaign against or break proslavery laws, Brown's militancy was much more severe. Brown held rigid religious views and was strongly evangelical in his Christianity. His upbringing had been with strict Puritans, and he felt a direct calling

[2] Mott (1793–1880) was a Quaker Preacher in early adulthood. She promoted abolition and electoral suffrage for all Black people, male and female. Her home was a stop on the Underground Railway for escaped slaves seeking freedom.

[3] Stanton (1815–1902) was an American suffragette and lead author of *The Woman's Bible* (1895/1898), an early statement of liberation theology.

[4] Frederick Douglass, the only African American at the convention, spoke strongly from the floor in support of women's franchise: "'In this denial of the right to participate in government, not merely the degradation of woman and the perpetuation of a great injustice happens, but the maiming and repudiation of one-half of the moral and intellectual power of the government of the world.'"

from God to "strike a death blow" to American slavery. He believed he was a chosen "instrument of God." While his first work against slavery was through speaking and nonviolent action, he began to take direct and violent action in the late 1850s when he moved with his sons and others to Kansas Territory. "Bleeding Kansas" was in the midst of a violent confrontation between pro- and antislavery groups each seeking control of what would soon become a recognized American state. After an assault and the destruction in 1856 of the antislavery town of Lawrence, Kansas, by proslavery forces that killed some 150 men and boys, Brown and his group massacred a group of proslavery supporters, then joined others in fighting the proslavery forces in the battles of Black Jack and Osawatomie.

Leaving Kansas territory, he began to plan a bold assault on slavery itself. To this end he led an attack, killing seven people, on the Federal Armory at Harpers Ferry, Virginia. His plan was to appropriate the extensive weaponry there in order to arm slaves in a revolt against their slaveholders. Only a few slaves joined the revolt, however, and he and his group were ultimately killed or captured by US Army troops. Brown was tried for treason, the murder of five men, and for inciting a slave insurrection – he was found guilty on all charges and was executed by hanging on December 2, 1859. He was the first American to be executed for treason. Brown's attack on Harpers Ferry, his trial, and execution were reported widely, generating both enormous support for his cause in some sections, and hardening the resolve of proslavery supporters, many of whom now felt that a wider armed conflict was inevitable. One historian put it this way: "Brown's raid succeeded brilliantly. It drove a wedge through the already tentative and fragile Opposition–Republican coalition and helped to intensify the sectional polarization that soon tore the Democratic party and the Union apart."[5] A growing fundamental and increasingly violent antagonism grew between those heavily invested in slavery and those who sought abolition.

After the Civil War (1861–1865), a long reinterpretation of the events leading up to the war, and the logic of the war itself, were altered in both public opinion and the historical accounts. This reinterpretation, growing mainly from Southerners, focused on honor, a lost cause marked by chivalry, a stable and happy system of masters and servants, and the crimes of perfidious Northern "Carpet Baggers" that exploited Southern

---

[5] Daniel W. Crofts, *Reluctant Confederates: Upper South Unionists in the Secession Crisis* (Chapel Hill, NC: The University of North Carolina Press, 1989), 70 ff.

families in the aftermath of the Civil War. It was a postwar campaign to bring white Americans into an acceptance of legal racial discrimination and exploitation, a reinvention of the religious and philosophical drivers of the conflict. Yet, the declarations of war made by Southern states in 1861 had made it clear that they felt the key issue, and ultimate conflict, was over the moral and legal right to enslave others. One rapid adjustment to abolition in Southern states was to establish an extensive re-enslavement, within a system known as "peonage," of thousands of African Americans through manipulation of the legal system. This state-supported enslavement lasted into the 1940s.[6]

A little discussed, but key, aspect of the American Civil War to end slavery was its enormous cost in lives and treasure. Original estimates suggested 620,000 soldiers died in the war, with an equal number of casualties and wounded. Some 50,000 civilians were thought to have died in the war and a further 80,000 slaves. More recent estimates range up to 1.5 million total casualties. A large part of the United States was put to the torch and extensively destroyed; the economic costs to the South were vast and the region was decades in recovery. If we are considering the human and financial costs of ending slavery, the Civil War was likely the most costly of all historical antislavery efforts by a significant margin. This war was also one of a number of conflicts in human history that aimed for the liberation of slaves (as contrasted to the much larger number of acts of raiding and war undertaken to take slaves and enforce slavery). In North America alone there were thirty-nine slave revolts between 1520 and 1859. One of these was the Haitian Revolution, the only known slave uprising in history that led to the founding of a state free from slavery and ruled by non-whites and ex-slaves.

6.1 THE FOURTH ANTISLAVERY MOVEMENT: 1885–1914

The fourth antislavery movement is possibly the least well known, though Adam Hochschild's remarkable book, *King Leopold's Ghost* (1998), brought it clearly and sharply into public awareness. It is a story that almost suggests a fictional origin – a young missionary couple who use cutting-edge technology to alert the public to horrific hidden crimes; a truly vile and heartless villain in King Leopold II of Belgium; the inter-woven lives of adventurers – the explorer Henry Stanley; the author of

---

[6] See Douglas A. Blackmon, *Slavery by Another Name: The Re-Enslavement of African-Americans from the Civil War to World War II* (London: Icon Books, 2012).

Heart of Darkness, Joseph Conrad; a British civil servant and superlative researcher, Roger Casement, who would later be hung for treason; and a lowly young shipping clerk, Edmond Morel, who conceived, organized, and launched a global antislavery movement.

As the nineteenth century was closing, the broad 400 year-long European conquest of most of the planet was coming to an end. In the "Scramble for Africa" (1885–1914), seven Western European states had dismembered, allocated, and colonized that continent. This period has also been termed the "New Imperialism" because of the nearly complete European control achieved over the continent between 1833 and 1914 – only Ethiopia and the small American possession of Liberia were not made European colonies. All the rest became colonies of the United Kingdom, France, Portugal, Spain, Italy, the German Empire, and the surprising late entry – Belgium.

Belgium was, and is, a small country, with a reasonable but not especially rich economy. However, the ruler of Belgium in the late nineteenth century, King Leopold, was keen to take part in the division of Africa. Without the armies and influence of the larger states he used dubious diplomacy to gain control of the last "free" part of Central Africa, the Congo. First, Leopold convinced his European neighbours that the great Congo basin could be best controlled and exploited if it were declared to be a "free state" – an area that belonged to no specific nation, but open for development and trading by any nation with a guarantee of no taxation on the traders. Leopold also argued that this would also support the suppression of the Arab slave trade in Central Africa, using this "human rights" approach to convince delegates to support the "free state." On the basis of lavish promises of access, and multiple resources to be exploited, the legal fiction of the free state was approved at the Berlin Conference of 1884–1885. In effect, and according to the fine print of the agreement, this vast area of Central Africa was not a colony of Belgium, but a registered charity, the International African Association (IAA), which was secretly the personal and legal property of King Leopold alone. Behind the scenes Leopold had bribed conference delegates and journalists and produced famous explorers and humanitarians to build his case. Through this subterfuge, he gained total personal control over just under 1 million square miles of Central Africa.

With the Congo under his control, Leopold launched a new vehicle of exploitation in the International Association of the Congo (IAC). The IAC appeared to be a registered charity but was actually a joint stock company and, again, secretly, Leopold's personal private property. The IAC was empowered to grant (sell) leases to land and resources in the Congo Free State – and it came into its own in 1884–1885 when it was recognized as a legal entity at the Berlin Conference, and then further recognized as a sovereign state by the United States and Germany. Convincing the world's leading countries to accept that a private company, wholly owned by a single individual, was to be treated as a sovereign state was both audacious and phenomenally lucrative for Leopold.

Leopold then hired the famous African explorer, Henry Morton Stanley, to "make treaties" with the Indigenous peoples of the Congo. Some 450 treaties were made with local "chiefs," none of whom knew what they were agreeing to. In fact, the crux of the written agreement was that "for one piece of cloth per month … [the inhabitants] give up all sovereignty and governing rights forever, to assist *by labor or otherwise* … any works, and assign to the Association [the IAC] all waterways and tolls, and all game, fishing, forest and mining rights, as absolute property."[7] These "treaties" handed over complete control of the Congo and its peoples to the IAC, and through it to rapacious and scrambling "agents" who paid the IAC for the right to exploit, totally and brutally, their assigned areas of land.

Even as these "treaties" were being forced on the Indigenous peoples of the Congo, Leopold launched yet another diversion in 1889 – an Anti-Slavery Conference, hosted in Brussels. While supposedly working to thwart the Arab slave trade, Leopold's true aim for the conference was to raise funds by selling "leases" and gain even greater control over Central Africa. After the conference, new "leaseholders" began spreading along the rivers and into the interior of the Congo. The leaseholders' aim was to get rich quickly, and the best way to do so was to harvest ivory and rubber. Uncountable numbers of elephants were slaughtered, and their ivory taken, but in many ways the future, and the source of greatest wealth, was rubber. Between the bicycle "craze" of the 1870s and the emergence of the first automobiles in the 1890s the demand for rubber was large and growing. Rubber grew wild and widely in the Congo, and fetched high prices in Europe and North America. To gather ivory and rubber, entire communities of Congolese were enslaved at gunpoint by the militias formed by leaseholders, then marched away to areas where they would be sold or used. The death toll on these marches was high,

---

[7] Adam Hochschild, *King Leopold's Ghost: A Story of Greed, Terror, and Heroism in Colonial Africa* (Boston: Houghton Mifflin, 1998), 72.

especially for children, the elderly, and anyone who resisted or attempted escape.

All of this was carefully concealed by Leopold's administration in Congo and his publicity machine in Belgium, but it could not be hidden forever. One of the very first clear denunciations of Leopold's system was mounted by a brilliant African American soldier, Baptist minister, historian, and member of the Ohio State Legislature – George Washington Williams (1849–1891). At age fourteen, Williams had enlisted in the Union forces and fought in the American Civil War. After the war he joined the African American "Buffalo Soldiers" (US 10th Cavalry) in Indian Territory. Wounded in combat, he was discharged, enrolled at Newton Theological Institution, and became the first African American to graduate there. He went on to pastor several churches, serve a term in the Ohio legislature, and ran his own law practice. He is best known as a historian; his book *The History of the Negro Race in America 1619–1880* was published in 1882 and is regarded as the first overall history of African Americans. He was, in short, a man of great intellect and energy.

In 1889, Williams traveled to Europe as the representative of an American news service. Granted an informal interview with King Leopold, he was, at first, impressed by the descriptions of what the Belgians were accomplishing in the Congo Free State. With support from the United States government, he traveled to the Congo to see this "development" firsthand. What he found was the abuse of local peoples, mutilation as a standard punishment, and an extremely high death rate among the inhabitants. He recorded this evidence carefully and in July 1890, published "An Open Letter to His Serene Majesty Leopold II, King of the Belgians and Sovereign of the Independent State of Congo." In his letter, which was republished widely, he was the first person to use the term and charge "crimes against humanity" in a public way and against public officials. The response from King Leopold was immediate and vicious – newspapers in Europe and America were ordered or bribed to attack Williams as an "unbalanced Negro" and a "so-called Colonel" to discredit his reports, while a counterreport was issued by the Belgian government. By the time of these attacks, Williams was dying of tuberculosis. He had left Africa via Cairo and reached England, where he died in August 1891. Williams' moral activism and ethical stands often placed him in great danger, but he never failed to attack greed and violence.

Despite Leopold's subterfuge and lies, the truth of the situation in the Congo began to emerge in glimmers and vague reports. There were

Belgian operatives in the Congo who were shocked by the cruelty and violence they witnessed, but most thought these to be isolated occurrences. Meanwhile, vast amounts of trade goods flowed North to Europe, enjoyed by consumers, enriching thousands of European investors, and especially enriching King Leopold. Remarkably, it was a young clerk in the office of a Liverpool-based shipping line who, in 1899, began to perceive the inner workings of this travesty, and who would go on to expose the attendant atrocities.

Edmund Dene Morel was in his mid-twenties and a junior shipping clerk in the Liverpool firm of Elder Dempster. He was also bilingual in French and so was selected to be sent to Belgium by his firm to supervise and record the arrivals and departures, loads and cargo, of the ships sailing to and from the Congo. Despite official reports as to the goods flowing to Congo and further goods flowing back, Morel realized that the official accounts could not be right. He first noticed that virtually all cargo sent to the Congo consisted of weapons and ammunition, at a level needed for a sizable army. Second, access to the actual accounts in shipments and payments clearly showed that someone was skimming vast sums off the top. Morel realized that "the amount of rubber and ivory brought home from the Congo ... greatly exceeded the amounts indicated in the Congo Government's returns."[8] His third discovery was the clear fact that, "Nothing was going in to pay for what was coming out." This meant that those doing the actual work weren't just being paid poorly, they weren't being paid at all. He later wrote, "It must be bad enough to stumble upon a murder. I had stumbled upon a secret society of murderers with a King for a croniman [accomplice]."[9]

When Morel showed his employers the accumulating evidence against their biggest client, they shut him out and tried to bribe him into silence. Morel took a moral stand. Now aged twenty-eight, he quit his job and devoted himself to exposing and combating the atrocities in the Congo. He researched and wrote constantly, sending articles and pamphlets to newspapers, magazines, and church and charity groups. As the truth of his investigations spread, Belgians and others working *inside* the Congo began to secretly send him further evidence. When Leopold denied hostage-taking and killing, Morel published official Belgian internal memos on how to take hostages and when to kill them. When Leopold

---

[8] Hochschild, *King Leopold's Ghost*, 180.   [9] Ibid., 181.

denied accounts of enslavement in the Congolese "army," Morel published the official Belgian price list for men and boy slaves sold to the army.

The British government was in a dilemma. They were not anxious to disrupt the profits flowing from their ally Leopold, but also did not want to be tainted by scandal. To get quietly to the bottom of things a cable was sent to their operative consul[10] in the Congo, Roger Casement, ordering him to go into the interior and investigate the claims and accusations. Casement chartered a small steamboat to go deep into the Congo, where he found and documented extensive slavery, murder, mutilation as punishment for men, women, and children, kidnapping, torture, and sexual assault. Writing to the Belgian Governor of the Congo, Casement described the Belgian rule as "Entirely wrong ... if persisted in, will lead only to their [the Congolese] final extinction."[11] Returning to London, Casement met and befriended Morel. Unable to campaign openly as a government official, Casement bankrolled the launch of a campaigning organization, the Congo Reform Association, with Morel at its head. Branches of the Association sprang up in other countries as more facts emerged about atrocities in the Congo.

This was especially the case after a young woman named Alice Seeley Harris (1870–1970) and her husband were sent to the Congo as missionaries in 1898. Once on site at their mission, they were shocked to find horrific mutilations, murders, enslavement, and starvation inflicted by Belgian agents. Aghast, Harris turned to her hobby as a photographer to capture the truth of the Belgian crimes. Using the new Kodak Brownie hand camera, she took hundreds of photographs in the Congo. When she and her husband returned to England, many of these photos were made into "Magic Lantern" slides – glass plates that could be projected onto very large screens in theatres, and then narrated by Seeley Harris. These images presented both the riches of the land and the humanity of the Congolese, but also made clear the atrocities visited on men, women, and children for lacking obedience or not fulfilling rubber quotas. Figure 6.1, a photograph by W. D. Armstrong included in Harris' presentations,

---

[10] A consul was the official representative of the British government. Casement was therefore a diplomat and employed by the British Foreign Office; he held that post and title for twenty years.

[11] David Lagergren, *Mission and State in the Congo: A Study of the Relations between Protestant Missions and the Congo Independent State Authorities with Special Reference to the Equator District, 1885–1903* (Uppsala, Sweden: Gleerup, 1970), 323–329.

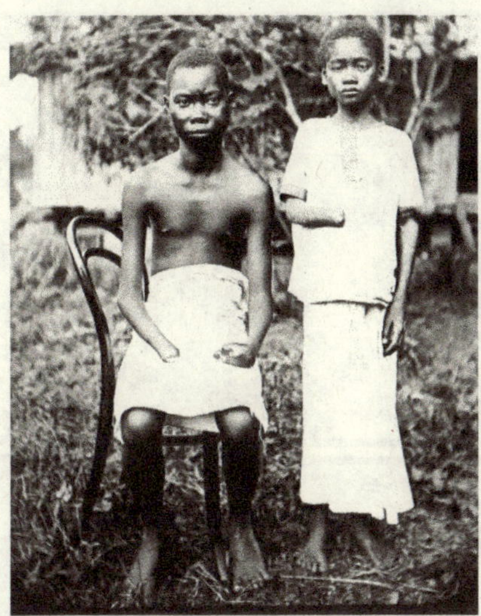

FIGURE 6.1 A young man and child with severed limbs. Photograph by W. D. Armstrong. Copyright retained by Anti-Slavery International.

shows a man and child whose hands were destroyed by soldiers enforcing rubber quotas.[12]

The impact of photography in a world with little experience of graphic and patently unaltered images of such atrocities was profound and galvanising. It is telling that the political cartoon in Figure 6.2, by David Wilson in the London *Daily Chronicle*, both reported and demonstrated the power of truthful photographic images with John Bull (the personification of England) challenging and then overcoming King Leopold.[13]

The fall of Leopold was precipitous. As his own crooked agents begin to turn on him, Leopold established an "independent" inquiry into the atrocities, only for it to turn on him as well. Further inquiries created a mountain of evidence of corruption and genocide. By 1905, Leopold gave in and sold the Congo to the government of Belgium, which established it

---

[12] See antislavery.nottingham.ac.uk/items/show/2061. The travelling *Congo Atrocity Lantern Lecture* was made up of 60 images. A full text of the lecture itself, as well as all the slides, and other materials and images, both historical and contemporary on the Congo can be found at the Anti-Slavery Usable Past website, Congo Section: antislavery.nottingham.ac .uk/congo.

[13] This cartoon, originally published in the (London) *Daily Chronicle*, is now held in the archive of Anti-Slavery International. It was entitled "Harrowing tales of torture from the Belgian Congo," and showed King Leopold II of Belgium and John Bull of Britain. It was later reproduced in the *Official Organ of the Congo Reform Association*, July 1906.

EFFECT OF THE KODAK.
(*Reproduced by kind permission of the* DAILY CHRONICLE.)

FIGURE 6.2 Harrowing tales of torture from the Belgian Congo. Originally published in the (London) *Daily Chronicle*, now held in the archive of Anti-Slavery International.

as a colony. A year later Leopold was dead. The Congo Reform Association was disbanded in 1913. The conflagration of World War I began within a year and little attention, or memory, survives of the fourth antislavery movement – though a reawakening of scholarship and interest in this period and the Congo campaign began to grow nearly one hundred years later.

For the most part religion did not play an overt role in bringing down Leopold; this was due to the rivalries among British and American denominations, and because of racial discrimination on the part of European clergy toward African American clergy who visited the Congo and attempted to play a role in exposing and reducing suffering. There was also a long-standing rivalry in Central Africa between Roman

Catholics (especially Belgians) and Protestant missionaries. This rivalry was to make worse the suffering of the Congolese in that it shifted focus and energies away from aid and support, and toward arguments and struggles over access and what was the "true" situation in Leopold's Congo. An early article by the historian Catherine Ann Cline, who would later write a book on E. D. Morel's political campaigns, set out the context of this rivalry:

When Christian Missionaries returned to the Congo in the 19th century, all traces of the promising Portuguese [Catholic] missionary effort of the late 15th and early 16th centuries had been obliterated. The Kingdom of the Congo which had produced several generations of Christian Kings, thousands of converts, even an African clergy and an African Bishop, had literally been swept away by the European slave trade.[14]

It is important to remember that the violent African slave trade did not begin with Leopold: Internal slavetrading and external slavetaking by Arabs and others had long existed. But the vast, and often genocidal, assault on Africa and the Americas by European countries beginning in the fifteenth century was of a much greater magnitude. These assaults continued until the end of the nineteenth century, at which point virtually all of Africa was under European control.

In the time of Leopold, the "discovery" of the Congo by European explorers simply fanned antagonisms between Roman Catholic and Protestant missionaries. Leopold himself angled to expel or limit Protestant missions, and enlisted Belgian Catholics to work "hand-in-hand with the State" for "the material and moral regeneration of the African people."[15] As a result, while the horrific exploitation continued, the religious bodies struggled against each other, and Protestants were often excluded or expelled. As Cline explains:

The competition among the Christians for the souls of the Africans had been far from friendly. Catholic missionaries resented the very presence of the Protestant in the Congo. Protestant missionary journals caricatured Catholic teachings and denounced their methods of proselytism. Catholic journals gloated over the small number of Protestant baptisms which they interpreted as indicating lack of success. Against this background of bitterness, Catholics rallied to the defence of a regime, which, whatever its weaknesses, had shown a marked preference for

[14] Catherine Ann Cline, "The Church and the movement for Congo reform," *Church History*, 32:1 (1963), 46–56, 46.
[15] Ibid., 47.

Catholic missionaries over the Protestant groups whom they mistakenly regarded as the motive force behind demands for reform.[16]

It is another example of the nefarious schemes and lies of Leopold that he was able to deflect attention from himself by stirring up conflict between religious denominations. Or, as Cline put it: "Indeed it might be said that King Leopold succeeded for many years in exploiting not only the Congo natives but also the habitual antagonisms and allegiances of his co-religionists."[17]

While the crimes of Leopold absorbed a great deal of attention and condemnation, other instances of enslavement to supply raw materials soon came to light in other parts of Africa and in South America. After the boom in chocolate production in the mid nineteenth century, especially in Great Britain, the Portuguese colony islands of Principe and Sao Tome (off the West African coast) were given over almost entirely to cocoa production. Local officials used press gangs to round up men and boys in Mozambique, charge and convict them of "vagrancy," and if they could not pay the requisite fine, hand them over to "recruiters" for delivery to Sao Tome and Principe. It was slavery, but accomplished through "official" channels and trickery. By 1908 these practices were becoming known in Europe and the brunt of the criticism was falling on the Quaker chocolate magnates who sourced their cocoa from the Portuguese colonies, some of whom were members or officers of the Anti-Slavery Society.[18] By 1912 the chocolate companies were sourcing cocoa from other countries, but clear facts about working conditions in Africa remained hard to uncover. A similar situation erupted in South American rubber, after being exposed by Roger Casement, who found evidence of atrocities and enslavement.[19] These instances of slavery in

---

[16] Ibid., 52.   [17] Ibid., 54.

[18] In 1908, the conservative British newspaper, *The Standard*, published an exposé of the slavery on Sao Tome and its links to the chocolate business of George Cadbury, a leading Quaker and supporter of the Anti-Slavery Society. Cadbury sued *The Standard*, resulting in a long and fraught trial and public debate. While Cadbury won his lawsuit, the jury showed their opinion of Cadbury and the larger situation by awarding him financial damages of 1 farthing (one-quarter of an English penny).

[19] For Roger Casement, the remarkable antislavery researcher, sponsor of the Congo Reform Association, and high-ranking British civil servant, the First World War opened the possibility of Ireland casting off the control of Great Britain. Soon after the war broke out, Casement enabled shipments of German arms to Ireland to be used in a revolt against the British. For this he was arrested, tried, and convicted of treason, and died by hanging on August 6, 1916, after converting to Catholicism on August 5. It was not until much later in the twentieth century that his reputation was repaired.

commodity production, very much resembling the same type of human exploitation present in the extraction of raw materials in the twenty-first century, ceased to hold public and government attention as Europe descended into World War I.

6.2 THE INTERWAR PERIOD

World War I dramatically altered cultures, economics, and political alliances and arrangements across the planet. The punitive nature of postwar diplomacy and the global depression of 1929 planted the seeds that would rekindle world war within twenty years – a global war that would be significant in terms of slavery. In the 1920s, however, antislavery activism tended to focus on diplomatic agreements and developments in international law, with a special focus on eradicating the slave trade in the Arabian peninsula and the Hejaz, even as European states were vying for control over that region.

An innovation that had little effect at the time, but would be important later, was the publication of the League of Nations 1926 Convention to Suppress the Slave Trade and Slavery. British diplomats and activists of what was then known as the Anti-Slavery and Aborigines' Protection Society[20] were central to writing, promoting, and promulgating the 1926 Convention. The Convention was occasionally called upon for diplomatic pronouncements in the late 1920s and 1930s, but rarely used or mentioned as the world descended into World War II. The content of the Convention, however, was and continues to be important in the legal interpretation and adjudication of slavery crime. This importance is linked to the logic and simplicity of the Convention – and helps to resolve the confusion of many national laws on slavery which are diverse and rarely in agreement.

The Convention (Article 1) defines slavery as: "the status or condition of a person over whom any or all of the powers attaching to the right of ownership are exercised." This definition harks back to Roman and later laws that ruled that slaves could be specified as *property*, and therefore could be treated and used in the same ways that someone might choose to use their property. This "use" could include buying, selling, loaning, renting out, use of property as collateral, the bequeathing of property on the owner's death, and ultimately, if the owner chose to do so,

---

[20] Another renaming of the British antislavery organization now known as Anti-Slavery International.

destroying one's property. The special power of this definition is that it serves as both a legal definition (within legal proceedings and rulings), and an operational or empirical definition (in determining if a specific act is, in fact, slavery, and allowing its identification and enumeration). In the early twenty-first century this would lead to the promulgation of the Bellagio-Harvard Guidelines, which set a global standard in determining and defining when slavery exists.[21] This standard has been crucial in ending debates about how to define slavery, while making possible clear and empirical measures of the extent and forms of slavery.

6.3 SLAVERY IN THE COLONIES

In the interwar years, however, the Convention to Suppress the Slave Trade and Slavery was used only occasionally, and with little legal impact. More concerning for most states and actors were the evolving relationships between colonies and European powers, relationships that ranged from active modernization to outright rebellion. As the European states began to build up their colonial administrations in the interwar period, they found themselves embroiled in long-standing political and commercial activities that included an extensive and significant traffic in slaves between colonies and protectorates. Preoccupied by World War I, European colonial powers had done little to investigate or interfere with the movement and markets for slaves – especially visible in the Middle East. The Indigenous rulers of Sudan and Ethiopia had carried out a lively slave trade along the Red Sea throughout World War I, including supplying slaves taken from Egypt, which became a British Protectorate in 1914. It was not until 1928 that this trade was "discovered" by the League of Nations, and hundreds of slavetraders arrested. A thousand slaves were freed, and significant numbers of firearms were confiscated. The follow-up care for the freed slaves, however, was sparse and disorganized, and many were taken back into slavery.

On the Atlantic side of Africa, the British colony of Sierra Leone had been founded in 1808 as a place of resettlement for slaves freed through the military intervention of the British Navy during its earlier assault on

---

[21] Research Network on the Legal Parameters of Slavery, "Bellagio-Harvard Guidelines on the Legal Parameters of Slavery." The Bellagio-Harvard Guidelines are available at: www .researchgate.net/publication/301671974_2012_Bellagio-Harvard_Guidelines_on_the_ Legal_Parameters_of_Slavery_-_from_Slavery_in_International_Law. On this website the Guidelines are available in English, Arabic, Chinese, French, Russian, and Spanish.

the transatlantic slave trade. Again, during World War I, the focus was drawn away from the plight of persons re-enslaved in Sierra Leone, and local laws were passed that enforced control of the enslaved. Much of this enslavement was concealed behind labels of "apprenticeships" for children, or the renaming of hereditary household slaves as "cousins." Local laws were altered and improved in the 1920s, but these were mainly window dressing, and little was altered in the lives of the enslaved. In 1929 the British reported to the League of Nations that they had fulfilled their legal obligations in Sierra Leone to those still in bondage – even as the fundamental exploitation and control continued.

In many ways the recognition of what had always been happening in the "free" colonies of Great Britain was being exposed not by governmental action but by journalists and other researchers. An example of this exposure were the investigations into the situation of the *mui tsai*, literally "little sister" in Cantonese, who were actually Chinese girls sold by poor parents to richer families. In theory, they were being adopted and would, in time, find suitable husbands. The reality was much worse, and the little girls were overworked, unpaid, and regularly abused domestic servants. Many were exported to overseas Chinese communities, including into the United States. They might also be sold into commercial sexual exploitation. Under the hybrid legal system of the British colony of Hong Kong slavery was illegal, but *mui tsai* could be exploited and disposed of by their "legal guardians" without hindrance.

In 1920 a campaign against the practice was launched by European missionaries and Christian Chinese and grew to have many supporters in Britain.[22] In 1922 the Anti-Slavery Society brought together a conference of twenty-two other, primarily religious, organizations that called for a government commission to be established. It was the relatively new Colonial Secretary, Winston Churchill (1874–1965), under a barrage of parliamentary questions, who intervened to shift policy. He stated: "No compulsion of any kind will be allowed to prevent these persons from quitting their employment at any time they like. I do not care a rap what the local consequences are."[23] New laws were written that attempted to make the *mui tsai* system illegal, but after compromises with local Chinese leaders the laws became very difficult to enforce. With the advent of an

[22] Harriet Samuels, "A human rights campaign? The campaign to abolish child slavery in Hong Kong 1919–1938," *Journal of Human Rights*, 6:3 (2007), 361–384: doi.org/10.1080/14754830701560764.

[23] Minute by Churchill, February 21, 1922, CO 129/478 p. 297, 8660.

Anti-Mui-Tsai Society in 1931 some 5,000 home visits were made to determine if *mui tsai* were still being held or abused, but odd cases were still being uncovered in the 1950s in Hong Kong.

The relatively constant sequence of events within the European colonies during the interwar years was, first, the official denial of slavery, followed by the proof of its existence, and ultimately a mild form of official response which tended to bring little change. For example, when the resident Commissioner of the Bechuanaland Protectorate (now the country of Botswana) was asked in 1923 to report on forced labor in the Protectorate, he replied that "Slavery is not known to exist in the Bechuanaland Protectorate" but did allow that "a modified form of hereditary service" existed.[24] The primary ethnicity holding the most political power in the Protectorate were the Tswana people. As they expanded under British control, they absorbed other Indigenous hunting and gathering groups which were held separate from, but controlled by, the Tswana. By all measures, these Indigenous groups or Malata were enslaved, held as property, and could be inherited, sold, offered in tribute, or given away. Their status was hereditary, and children "belonged" to their mother's owner.

The British colonial administration maintained a strongly "hands-off" policy that allowed the Tswana to rule with "native law and custom" – and asked no questions about the status of subgroups such as the Malata. Yet, again, journalists intervened. Just as the British government was about to sign the League of Nations Anti-Slavery Convention, Bechuanaland was in the newspaper headlines due to conflict among the Tswana elite over the *ownership* of some Malata girls. This case opened the issue to both further inquiry and government obfuscation. Official investigations were undertaken that found little, while journalists continued to document cases of enslavement. Questions were asked in Parliament "regarding the existence of more than 10,000 slaves within the Bechuanaland Protectorate; and what is being done to terminate such slavery in British territory?" The official reply simply referred to a previous answer by the Government. What is clear from the official records is that racism played a large part in the official position on slavery in Bechuanaland.[25] The Resident Commissioner of the colony, Colonel

---

[24] Resident Commissioner to High Commissioner, April 21, 1926, BNA S 43/7.

[25] Suzanne Miers, *Slavery in the Twentieth Century: The Evolution of a Global Problem* (New York: AltaMira Press, 2003), 161–164.

Rey (1877–1968), summed up perhaps the most prevailing opinion of the 1930s on the Malata minority:

I can conceive no useful object in the world in spending money and energy in preserving a decadent and dying race, which is perfectly useless from any point of view, merely to enable a few theorists to carry out anthropological investigations and make money by writing misleading books which lead nowhere.[26]

The links between racism, imperialism, nationalism, and militarism were not restricted to the British colonizers – Germany and Japan and their allies would wage war to "cleanse" their territories of "perfectly useless," or "dangerous," ethnicities, "races," and groups. The result would be a vast and intentional destruction and genocide, in which the first step would often be enslavement.

6.4 WORLD WAR II: JAPANESE AND GERMAN CONTROL OF RELIGIOUS GROUPS

The intentions of the Nazi regime in Germany and the State Shinto government of Japan toward religious groups are rarely mentioned in the larger consideration of World War II, but there was a common pattern of extreme governmental control over religious expression in both countries. In Japan, State Shinto was established as the national state religion in the Meiji Restoration in 1868, resting on the concept of "*saisei itchi*," the unity of religion and government. The Emperor was considered divine, with personal access to the Gods and therefore holder of sacred powers. In the early twentieth century, the Japanese state institutionalized Shinto, making it the "true" and only fully legal faith. Teaching Shinto was compulsory in all schools, and the government controlled and supported the 100,000 Shinto shrines around the country.

When Japan began its military conquest of China and the Pacific region, the military and occupation administrations established Shinto shrines across much of China and the Larger Pacific Region, especially in areas of military and economic importance.[27] In occupied areas the Japanese military made devotion to the God-Emperor a key focus in its military training and practice, to the extreme of suicide missions in combat. Not unlike Nazi racial beliefs, Shinto promoted a strong sense

---

[26] Botswana National Archives S.469/1{1.

[27] Ahmet Murat Kadıoğlu, "The use of Shinto for the legitimization of Japanese aggression in East Asia," *Nevşehir Hacı Bektaş Veli Üniversitesi SBE Dergisi*, 11:2 (2021), 492–500.

of racial superiority across Japanese culture and throughout the military, mirrored in a denigration and abuse of the inferior 'races' in occupied areas.

In Germany, the Nazi government made the subjugation of churches an important part of its efforts to attain total control over the populace. When Hitler took power in Germany in 1933, the population was 95 percent Christian (63 percent Protestant and 32 percent Catholic). The Reichstag Fire Decree of that same year was an emergency act passed by the Reichstag that restricted all civil liberties, including the right to speak, assemble, protest, and the right to due process. The Decree served as the basis and rationale for violent attacks on any groups or individuals that opposed the Nazis. By late March 1933 the Reichstag had also passed an Enabling Act which, among other provisions, gave the Nazi Party and the Chancellor (Hitler) complete and total control over not just the government but the entire national state. Article 2 of the very short Enabling Act read: "Laws enacted by the government of the Reich may deviate from the constitution as long as they do not affect the institutions of the Reichstag and the Reichsrat."[28] With total freedom to act, the Nazis began a nationwide program to take control of all religious institutions. As a historian of the period summarizes, churches in Germany "were constantly assailed with propaganda or police measures, designed to cajole or enforce their submission."[29] Church properties were seized, church communications and educational efforts suppressed, many lay religious groups were prohibited from meeting, and clergy critical of Nazi ideology were removed from their positions or arrested and sent to prison camps. Smaller sects that resisted Nazi control, such as the Jehovah's Witnesses, were shut down completely and many adherents died in concentration camps. The Nazi plans for German (and other) Jews were especially extreme and deadly. .

At least five years before the beginning of World War II, both the Nazis and the Shinto State of Japan had established a high degree of control over religious practice and had largely suppressed all but the approved expressions of "faith."[30] In both countries this control over faith groups supplied a political and cultural foundation on which enslavement and

---

[28] The upper house of the German Parliament.

[29] J. S. Conway, *The Nazi Persecution of the Churches: 1933–1945* (New York, Basic Books: 1968), xxx.

[30] Christopher Tatara, "Hitler, Himmler, and Christianity in the early Third Reich," *Constructing the Past*, 14:1, article 10: digitalcommons.iwu.edu/constructing/vol14/iss1/10.

extermination would grow to an extraordinary extent and deadliness. The suppression of independent religious groups was both a strategic and tactical aim that paved the way to enslavement and worse, through the branding of targeted or "enemy" populations as less than human.

As nationalism, militarism, and fascism grew in the 1930s, the links between national antislavery organizations broke down, and the pressure of emerging deadly conflicts took precedence and attention. Slavery and other forms of forced labor proliferated within imperialist expansion, often concealed behind dictatorial political facades. As regional land grabs and ethnic conflicts increased and began to merge into World War II, slavery grew as a component in waging war. Amid widespread conflict the sheer size of enslavement in the Axis-controlled countries was difficult to perceive, while addressing large-scale enslavement was not necessarily seen as a war aim by the Allies.

In contrast, early in the war the Nazis instituted the policy of "extermination through labor" (*Vernichtung durch Arbeit*) – a policy aimed at maximizing labor exploitation of prisoners and others, but with the specific and intentional result of their deaths. While such prisoners were not owned as property by individuals, they were treated as the property of the state, insofar as the state acted as if it had two key rights of ownership over the prisoners: the right to possess (i.e. the right to have physical control over a thing) and the right to use (i.e. to use the labor of the prisoners). For example, each of Germany's twenty-three main concentration camps had many "satellite camps" – totalling around 30,000 hard-labor subcamps that were notable for their very high mortality rates.[31] Japan also used captured and enslaved labor – from Korean "comfort women" used for systematic rape by Japanese soldiers in "comfort stations," to local populations in the Philippines or Indochina, as well as Allied prisoners of war, all forced to carry out heavy labor.[32]

After the end of World War II there was little investigation or charging of war crimes against those who ran the extermination through labor

---

[31] Christian Goeschel and Nikolaus Wachsmann, "Before Auschwitz: the formation of the Nazi concentration camps, 1933–9," *Journal of Contemporary History*, 45:3 (2010), 515–534: www.jstor.org/stable/20753613. See also United States Holocaust Memorial Museum, "Concentration Camp System: In Depth," Aug. 22 2023, in *Holocaust Encyclopedia*: encyclopedia.ushmm.org/content/en/article/concentration-camp-system-in-depth.

[32] See, for example, Yoshiaki Yoshimi, *Comfort Women: Sexual Slavery in the Japanese Military during World War II*, rev. ed., trans. Suzanne O'Brien (New York: Columbia University Press, 2002).

camps and work gangs. These issues were a low priority in postwar rebuilding, overshadowed by the genocidal Holocaust that occurred in the industrial-level death camps. There was an assumption that labor camp survivors would rehabilitate. The extreme tension between the Soviet Union and the United States-led Allied forces also worked to distract attention from enslavement in the recent past. The two superpowers settled down into fixed positions: the United States and allies asserted that most of the communist-bloc countries practiced widespread enslavement of their populations.[33] The Soviet Union and allies retorted that slavery could only occur in a capitalist state and economy, and so was rife in the West.[34] These two positions tended to exclude possible inquiry into the realities of forced and enslaved labor on either side. In many ways, the Cold War froze the world's antislavery movements, as well as many of the linked religious actors. It would be fair to argue that the fifth and current antislavery movement began in earnest only when the Iron Curtain fell in 1989.

6.5 THE FIFTH AND CURRENT ANTISLAVERY MOVEMENT

To systematically relate and analyze the history of the current global antislavery movement that emerged after 1989 would require, at least, another volume. This is due in part to the fact that this movement is the best documented of all, and in many ways the largest and most globalized of all antislavery movements. The current movement grew in parallel with the growth of personal computing and the World Wide Web. The ability to retrieve and preserve virtually all communications and records is enormously helpful but also overwhelms the historian and researcher. Meanwhile, this historically brief period of forty years has been one of explosive growth, both in the fifth antislavery movement, and in the promulgation of laws, programs, organizations, and events, as well as controversies. It has been an ongoing period of movement growth and change. This movement, however, has not reached common agreement or resolution on goals, direction, or social and legal intentions. For those reasons we will not attempt to offer a history of the current antislavery movement; it is too soon, too much in motion, and, at times, opaque and

---

[33] In 1949, delegates to the United Nations Economic and Social Council criticized the Soviet Union for exploiting in its camp and colonies up to 14 million people as "slaves."

[34] See, for example, Allan Kulikoff, *Abraham Lincoln and Karl Marx in Dialogue* (Oxford: Oxford University Press, Jan. 2018).

controversial. Instead, we will point to the size and forms of this movement, noting some successes and some failures, particularly in the roles of religious actors.

The 1990s were a time of significant and dramatic growth of antislavery/antitrafficking groups. When the Iron Curtain fell in 1989, the pent-up desire for freedom of movement in the former communist countries fed an explosive migration of people westward into Europe and the Americas. Not surprisingly, there were two insidious countermovements within these mass dislocations. The first was the luring and exploitation of young women from Eastern Europe and Russia into forced commercial sexual exploitation in the West. The second, though less visible at the time, was a parallel movement and exploitation of men eastwards to Russia, Kazakhstan, and other ex-Soviet states, with the promise of jobs that turned out to be brutal and enslaving. Criminal organizations in former Soviet countries grew rapidly, often arising from or in parallel with the existing security bureaus like the KGB, that had begun a vast asset-stripping sell-off of what had been state property – including those persons tricked and pressed into forced labor.[35]

The sudden appearance of large numbers of exploited persons in the West led to an immediate, if confused, reaction to what was termed "human trafficking" or "sex trafficking." Many of the key emergent antitrafficking actors were local and religious groups that proliferated globally. By 2002, when a UK-based antitrafficking group attempted to locate and catalogue voluntary sector/charitable groups engaged in antitrafficking work, they listed some 900 active antislavery/trafficking organizations spread worldwide.[36] From the beginning of the 1990s, as reports of enslavement spread, there was a slow, then rapid, recognition of the crime. Most of the public in Europe and North America had assumed slavery was a thing of the past, but as more articles, reports, books, and films illuminating "modern" slavery emerged, many religious groups began to respond. For the rich countries of North America and Western Europe the focus among religious groups was especially on "sex trafficking."

In the late 1990s, a particular issue kept the field from growing when a vituperative controversy broke out between antislavery/trafficking

[35] Alexandra Lewis and Brad K. Blitz, "The Ru.Lag: the Kremlin's new empire of forced labor," *Journal of Modern Slavery*, 8:1 (2023), slavefreetoday.org/journal_of_modern_slavery/v8i1a9-the-ru-lag-the-kremlins-new-empire-of-forced-labor.pdf.

[36] F. Luckoo and M. Tzvetkova, *Combating Trafficking in Persons: A Directory of Organizations* (London: CHANGE/Anti-Trafficking Programme, 2002).

groups. Several groups, primarily women's groups, argued strongly that the most important issue and the worst form of slavery was sex trafficking (human trafficking and enslavement into commercial sexual exploitation). Other groups took a wider view and sought to expose and address other forms of slavery in addition to enslavement into commercial sexual exploitation. In the late 1990s conferences were convened, sometimes by NGOs and sometimes by international bodies such as the United Nations, on "modern slavery and human trafficking" only to collapse in anger and accusations around the issue of what was the "worst," or most important, form of slavery. The public was largely unaware of this controversy or was dismissive of groups that seemed to focus only on definitional arguments. Meanwhile, most nations lacked laws that were applicable to slavery and trafficking, and the wider public had little awareness of the issue. At the same time, ancient and traditional forms of slavery continued in countries such as Mauritania and India, often as newer adaptations of slavery grew within the same countries as they engaged the processes of economic globalization. Figure 6.3 shows four teenagers from Mali in 2000, who had crossed into Ivory Coast looking for work, and then been tricked and enslaved on a cocoa farm.

FIGURE 6.3 Teenagers enslaved on a cocoa farm. Courtesy of True Vision | Brian Woods.

As the twenty-first century unfolds, we can state several key facts about slavery around the globe. The first is that slavery is pervasive: It is present in all countries and regions. Second, it appears to be growing in parallel with the unprecedented increase in the global population. With more than 8 billion people on the planet, criminals have found a "surplus" of exploitable persons who are often free for the taking, and are then treated as disposable inputs in the exploitation in which they become trapped. The third theme is that while slaves are a very small part of the global population (at an estimated six out of every 1,000 people on the planet), their situation results in a significant, negative, and outsized impact on climate and the environment through their use by criminals in destructive crimes such as illegal deforestation and destructive illegal mining. A fourth theme is that religious groups are central to addressing slavery and human trafficking in the twenty-first century. As we will discuss in Chapter 8, religiously inspired or affiliated work worldwide mobilizes thousands in freeing and supporting enslaved and formerly enslaved people. But even as these faith groups work to free slaves, there are other religious groups that practice and exploit enslavement, such as Boko Haram, ISIS, Al-Shabab, and semireligious states such as the country of Mauritania. It is to this issue that we now turn.

7

False Prophets: Exploiting Faith to Enslave

As the Sunni Jihadist armed forces of ISIS approached the Sinjar District in northern Iraq in 2014, they faced a thorny theological question. The invasion led by the United States in 2003 had created a power vacuum and brought about the disintegration of the structures of governance that had existed under Iraqi President Saddam Hussein. The United States' evacuation of most of its armed forces in 2011 had precipitated a multi-sided civil war, pitting armed groups against each other along the lines of both religion and ethnicity. In 2012 the Shia-dominated government of Iraq reneged on promises to include and support Sunni Muslims, leading to the rapid growth of a Sunni underground extremist movement. By 2013 this movement extended into Syria and had named itself as the Islamic State in Iraq and Syria (ISIS). By late June 2014 ISIS had rapidly occupied a large part of northern Iraq. After capturing the provincial capital of Mosul, the ISIS leader Abu Bakr al-Baghdadi declared the creation of an Islamic state (a Caliphate) and named himself Caliph. Within the city of Mosul a reign of terror unfolded that included rape, abductions, mass executions, pillaging, extortion, and seizure of state resources.

The unanswered theological question troubling ISIS leaders concerned the Yazidi population living in Sinjar District west of Mosul. Sinjar and particularly Mount Sinjar, is the ancient centre of Yazidi ethnicity, culture, and identity, and is seen by all Yazidis as a sacred homeland. The crucial question for the ISIS leadership was how to classify the Yazidi people in religious terms. ISIS had strict rules, based on their study of the Qur'an, on how each religious group they encountered should be understood and treated. ISIS then initiated a process of religious classifi-cation that would determine how the entire Yazidi ethnicity would be treated.

The Yazidis are a small ethnic group, numbering some 500,000 in Iraq. They have their own unique religion, not formally linked to Judaism, Christianity, or Islam. Yazidis assert that their religion is both the oldest on the planet, and the first monotheistic faith. Their calendar indicates that their religion, as well as the universe itself, began some 7,000 years ago. Over time, the Yazidi faith has incorporated influences of Zoroastrianism, Manichaeism, Gnosticism, Christianity, and Islam, with-out abandoning its original and holistic faith tradition.

Yazidis believe that God is omnipotent, omnipresent, and omniscient, and grants free will to human beings. While this description of the deity is similar to that held by Muslims, Yazidis depart radically from Islam and Christianity in their belief in a specific and unique Holy Trinity. The Yazidi Trinity does not include God, who is seen as complete in his oneness, and who is benevolent, forgiving, and merciful. Instead, the Yazidi Trinity is seen as an extension of God, tasked with instructing and guiding the Yazidi people. This Trinity is comprised of two deified humans, Sheikh 'Adi and Sultan Êzî, who were key early founders of the Yazidi faith, and a specific and special angel, the Tawusi Melek, or Peacock Angel. The Peacock Angel is the primary member of the Trinity, God's only earthly representative, and an omniscient being who is able to predetermine the future.

This unique feature of the Yazidi faith tradition has had two distinct outcomes for the Yazidi people. The first is that their faith has often made them a target as various peoples and religious groups moved through the liminal terrain and mountains of what is today northern Iraq. Restless expanding empires, or migrating ethnicities, often persecuted and abused the Yazidis over centuries, but as their religion is deeply tied to the holy sites around Mount Sinjar, they remained throughout the assaults. If forcibly displaced, the Yazidis returned there as soon as they could. This repetitive history of invasion and persecution led, in part, to a second key feature of Yazidi culture – the creation of a tightly knit and tightly structured society reinforced by an intensive double endogamy. Yazidis must marry other Yazidis, and they must also marry within the specific hereditary "castes" that make up the larger Yazidi society. Not surpris-ingly, there is a deep sense of close relatedness among all Yazidis, reinforced by an annual autumnal pilgrimage to Mount Sinjar attended, whenever possible, by Yazidis from around the world.

It was specifically the belief in the Peacock Angel, however, that often brought persecution and genocide to the Yazidi people in the past. Muslims tend to equate the Peacock Angel with Satan, mainly due to the Peacock Angel's refusal to bow or submit to Adam in Yazidi theology, just as Satan refused to submit to Adam in Islamic theology. While the Yazidi faith has no concept for Satan, this assumed identification of Satan with the Peacock Angel led many Muslims and Christians to accuse Yazidis of being "devil worshippers." For ISIS, the thorny question was how to classify the Yazidi within their specifically Islamic theological universe. Were they "people of the book"? Had they originally been Muslims and then apostatized? Or were they, indeed, "devil worshippers"? The resulting classification would determine their treatment, and ultimately whether the Yazidis in Sinjar would live or die.

The military leaders of ISIS were supported by a deep cohort of religious bureaucrats. While their military planning might be arrived at through decision-making by the ranking military leader, policy and planning could also be derived directly from Qur'anic Scripture and its specialist interpretation by ISIS leaders and theologians. To address the question of the status of the Yazidis, teams of religious researchers were deployed in search of an answer. As explained in the ISIS online magazine *Dabiq* (English language edition):

Upon conquering the region of Sinjar ... the Islamic State faced a population of Yazidis, a pagan minority existent for ages in the regions of Iraq and Sham [Syria]. Their continual existence to this day is a matter that Muslims should question as they will be asked about it on Judgment Day. ... Prior to the taking of Sinjar, Shari'ah students in the Islamic State were tasked to research the Yazidis to determine if they should be treated as an originally *mushrik* [pagan, devil-worshiping] group, or one that originated as Muslims and then apostasized, due to many of the related Islamic rulings, that would apply to the group, its individuals, and their families. Because of the Arabic terminologies used by this group to describe themselves or their beliefs, some contemporary Muslim scholars have classified them as possibly an apostate sect, but upon further research, it was determined that this group is one that existed since the pre-Islamic *jahiliyyah* [literally, "the age of ignorance" – that is, the time before the revelation of Islam], but became "Islamized" by the surrounding Muslim population, language, and culture, although they had never accepted Islam nor claimed to have adopted it. The apparent origin of the religion is found in the Magianism of ancient Persia, but reinterpreted with elements of Sabianism, Judaism, and Christianity, and ultimately expressed in the heretical vocabulary of Sufism. Accordingly, the Islamic State dealt with this group as the majority of *fuqaha* [religious scholars] have indicated how *mushrikin* should be dealt with.[1]

---

[1] *Dabiq* 1435, Online Magazine, Issue 4, 14–16. With a registered account, this article can be accessed at: jihadology.net.

The *Dabiq* article goes on to explain the appropriate and permissible treatment of the *mushrikin* Yazidis: They are not allowed, like Christians and Jews, to make a *jizyah* payment in cash or goods to avoid enslavement or death. In other words, Yazidis could be killed with impunity. "Also," state the religious commentators, "their women could be enslaved." The *Dabiq* article then describes what happened after ISIS moved against the Yazidi:

After capture, Yazidi women and children were divided according to the *Shari-ah* among the fighters of the Islamic State who participated in the Sinjar attacks, after one-fifth of the slaves were transferred to the Islamic State's authority to be divided as "*khums.*"

(Muslims are required in certain circumstances to donate one-fifth, "*khum,*" of acquired wealth, in this case slaves, to the religious hierarchy.) In the eyes of ISIS the long history and tradition of the Yazidi counted for nothing once they were classified, symbolized, and segregated as *mushrikin* devil worshippers. ISIS dehumanized the Yazidi in a series of religious rationalizations cherry-picked from the breadth of Islamic legal opinion. They also ruled that enslaved Yazidi mothers with small children should not be killed, with the result that mothers with small children were subsequently taken as household slaves or, sometimes, second or third wives. After the assault ISIS propaganda reported that "Many of the *mushrik* women and children have willingly accepted Islam and now race to practice it with evident sincerity after their exit from the darkness of *shirk* [sin and disbelief]."

Once these rulings on the religious and existential status of Yazidis were in place, the marching orders to the ISIS fighters were clear: It was time to cleanse the newly conquered territories of the Caliphate of the heathen Yazidis. This assault would follow the religious rulings that further subdivided the Yazidi into specific categories for exploitation and/or extermination. Broadly, this categorization by ISIS of subgroups within the captured Yazidis was manifested through a sorting process that determined who could or should be killed immediately, and those who might be enslaved or put to other tactical uses.

On the night of August 2, 2014, ISIS forces began a closely coordinated attack into Sinjar District and the Yazidi homeland. Many Yazidis had taken up arms and set patrols around their villages and towns. They waited to act on the assumption that the Kurdish armed forces in the area would engage ISIS as needed. But faced with a large-scale invasion, the Kurdish Pushmerga, the only organized military force defending

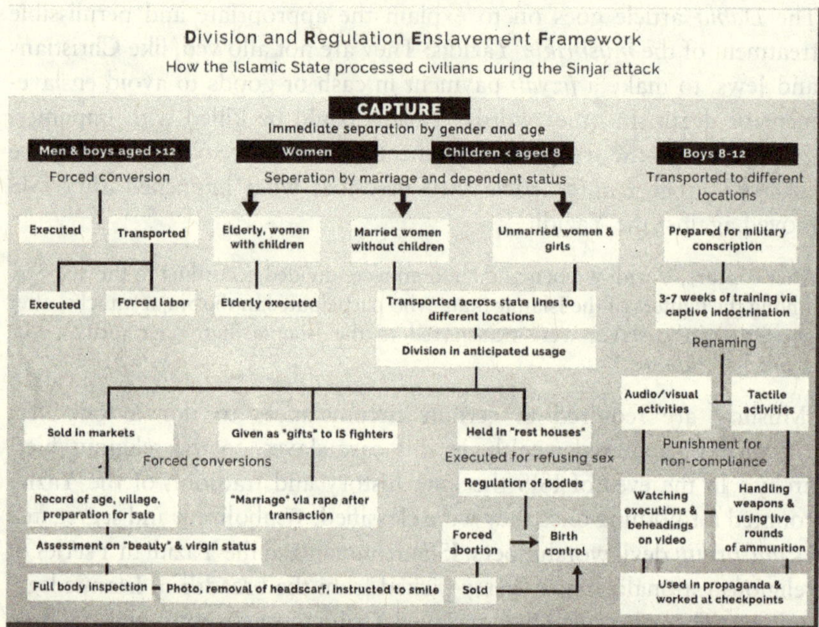

FIGURE 7.1 Division and regulation enslavement framework. Used with permission – drawn from: Nadia Al-Dayel, Andrew Mumford, and Kevin Bales, "Not yet dead: the establishment and regulation of slavery by the Islamic State," *Studies in Conflict & Terrorism*, 45:11 (2020), 12: doi.org/10.1080/1057610X.2020.1711590.

Sinjar, withdrew that night from the area, leaving it undefended. In darkness villages or towns were surrounded and taken by the ISIS fighters. At dawn the civilian populations were forced from their homes and hiding places and taken by ISIS fighters to a public square or similar open space. Acting on predetermined orders, the ISIS troops divided the captive population by age and gender. Most of the captured men and male teenagers were executed immediately by gunfire and usually in public. Some men were taken away, with the expectation of execution at a later date, and used, in the meantime, for forced labor. Older women, those deemed past childbearing, were separated, and then marched away from other captives. Once segregated these older women were also executed *en masse,* then buried in a common pit. Figure 7.1 shows the division and regulation of captives by ISIS, and the typical outcomes for each subgroup.

As can be seen in the flowchart, most men, older boys, and older women were immediately executed. Younger boys, aged eight to twelve, were separated and taken away for indoctrination and military training.

Married women without children, and unmarried women and girls, entered a more convoluted set of pathways leading to different forms of enslavement, with the added ISIS aim of forced impregnation. Women with small children were distributed to fighters as second or third wives.

Forced impregnation was a key aim in this process of capture and use. It had been carefully discussed within ISIS and the *Dabiq* article explained the rationale:

It has been stated that the conquests of the lands of *kufr* [unbelief] multiply as well enslavement, and thereby concubines increase in numbers, until the slave women give birth to their masters, this is because the child of the master has the status of the master – meaning he is a free man like his father – and thereby she has given birth to her master from this angle.[2]

Within ISIS, then, was the intention to achieve both a *tactical* and *strategic* use of enslavement and rape. Enslaved Yazidi women were to be impregnated, and their offspring would not be Yazidi but ISIS Muslims. New infants would hold the same status as their ISIS fathers, thus becoming "masters over their mothers." This is not precisely "ethnic cleansing," but an *ethnic transformation through rape* which is best understood as a strategic aim. It is an act that Fisher terms "forced impregnation as genocide."[3]

There was one further, theological, motivation for the practice of enslaving *mushrik* women and girls. A key existential belief and aim of the religious leaders of ISIS is to bring about the apocalyptic end of time and history, thus ushering in a new Islamic creation. A key ISIS belief is that a "great battle before the Hour" will usher in a new postapocalyptic reality ("the end of time") in which Islam is triumphant and universal. Published ISIS pronouncements make clear that one of the "signs of the Hour," that is, indications that the end of time is near, is that the "slave girl gives birth to her master." A revival of slavery is seen as both a sign predicting, and a trigger of, the *al-Malhamah al-Kubra* (the final apocalyptic battle).

Beyond these theological motivations was the tactical need for resources including hard cash. What was unique to the ISIS program was the large-scale sale of enslaved women and girls in both public and online auctions. While a fundamental goal of ISIS was to exterminate the

---

[2] *Dabiq* 1435, Issue 4, 14–16.
[3] Siobhan K. Fisher, "Occupation of the womb: forced impregnation as genocide," *Duke Law Journal*, 46:1 (1996), 91–133.

mushrikin Yazidi, a parallel goal was to convert women and girls into cash that would be used to support the ISIS war effort. This is fundamentally a tactical use of enslaved persons and was by all accounts very successful in generating significant amounts of money for ISIS. The lived outcomes of this group of women and girls is largely unknown. Once sold at auction they disappeared from ISIS monitoring and their whereabouts were further clouded by the fog of war.

The extensive, yet well documented, processes and practices used by ISIS to achieve goals both strategic (extermination of the Yazidi, and the furthering of the aim to bring about the end of time) and tactical (raising funds, training captured children to become fighters, and other uses of enslaved labor) highlight the extent to which religious practice can be deeply exploitative, destructive, and deadly. A significant number of Yazidis are still held in slavery, and those, mainly young women, including those who were sold in online auctions, have essentially disappeared. The offspring of women enslaved and "married" to ISIS fighters are also lost to any estimation.

If we have gone into detail on the specific case of ISIS, it is because their theological justifications and rationalizations are so clearly available in their own words. Their extensive records, now captured and available for analysis, provide sharp details of their plans and processes. Their own public pronouncements and published works, as well as their well-documented and independently reported actions, paint a clear picture of their intentions and goals. Altogether, these describe a faith group that clearly rationalizes and practices slavery, as well as genocide, openly, tactically, and strategically. Other religious groups that practice enslavement are less blatant, less aggressive and militant, and less organized than ISIS, but the impact on the lives of those enslaved can be equally severe. The control, manipulation, and exploitation of women and girls is repeated within a number diverse religious groups, each with their own unique religious justification.

7.1 "TROKOSI" IN WEST AFRICA

The religious system of *trokosi* (a compound of two Ewe words: *tro*, meaning "deity" or "god," and *kosi*, meaning "slave") is prevalent among two patrilineal ethnic groups, the Ewes of Tongu and Anlo, and the Dangmes of Greater Accra. These two ethnic groups total about 10 million people across West Africa with the majority living in Ghana. About 90 percent of these ethnicities have converted to Christianity, but some also continue to practice the rituals of their previous religions.

This "ritual" slavery appears to be more prevalent in rural areas and revolves around a specific practice of atonement. The *trokosi* priests, who control the fetish shrines, insist that a family can only gain atonement for offenses committed by male relatives or ancestors by giving a virgin daughter to the shrine – typically aged between eight and fifteen. Offenses committed by male relatives might range from petty theft to murder. Once a girl is handed over to the shrine, she is put under strict control, enslaved, and used for both domestic and agricultural labor, as well as for sexual exploitation. Any babies born to the *trokosi* become the property of the priest and shrine. Generally, *trokosi* girls are denied education, sufficient food, and basic health care. There is severe punishment if *trokosi* attempt to escape. Most remain in slavery for between three and ten years, but some remain in bondage for their whole lives. If a girl or young woman dies, her family must offer another virgin daughter. If *trokosi* are released or gain freedom, they are considered unmarriageable. *Trokosi* status is hereditary, and the *trokosis* themselves are passed on to another priest when the priest who holds them dies. South African scholar D. Y. Dzansi interviewed one ex-*trokosi* who described her experience:

I did domestic and other services to the priest. My duties included the performance of domestic chores such as cooking, washing, sweeping, fetching water and taking care of visitors. On a regular basis, I had to do farm work. More often than not, I worked from dawn to dusk, sometimes without food. At times while on the farm, we lived on palm kernel or ate pepper and drunk water on it as food. I was never remunerated, neither did I ever get a share in the farm produce of my labour. The priests had absolute sexual control over us, which often resulted in pregnancy and childbearing. I may be free now but inside me I feel hollow. Worst still I am struggling to look after my "fatherless" three children.[4]

The mechanism for achieving "atonement" creates the religious justification on which the *trokosi* is founded. Crimes committed or conflicts engaged in by male family members – for example, assault, theft, adultery, murder, falsehood/fraud, litigation and disputes over land, and the nonpayment of debts – can lead to the need to atone. Nearly all the young women or girls sent to be *trokosi* are the younger female relatives of the perpetrators of such crimes. Aggrieved parties, victims of these crimes, will go to the shrines to ask the priests to call upon the gods to search out the wrongdoers and punish them. As Wisdom Mensah explained, "People

---

[4] D. Y. Dzansi and P. Biga, "'Trokosi' – slave of a fetish: an empirical study," *Studies of Tribes and Tribals*, 12:1 (2014), 1–8, 6.

who feel an injustice has been committed against them, will go to the shrine and place a curse on the offender so that they will be punished by the gods. These curses take several forms: strange sicknesses, unexplained deaths, incurable diseases, or successive deaths within a family."[5]

When divine power is invoked in this way against a perpetrator, it is believed to produce devastating effects and repercussions. As Dzansi[6] and others report, all shrine priests attest to this destructive power as a fundamental tenet of faith, which in turn supports a strongly held general belief that catastrophe will envelop the family of a perpetrator unless atonement can be achieved. Handing over a girl or young woman is deemed necessary to appease the gods and gain atonement. Oral tradition asserts that family or community members will keep suffering and dying until the perpetrator admits his guilt and makes amends to the gods by bringing a girl or young woman into servitude at a *trokosi* shrine. This appeasement is both for the good of the wider family (and community), and to protect innocent family members who could become victims of divine retribution. Other ethnographic accounts confirm this process of offense and atonement.[7]

While the tradition of *trokosi* was banned by law in Ghana in 1998, there has been little reduction in the practice. This is, in part, due to the fact that many African countries, including Ghana, have what are known as "plural (or parallel)" legal systems.[8] In these countries there are *national laws* (normally based on a constitution which includes a list of rights and responsibilities), but parallel legal standing is also afforded to *religious laws and legal structures*, such as Muslim *shari'a* law, as well as to *tribal laws* as practiced by groups such as the Ewe and Dangme tribes.

---

[5] Wisdom Mensah, "Girls in West Africa offered into sexual slavery as 'wives of gods,'" *The Conversation*, Oct. 29, 2018: theconversation.com/girls-in-west-africa-offered-into-sexual-slavery-as-wives-of-gods-105400.

[6] Dzansi and Biga, "'Trokosi.'"

[7] See Jonathan C. Goltzman, "Cultural relativism or cultural intrusion? Female ritual slavery in Western Africa and the international covenant on civil and political rights: Ghana as a case study," *New England International and Comparative Law Annual*, 4 (1998), 53–72; Sarah C. Aird, "Ghana's slaves to the gods," *Human Rights Brief*, 7:1 (1999), 6–8, 26; Sofia Wiking, "From slave wife of the gods to 'ke te pam tem eng': Trokosi seen through the eyes of the participants," unpublished Master's thesis, Malmo University, Sweden (2009); Rhonda Martinez, "The Trokosi tradition in Ghana: the silencing of a religion," *History in the Making*, 4:5 (2011): scholarworks.lib.csusb.edu/history-in-the–making/vol4/iss1/5.

[8] Jody Sarich, Michele Olivier, and Kevin Bales, "Forced marriage, slavery, and plural legal systems: an African example," *Human Rights Quarterly*, 38:2 (2016), 450–476: doi.org/10.1353/hrq.2016.0030.

Which of these legal systems takes precedence in a given situation is often unclear and varies from place to place. This is especially the case when a legal question concerns the practice of religion or the practice of marriage – both of which are central to *trokosi*.

Forced and child marriage in general has been shown to be highly correlated with plural legal systems. One study explained the tensions arising from plural legal systems this way:

> This raises the question: which legal rules do citizens acknowledge as binding – those coming from a supposedly democratic or undemocratic legislature, or those they believe to be endorsed by religion or custom? Human rights instruments rightfully acknowledge the validity and value of diverse cultures, religions, and traditional practices while condemning those practices that are considered "harmful," broadly defined. The preservation of minority rights, particularly culture and a traditional way of living, is also well documented in international law.[9]

The result is a highly contested space in which apparently gross human rights violations are deemed appropriate within specific religious practices.[10]

Between 1996 and 2006, the nongovernmental organization International Needs-Ghana freed some 3,500 slaves from more than 130 shrines in the Volta and Greater Accra regions of Ghana. But close to 90 percent of the 2,000 *trokosis* liberated between 1997 and 1999 returned to the shrines.[11] Facing stigma from their families and communities, and boycotted if they tried to sustain themselves economically, their independence meant starvation. At the same time, some *trokosi* chose to remain in the shrine, fearful of repercussions for disobeying the gods. For the large part of the Ghanaian population who do not practice *trokosi*, it is seen as a strange, but debatable, local practice. Some Ghanaians argue that the children of *trokosis* are destined to redeem mankind. Others assert that the *trokosi* system maintains order in place of official law enforcement. Still others insist that *trokosis* are priestesses, not slaves. Viewed as a traditional tribal practice, and thus protected as a

---

[9] Ibid., 470.

[10] More broadly, this area of inquiry is understudied. The interaction of law and religion (and religious "law") is complex and varies from culture to culture, nation to nation, and often community to community. It is currently a matter of significant concern and political activity in the United States, just as it is, in very different manifestations, in China, Iran, Brazil, Afghanistan, and a host of other countries.

[11] Deann Alford, "Sex slaves' slow freedom," *Christianity Today*, 49:2 (February 2005), 22.

cultural right,[12] it is unlikely that *trokosi* will be reduced or eradicated without significant political will and broad societal agreement. What *trokosi* has in common with many other antisocial or damaging practices of religious groups worldwide is that the most common demographic group to be exploited is that of young women and girls.

7.2 DEUKI AND DEVADASI IN NEPAL AND INDIA

Two religious systems similar to *trokosi* exist in South Asia. In Nepal a girl becomes a *deuki* ("a girl offered to god" – derived from "Debkanya" in the Sanskrit language, meaning "daughter of God"). Well-off families without daughters buy young girls from impoverished rural families in order to offer them to Hindu temples as their own – with the intention of gaining benefits and favors from the gods. These young girls are then dedicated as servants to the temple deities, they are prohibited from marrying, and, normally without other support, are forced into prostitution to support themselves. A key religious justification for the sexual exploitation of *deuki*, one that mirrors the exploitation of *trokosi*, is the belief that men can be cleansed of their crimes and other sins by having sex with a *deuki*. While this practice is thought to be in decline,[13] estimates range from 2,000 to 30,000 girls held as *deuki* in Nepal. According to some accounts, the role of *deuki* in the past "as a caretaker of the temple was valued and respected. For their service, women were granted a parcel of temple property and accumulated wealth through donations to God."[14] The situation today displays none of those positive outcomes.

Once given to the temple to be a *deuki*, the young women are regarded as unmarriageable but can and are expected to have sexual relations with anyone who comes to the temple. Without any other form of livelihood, the result is that they practice what is often referred to as "survival sex," that is, sexual exploitation in exchange for food, clothing, and other necessities. Once engaged as a *deuki* in commercial sexual exploitation

---

[12] Article 21 of the Ghanaian Constitution (guaranteeing freedom of religion), "upholds the religion of their forebears."

[13] Anju Gautam Yogi, "Women sacrificed to gods struggle to rehabilitate, Deuki tradition wanes in Nepal,, Sep. 10, 2012, *Global Press Journal*: globalpressjournal.com/asia/nepal/women-sacrificed-to-gods-struggle-to-rehabilitate-deuki-tradition-wanes-in-nepal/.

[14] Robynne A. Locke, "Rescued, rehabilitated, returned: institutional approaches to the rehabilitation of survivors of sex trafficking in India and Nepal," Master's thesis, University of Denver (2010): digitalcommons.du.edu/etd/378.

they are considered otherwise unemployable. All *deuki* report the regular occurrence of rape and sexual violence in addition to the practice of prostitution.

Nepali government programs, particularly those based in the Ministry of Women, Children and Social Welfare, and sometimes linked to foreign NGOs, are making some progress in both reducing the practice and rehabilitating and supporting *deuki* women and girls. The Constitution of Nepal (1990) made illegal any human trafficking and exploitation in the name of religion, though enforcement is slight at best, meanwhile secularization and lower attendance at temples has reduced the demand for *deuki*. That said, any female children born to *deuki* are expected to become *deuki* as well, and male offspring, known as *deuka*, are given to temple priests to serve as servants.

A 2020 qualitative research project surveyed *deuki* in Nepal. They noted that while the practice seems to be diminishing in Central Nepal, it is still prevalent in the more rural areas of western Nepal. Interviewing *deuki* they reported that:

The *Deukis* admit that the perception of society towards them has changed from reverence to hatred. The moral, religious, and cultural importance of *deuki pratha* has been worsened. . . . With the growing hatred and humiliation in the society, the *Deukis* had started to feel that the deity did not possess them. *Deukis* expressed that the prohibition of legal marriage and complete devotion to the service of God had nothing to offer them rather just trauma, hardships, devoid of basic human and women rights.[15]

More widespread than the *deuki* system in Nepal is the *devadasi* ("servant to the gods") system in India, again part of Hindu tradition. Prepubescent girls are dedicated to the goddess Yellamma by family members and village elders, then given to temple priests and enslaved into sexual exploitation. They begin sexual servitude between the ages of eight and twelve, and remain the property of the temple priests well into adulthood. Family members dedicate girls out of devotion to the goddess, through fear of the goddess' disapproval, or hope that the offering will ease a family crisis. The practice is prevalent in two Indian states in particular: Andhra Pradesh, where there are currently estimated to be around 17,000 *devadasis*, and Karnataka, where there are estimated to be around 23,000. The practice was banned in Karnataka in 1984 and in Andhra

---

[15] Dipendra Bahadur K.C., "Deuki Pratha in Nepal: problems and changing beliefs," *Tribhuvan University Journal*, 35:2 (2020), 89–102, 96: doi.org/10.3126/tuj.v35i2 .36194.

Pradesh in 1988, after which the total number of *devadasis* declined. But in the early 1990s there remained around 50,000 *devadasis* in Karnataka alone.

Declared to be "wives" of the gods, *devadasis* are prohibited from entering into normal marriages. Instead, they are available for sex with the deity's priests or devotees and become the temporary concubine of one man after another. This temporary "husband" is under no formal obligation to support his *devadasi* or any children he might sire. Some "husbands" may provide temporary lodging, but most *devadasis* live with their parents. Traditionally, *devadasis* lived within the temple grounds, but this is no longer a common arrangement. *Devadasis* are not paid for their sexual exploitation and instead must support themselves through low-skilled labor in agriculture or construction. When the period of sexual activity is over, by middle age, the stigma remains. The *devadasi* status can never be cast off and the inability to enter into an ordinary marriage normally means extreme poverty throughout the *devadasi*'s life. Children of *devadasis* also suffer discrimination because they have no recognized fathers. Sometimes the *devadasi* role is passed on to the new generation, but more often the children simply become vulnerable to other forms of commercial sexual exploitation.

Nearly all of India's *devadasis* belong to "scheduled castes" – people in the lowest social categories and who exist outside the formal *varna* caste system. Previously known as "untouchables," they are also known as Dalit (from Sanskrit *dalita*, meaning "broken/scattered"). The term "scheduled castes" is a product of government obfuscation and is used to replace other pejorative and demeaning terms in government documents. No *devadasi* comes from an upper caste. And in fact, beyond this supply of *devadasis*, India's caste system, rooted in Hindu theology, creates a ready-made hierarchy for numerous other forms of enslavement.

7.3 THE IMPACT OF RELIGIOUS AND ETHNIC HIERARCHIES IN SOUTH ASIA

A pervasive characteristic of Indian society is the Hindu "caste" system – a hierarchy of social differences ascribed at birth and passed from parent to child. Several segments of the population are excluded from this *varna* caste system such as the *Adivasis,* or the Indigenous peoples of the subcontinent, sometimes termed the "scheduled tribes" who make up 9 per cent of the population, some 104 million people according to the 2011 census. Another group, the "untouchables" or Dalits, are now officially termed the "scheduled castes." This oppressed and exploited Dalit minority makes up close to 200 million persons, constituting around 16 per cent of India's total population.

The prejudicial assumption that Dalits are "unclean" or "polluting," in a religious as well as physical sense, is part of a vicious cycle of control and exploitation. Dalits are refused jobs in all except "unclean" work: as sanitation workers, manual scavengers, cleaners of drains and sewers, garbage collectors, removers of animal and human waste, and so forth. Restriction to these precarious, poorly paid, and often dangerous forms of work means that Dalit families are in general extremely poor, cut off from civic participation and social protections, and recipients of prejudicial treatment, normally without any chance of legal recourse. It is a small, but telling, indication of the religious discrimination Dalits face to note that, like African Americans in the 1950s, Dalits are forbidden to drink from public water fountains and face public violence if they do so. One result of this discrimination and separation is a significant vulnerability to enslavement. A report by Anti-Slavery International found that Dalit people form a large proportion of India's slaves.[16] Some 80 per cent of all enslaved bonded laborers in India are thought to come from the castes most discriminated against, as are most child laborers trafficked from the state of Bihar, 70 per cent of child domestic workers in Chennai, and around 60 per cent of Indian victims of forced commercial sexual exploitation.

Rural states, such as Uttar Pradesh and Bihar, remain "traditional" on the religious ideology of caste. Many rural Dalit families are caught in hereditary forms of collateral debt bondage slavery. This means that at some date in the past an ancestor was advanced funds or food and went to work for a rural landowner. Being illiterate they were unable to contest the landowner's assertion that they have never repaid the original debt and must continue to work under the landowner's control. Such control means they are forbidden to leave their master's land, their children must work and cannot go to school even if one is available, and the girls and women are assumed to be available for sexual assault by the landowner and his male family members. Since the families are held in isolation, after one or two generations in this form of hereditary collateral debt bondage

---

[16] Krishna Prasad Upadhyaya, *Poverty, Discrimination and Slavery: The reality of bonded labour in India, Nepal and Pakistan* (London: Anti-Slavery International, 2008): www.antislavery.org/reports/poverty-discrimination-and-slavery-the-reality-of-bonded-labour-in-india-nepal-and-pakistan/.

FIGURE 7.2 Hereditary debt slaves at work in a quarry. Courtesy of Supriya Awasthi | Free the Slaves

slavery there is little or no memory of freedom. The small community of Dalits is "institutionalized," without knowledge of the outside world, their rights, or any other way of life. The only form of "payment" to the enslaved families is a meager daily ration of food. The photograph in Figure 7.2, taken in 2004, shows an upper caste Hindu pointing to the families he "owns" and who have worked in his family's quarry for generations.

In a similar way, families who are members of other religious minorities are enslaved in brick kilns across South Asia. Brickmaking in Nepal, India, and Pakistan is a vast industry; there are more than 50,000 brick kilns in the region. These primitive kilns manufacture bricks using methods similar to the brickmaking described in the Old Testament (Exod 5), but with the dangerous addition of large makeshift firing kilns that are a major cause of death and injury.[17] Figure 7.3 shows an enslaved

---

[17] For a detailed description and analysis of the South Asian brick industry see Bales, *Disposable People*, chap. 5. For the identification of brick kilns from space, see Doreen Boyd, Bethany Jackson, Jessica Wardlaw, Giles Foody, Stuart Marsh, and Kevin Bales, "Slavery from space: Demonstrating the role for satellite remote sensing to inform

FIGURE 7.3 Enslaved girl at work in a brick kiln. Courtesy of Leslie Roberts | Anti-Slavery International (UK).

child worker in a brick kiln in Pakistan, and Figure 7.4 shows laborers, likely enslaved, working in a brick kiln in northeastern India.

Figure 7.5 is a picture taken in 2023 of a mother and her children in Uttar Pradesh, India. The mother has been trapped in debt bondage for years and both she and her children are forced to work without pay in a brick kiln.

Dalits and Muslims are lured with promises of work and enslaved in brick kilns in India; in Pakistan the enslaved workers are more often Christians or members of the oppressed Ahmadiyya Muslim minority. The fundamental pattern is that families and individuals who are part of one of the beleaguered religious minorities in South Asia are easy prey for employers and criminals who illegally control and abuse workers.

7.4 TRADITIONAL RELIGIOUS JUSTIFICATIONS FOR ENSLAVEMENT

In many countries and cultures around the world, religion forms the dividing line between slave and free without specifically defining the system of bondage. Beyond its role in creating social exclusion and economic vulnerabilities, as in India's Hindu caste system, or in shaping

evidence-based action related to UN SDG Number 8," *ISPRS Journal of Photogrammetry and Remote Sensing*, 142 (2018), 380–388.

FIGURE 7.4 Laborers at work in a brick kiln. Courtesy of Peggy Callahan | Voices4Freedom.

FIGURE 7.5 Enslaved family in Uttar Pradesh, India, 2023. Courtesy of Miranda Penn Turin | Voices4Freedom.

ritual slavery such as that of the *trokosi* in Ghana and the *devadasi* in India, religion can be a tool and weapon used by human traffickers and slaveholders adept at exploiting religious beliefs and prejudices. In Pakistan, for example, religion is not the sole defining factor in enslavement, yet a large proportion of families and individuals enslaved in brick kilns are socially and legally oppressed Christians while the slaveholders are Muslim. In Hindu-dominated Nepal, cases of slavery are higher in Muslim areas – not because local Islamic doctrine supports a slave system, but because divorced Muslim women are seen as outcasts and can easily be coerced away from their villages and forced into commercial sexual exploitation. In Nepal 81 percent of the population is Hindu, 4.4 percent is Muslim, a ratio that means it is Muslims who are often denied full participation in civic life and hence can be exploited and enslaved with little public concern.

In Thailand, slaveholders often rely on Buddhism to justify and exert control. One interpretation of Theravada Buddhism, widely practiced in Southeast Asia, justifies male promiscuity and the use of those women and girls held for commercial sexual exploitation. The *vihaya*, or rules for Theravada monks, lists ten categories of "appropriate wives" and the first three are "those to be enjoyed or used occasionally." Theravada Buddhism clearly positions women as inferior to men. Women cannot reach the state of *nirvana*, and being born a woman implies a particularly sinful previous life. Slaveholders encourage women and girls to believe that they must have committed terrible sins in a past life to deserve their enslavement and abuse. Adapting another Thai cultural belief based on Buddhist teachings – that of acceptance and resignation in the face of life's pain and suffering – slaveholders urge the women they have enslaved to accept their karmic debt, to come to terms with it, and to reconcile themselves to their fate. Human traffickers prey on young women even more effectively when these applications of religious tradition combine with the view of some parents in poor, rural areas that their daughters, being tainted by their past lives, may be treated as commodities and sold if the proceeds can further the well-being of the extended family. This sacrifice is supported by the belief inculcated and deeply held by Thai children, especially girls, that they owe their parents a profound cosmic and physical debt.

The use of religion by slaveholders to encourage acceptance of enslavement in Thailand is repeated by Nigerian human traffickers. These traffickers apply West African *voodoo* to discourage women from attempting escape. After accepting an "offer of work" in Western Europe, and before leaving Nigeria, women and girls must undergo an initiation ritual. This can include the marking or scarification of their faces and hands, the laying of hands on a *juju* (statue), and the drinking of blood. Their hair and nail clippings are placed in a magical pouch said to give the slaveholder control over their soul. They are forced to swear to the gods that they will work hard for their employers, and will never mention their real names, run away, or contact the police. Once they have arrived in Europe they are often drugged and sold, most often to brothels. If the women are not cooperative after arrival, they are exposed to a mixture of physical violence and new, enforcing, rituals. Captors, usually the brothel "madams," threaten the women with death or punishment by the gods for disobedience, and warn that any attempt to escape will awaken a curse on their families.

An orphan who was tricked into leaving her village in northern Nigeria in 1998, Joy Ubi-Ubi, remembers that she drank blood during a voodoo ritual before leaving Africa. Afterwards, once she was in Europe, her captors said this ritual meant the *juju* would kill her if she tried to escape. As Joy explains, she was forced to become a prostitute through both the threat of death and religious coercion:

We went very far – before, I had only been to the next village or to the market. When we got there I met some men in white clothing. There was a woman there too, a priestess … They asked me to pull off my shoes, and they brought blood for me to drink. They asked me to drink it for my own good, and said that it wasn't going to kill me. I drank it, and they marked my body and my hand. Then they gave me a sheep's eye and said I had to eat it … They said that anybody who was going to Europe had to do this … When I was finished, they asked me to put my hand on the juju … Then they took me away in a car, and straight into a ship … In the Red Light District [in Europe] I said: "what kind of job is this?" They said, "prostitution" … One man said that if I went to the police, or if the police arrested me, they would deport me to Nigeria, and then he would come to Nigeria by himself to kill me … They said that because of everything I drank before coming, and because I had put my hand on the juju, if I went to anybody or tried to run away, the juju would kill me. So I was forced to do the work.[18]

Joy was enslaved for three years in the deprived Bijlmer district of Amsterdam, home to many West African immigrants. After she became pregnant and was told to abort her pregnancy, she courageously escaped her captors and found help from "a West African Pentecostal minister who operates mission houses in Amsterdam."[19]

7.5 CHILD AND FORCED MARRIAGES

Child and forced marriages, driven by religious marriage practices, often linked to "honor"-related violence, occur at low levels across Europe. Norway, for example, has opened five refuge centers (their locations undisclosed) for girls and women fleeing forced marriage or the threat

---

[18] Narrative of Joy Ubi-Ubi, in Kevin Bales and Zoe Trodd (eds.), *To Plead Our Own Cause: Personal Stories by Today's Slaves* (Ithaca: Cornell University Press, 2008), 170.
[19] Ibid., 169.

of "honor"-based assaults. A project leader at the Norwegian Institute for Social Research, Julia Orupabo, noted that "Many of the young people residing in these state-run facilities have shocking tales of violence to tell. Some are under the shadow of extreme threats. They have had to move away from their families, friends and networks and take on new identities."[20]

Slavery linked to religion occurs in the United States, as well – sometimes in the guise of marriage. While there are a number of international conventions,[21] bearing on child and forced marriage, they are difficult to enforce. The United States may be especially problematic in that, measured against international conventions, forty-four of the fifty American states allow child marriage, that is, marriage by a person under the age of 18. In some US states early marriage is allowed with parental consent or court approval. A 2021 study of child marriage in the United States presented this overall picture:

[S]ome 297,033 children were married in the U.S. between 2000 and 2018: 232,474 based on marriage-certificate data plus 64,559 based on estimates. A few children were as young as 10 years when they married, but of those for whom age information was available, nearly all – 96% – were aged 16 or 17 years. Of those for whom age, gender, and spousal information was available, 78% were girls (under 18 years of age) wed to adult men (aged 18 years or older). The national number of children wed decreased each year – from 76,396 in 2000 to 2,493 in 2018 – but is unlikely to get to zero without legislative intervention.[22]

Some child "marriages" occur in the context of schismatic, polygynist, break-away branches of the Church of Jesus Christ of Latter Day Saints (LDS or Mormons). These schismatic groups are often referred to as the

---

[20] Siw Ellen Jakobsen, "Out on a limb after forced marriage," *Sciencenorway.no*, Mar. 10, 2015: sciencenorway.no/forskningno-immigration-norway/out-on-a-limb-after-forced-marriage/1415065.

[21] United Nations (UN) Convention on the Rights of the Child, 1989; Universal Declaration of Human Rights, General Assembly Resolution 217 A (III), 1948; UN Supplementary Convention on the Abolition of Slavery, the Slave Trade, and Institutions and Practices Similar to Slavery (Slavery Convention), 1956; Convention on Consent to Marriage, Minimum Age for Marriage and Registration of Marriages, 1964; The UN Convention on the Elimination of All Forms of Discrimination against Women (CEDAW), 1979; International Covenant on Civil and Political Rights (ICCPR), 1966; African Charter on the Rights and Welfare of the Child, 1990.

[22] Fraidy Reiss, "Child marriage in the United States: prevalence and implications," *Journal of Adolescent Health*, 69:6, Supplement (2021), S8–S10: doi.org/10.1016/j.jadohealth.2021.07.001.

Fundamentalist Latter Day Saints (FLDS)[23]. One recent FLDS leader, Warren Jeffs, now imprisoned, had seventy-eight wives, many of whom were minors, some as young as twelve years old. They lived in a closed compound under strict control by male members of the sect. "Brides" would sometimes be taken from one man and given to another by Jeffs. This group was small in numbers, but had a significant and traumatic impact on many of the girls born into the sect. There are other small communities in the western United States that practice polygyny, nearly all of them rooted in FLDS practice. Given their isolation, it is difficult to document the extent of child "marriage" in such communities.

7.6 RELIGION AS A DRIVER OF ENSLAVEMENT TODAY

The cases and groups described above represent only some of the instances of slavery being justified through religious prejudice, dogma, or rationalization. Some religious groups are linked to slavery within armed conflict, such as ISIS, Boko Haram (Islamic), and the Lord's Resistance Army (Christian). Other types of slavery, such as the endemic and customary hereditary slavery practiced in Mauritania,[24] are supported by both dubious interpretations of the Qur'an and powerful traditions based in genetic or tribal difference.

How does one person decide to enslave another? How likely is it that slaveholders are bringing religious rationalizations or justifications to this decision? For most criminals, the key motivation is the profit (of whatever sort) that they will derive from the person they enslave. To this will be added the intention of controlling the person they enslave well enough and long enough to realize that return. Around the world this simple calculus of control and exploitation is played out daily – with the result that at a conservative estimate 45 million people are currently held in slavery.

That calculus, however, is often shaded with other views. The human trafficker in Romania, while working through a criminal plan for economic sexual exploitation of a young person, might bring the prejudice of race, class, or ethnicity into the equation. A young person from the ethnic Roma community, already facing social discrimination and treated as a

---

[23] The FLDS split from the Mormon Church in 1890, when Mormon leaders renounced polygamy. See fldsmormons.com.

[24] For a detailed description and analysis of the slavery system practiced in Mauritania see Bales, *Disposable People*, chap. 3.

second-class citizen, will likely be easier to acquire and control than a non-Roma, and less likely to generate an adequate response from state law enforcement. Religious confession might also be part of this calculation. Christians in Pakistan, Uyghurs in China, Muslims in India or Myanmar, Bahai's in Iran, Yazidis in Iraq, and other religious minorities worldwide are treated as second-class citizens and are therefore more vulnerable to discrimination and exploitation, and sometimes enslavement. Their potential enslavers likely care nothing about their religious faith or affiliation except that their faith and affiliation marks them as people less likely to be protected by law enforcement and more likely to be isolated within the larger community. For slaveholders, religious affiliation can be simply one factor that adds to the vulnerability of potential victims and diminishes their ability to resist coercion, capture, and control.

The next step along this continuum occurs when slaveholders rationalize their enslavement of others through religious beliefs or practice. This might occur at the level of atomized criminal activity all the way up to the level of government policy and practice, and this justification for exploitation based on religious membership can be mixed with other markers – ethnicity, nationality, or sexuality. Consider the Holocaust as an example. The focus within this particular genocide has been on the 6 million Jews, and several million other people, who were killed outright. Those less considered are the estimated 13.5 million persons enslaved by the Nazis, a significant proportion of whom died in concentration camps, through the specific Nazi policy of "extermination through labor." This state-sponsored slavery, in much the same way it was used on a smaller scale by ISIS in Sinjar, or is currently used in China to control and suppress the Uyghur population in Xinjiang, was both of tactical and strategic value to the Nazi war effort.

Today, the practice of enslavement in conflict rationalized by religious difference is repeated across a number of small wars. For example, Muslim Rohingya are pressed into forced labor and often later executed by the armed forces of Myanmar. The official State Religion of Myanmar is Theravada Buddhism. Other examples are the capture, enslavement, and "marriage" of Christian girls and young women in Nigeria by the Islamist group Boko Haram; and the recent use of terror and enslavement, including forced "marriages" by the Christian Lord's Resistance Army in Uganda, South Sudan, the Central African Republic, and the Democratic Republic of the Congo.

The three-year war precipitated by the breakup of Yugoslavia in 1995 was fought mainly along religious lines – Catholic Croats, Muslim

Bosnians, and Orthodox Christian Serbs. The 1995 Srebrenica Massacre involved the killing of 7,000–8,000 Muslim boys and men by Orthodox Christian Serbian troops over a period of eleven days. It is regarded as the worst atrocity in Europe since World War II. Parallel to such massacres, enslavement grew rapidly within the war zone and the countries around it. This especially involved the capture and human trafficking of women and girls within the former Yugoslavia, and outward to other countries, according to their religious affiliation. Within Bosnia, Orthodox Christian Serb forces captured and held Muslim women and girls in separate camps or buildings for sexual exploitation for long periods. In 2019, this led to 321 defendants being charged with 203 war crimes, specifically rape and sexual enslavement.

Though it is little studied, there seems to be a tendency to commit human rights violations linked to religious profession, and in many cases the victims of these violations are members of other, targeted, religious groups. While there are strong antislavery and antitrafficking organizations and movements rooted in religion, we have much less understanding of religion as a *driver* of enslavement – the contemporary situation alone would require a full volume, and it is our hope that others will join in such research.

If there is an irreducible truth in the explication of slavery and religious belief and practice, it is that those who enslave others assign to themselves God-like powers – of subsistence, of life and death, of procreation or its termination, of the crushing of spirit and consciousness, even to the severing and sale of body parts. The full destructive repertoire of enslavement is ever elaborated as cultures change and grow. The antidote is fragmented and weak, yet at the core of the forces of liberation are those giving their all to bring freedom, through the inspiration and intention to serve the divine – as we explore in the next chapter.

8

Religion's Role in Freeing Slaves Today

How is religion helping in the fight against contemporary slavery? And how might it help more? All of the four largest religions, Christianity, Islam, Hinduism, and Buddhism, which together have something in the order of 6 billion adherents in the global population of 8.2 billion, have members who are soundly antislavery, many adherents that have little understanding of the issue, and a very small minority of groups and believers that accept and exploit enslavement, as we have seen in the previous chapters.

The authors of this book come from what might be thought of as opposite ends of Christianity – one a Roman Catholic, the other a Quaker. Yet both of their religious traditions have fostered significant antislavery acts and movements in the past, even as they struggled to achieve unity against slavery. That said, as both of their wider faith groups continue to work against slavery, they rarely do so in concert. The same can be said for other large faith traditions, even as we recognize the vast potential that exists if religious, secular, and political alliances work together to confront the complex and pervasive slavery of today. Virtually all agree on the self-evident truth that slavery is a fundamental violation of human life and liberty – yet there is little agreement, both within and between religious bodies, as to how slavery should be identified, confronted, and brought to an end.

Unfortunately, the current national and global antislavery movement (s), as well as national governments, have not reached agreement or resolution on goals, direction, or social and legal intentions. The current movement is both enlightened and challenged by a deeper understanding of how slavery influences wider issues, often in ways that are critical and crucial to addressing our most pressing global challenges. Yet the wider religiously based movement is disorganized, still grappling with how to address contemporary slavery as it intersects and influences those same pressing global issues.

For example, we now know that there is a strong and extremely destructive intersection between slavery, climate change, and environmental destruction.[1] There is also a deep and dangerous interaction between slavery and the many armed conflicts raging around the world.[2] There is something of a paradox in the fact that the exploitation of the approximately 50 million slaves on Earth leads to such an outsized, negative, and destructive impact on the lives of the 8.2 billion people on the planet – especially given the fact that the enslaved represent only one-half of 1 percent of the global population. Earlier in this book we explored the links between slavery and forced early and child marriage – and the fact that some religious groups practice early and child marriage. Meanwhile, the products of slavery, from food to clothing to electronics, flow through global supply chains and into our homes.[3]

For people in the well-off countries of the world, slavery tends to be seen as something that happens somewhere else. That "somewhere else" may be a household, a farm, a factory, a mine, a forest, or a battlefield. The deeply hidden nature of slave-based production of commodities means that it is unlikely that a person in a well-off country would ever be able to discern or identify the slavery in their food, clothing, electronics, vehicles, household goods, or any of the thousands of products and consumables that feed, cloth, house, transport, and intoxicate those of us who live in the richer countries. The constant flow of slave-made goods and products into our lives is difficult to avoid because criminals whitewash slave-tainted goods to conceal their origins. Meanwhile, many large and well-known Western businesses and corporations put little effort into closely tracing the goods that they ultimately sell – and slave-produced products and commodities slip into our homes.

Part of this puzzle was made even more inscrutable by the great economic "globalization" of the late twentieth century. When factories and farms in the countries of the Rich North were shuttered and their

---

[1] Kevin Bales, *Blood and Earth: Modern Slavery, Ecocide, and the Secret to Saving the World* (New York: Spiegel & Grau, 2016).

[2] Smith, Datta, and Bales, "Contemporary slavery in armed conflict."

[3] Monti Narayan Datta and Kevin Bales, "Slavery is bad for business: analyzing the impact of slavery on national economies," *The Brown Journal of World Affairs*, 19:2 (2013), 205–223.

production lines shifted to the developing world, the supply chains leading to our homes became complex, extended, tangled, and opaque. Clearly there can be no religious disagreement over the fact that global supply chains bring slavery into our homes. Clearly there is potential for collective and effective action to unite faith traditions to trace and expunge slavery in our shared supply chains. In fact, many religious groups in well-off countries work hard to illuminate slavery and exploitation in their supply chains with some success. The long and deep relationship between the Church of England and the FairTrade Foundation[4] that traces and supports clean supply chains is a superb example of effective collaboration. But it is also true that criminals are remarkably adaptive (they must be to be successful), and the exposure of one rotten supply chain simply and quickly reroutes tainted goods to another. Many countries have now passed supply-chain "transparency" laws, but these are in their infancy and difficult to apply and enforce. Supply chains touch us all, but they are also one of the most challenging areas of antislavery action. In other areas, particularly in social organizing and direct liberation work, the success rates of antislavery groups, including religious groups, are increasing.

8.1 EXAMPLES OF SUCCESSFUL ANTISLAVERY WORK

The wider antislavery movement has learned a great deal about the nature of liberation and the reintegration of ex-slaves into lives of freedom. For example, in northern India, in the state of Uttar Pradesh (population 241 million), it has long been the case that most of the inhabitants of many rural villages are held in hereditary collateral debt bondage – a type of slavery not far removed from the legal slavery of the American South before the US Civil War. The "collateral" held by landowners is the bodies and persons of the families they control, families that are treated like livestock and who are "owned" in perpetuity. The process of enslavement is powerful and long-lasting. Some time in a previous generation, the families were "recruited" to work in agriculture, quarrying, or brickmaking by the hereditary landowner – normally a higher caste Hindu. These poor migrant families tend to have originated from one of four possible religious subgroups: Muslims, Dalits, subcaste Indigenous "Tribals," or, more rarely, Christians.

---

[4] FairTrade Foundation: www.fairtrade.org.uk.

On the arrival of the "recruited" families, small sums of money, along with rudimentary food and shelter, were advanced to the migrants. Yet again and again, the families find that however hard they work, they end the year in significant, though fallacious, debt. Being illiterate and under physical threat, they are easily tricked by these false debts and then brutally subjugated by the landowners. Within a generation or two there is little or no memory of freedom among the worker families. Regular physical and sexual assault on the enslaved families by the landowner and his family, coupled with starvation rations and no health care, means lives lived in significant trauma, hopelessness, and exploitation. Current estimates of the number of people trapped in debt bondage slavery in India ranges from 8 to 18 million. International Justice Mission puts the number in debt bondage at 15.5 million.[5]

From the 1980s, antislavery activists in India, along with other human rights workers, began to seek the liberation of these villages. The first attempts were difficult and dangerous, to the point that some lives were lost to violence. Over time a systematic approach emerged that focused on inserting a school for children into a debt-bonded village, purportedly there by order of the government. In fact, the trained teachers that set up and opened the school were themselves ex-slaves from similar villages, who having escaped then gained education and training. A free lunch program for the children and most of the mothers (who help prepare the food), normally assured the acquiescence, or at least the tolerance, of the slaveholders, who tend to be pleased that someone was providing food and feeding their slave workers at no cost to themselves.

For the teachers and the mothers, the time spent cooking together every day opens the door to conversations about life, both within the village, but also about the wider world – allowing the enslaved families their first glimpses of lives in freedom. In time, the teachers reveal that they, too, had grown up in a village in bondage, and from that moment the mothers of the village are very keen to know: How did they come to freedom? The full answer has many parts, but all arrive at the same result, a moment in which the villagers, altogether, stand up to the enslavers and declare that they are taking their freedom. This conversation between the mothers and the teachers takes about two years to bring to fruition; it takes at least that long to overcome the deep fear and trauma suffered by the villagers.

---

[5] See International Justice Mission, "What is bonded labor?": www.ijm.org/news/what-is-bonded-labor.

The "teachers" and their colleagues in the supporting antislavery organization ensure that on the day of the declaration of freedom, the village will be visited by honest officials, supportive police, and many people, especially women, from other villages who have previously declared their own freedom. Occasionally, the slaveholders threaten reprisals, but local officials and police make clear the risks of that. With freedom of movement assured, the NGO workers escort the newly freed families to government offices where they can register as freed bonded laborers. This registration allows them to take advantage of programs that provide tools, money grants for subsistence, for learning a trade or business, or to buy livestock. The freed slaves' new government identity cards give them access to education and health care, and allow them to register to vote. The support grants are especially important as they open the door to new ways to make a living, away from the fields or brick kilns, mines or quarries, and away from the slaveholders.[6]

Today, there are "teachers" launching schools and organizing in villages of bonded workers, yet there is a rough estimate of hundreds of such villages still needing to be helped toward self-liberation. What is remarkable is the low financial cost of this intervention. The overall cost of the two-to-three-year process of bringing a village to freedom is around £25,000/$30,000. These villages normally have around 150 inhabitants in bondage – putting the "cost of liberation" over the two-to-three-year liberation process at about £165/$200 per person coming to freedom.[7] Once liberated, there is significant further investment through government assistance and business grants, which tend to multiply and solidify the achieved liberation. Organized and educated, with health care and jobs, the villages flourish.

Globally, the cost of liberation from slavery varies widely: In the poorest countries the cost can be very low, in the richest countries relatively high. But if the world's 50 million slaves could be liberated at the cost of the village liberation method described above the total cost to assist all the world's slaves to freedom would be around £8.25 billion/$10

---

[6] The Indian Bonded Labour System (Abolition) Act (1976) and its subsequent updates describe the crimes inherent in bonded labour slavery and set out rehabilitative provisions that support education, training, the provision of land or tools, and support for children and the elderly. For a general description see National Human Rights Commission, India, *The Bonded Labour System (Abolition) Act, 1976 And the Prohibition of Employment as Manual Scavengers and Their Rehabilitation Act, 2013* (New Delhi: National Human Rights Commission, 2021): nhrc.nic.in/sites/default/files/Bonded%20Labour.pdf.

[7] See www.voices4freedom.org/ for examples of this liberation process.

billion – which, while it does sound like a vast sum of money, in global terms is very small. For example, the UK book publishing industry's revenue in 2023 was £7 billion/$8.8 billion. Meanwhile, Google had revenue of $305 billion in 2023 – about the same amount that Great Britain spent on COVID-19 measures in 2020/2021.

These sums indicate that global slavery could be dramatically reduced if there were sufficient resources and training for antislavery workers in the same way that public health workers are trained and deployed to face health threats. A significant gap in our understanding is exactly how best to address and stop enslavement in its different forms. Again, drawing a parallel with the science and practice of public health is appropriate. The enormous growth of public health knowledge and practice in the late nineteenth and early twentieth centuries transformed human life – no longer were vast sections of the world's population regularly ravaged by disease. If we are serious about the impact of slavery on our world and our lives, we need to think in the same large-scale terms. That means evolving from a focus on rescuing individuals to planned and systemic large-scale interventions. And while that may sound costly, there is a significant "freedom dividend," both economic and social, manifest in every liberation that tends to exceed the original investment.[8]

8.2 THE EMERGENCE OF "MODERN SLAVERY"

As noted in Chapter 6, the sudden appearance of large numbers of exploited persons in the West led to an immediate, if confused, reaction to what was termed human trafficking or sex trafficking. From the beginning of the 1990s, as reports of enslavement spread, there was a slow, then rapid, recognition of the crime. Most of the public in Europe and North America had assumed slavery was a thing of the past, but as more articles, reports, books, and films illuminating "modern" slavery emerged, many religious groups began to respond. For the rich countries of North America and Western Europe the focus among many religious groups was especially on sex trafficking. Many of the emerging antitrafficking actors were local and religious groups that proliferated globally, such as International Justice Mission, the Coalition Against Slavery and Trafficking (CAST), and Love146. By 2002, when a UK-based antitrafficking group attempted to locate and catalogue these voluntary sector/

---

[8] See Kevin Bales, *Ending Slavery: How We Free Today's Slaves* (Berkeley: University of California Press, 2007).

charitable groups globally, they listed some 900 active antislavery/trafficking organizations spread worldwide.[9]

A tipping point, at least in the rich countries of North America and Europe, came with the new millennium. In 1999 the book *Disposable People*[10] was published, exposing and analyzing forms of slavery, and their economic basis, in Pakistan, India, Mauritania, Brazil, and Thailand. Soon after, the book was adapted into a documentary film for Channel 4 in the UK and HBO in the United States. The documentary film, *Slavery: A Global Investigation*,[11] was shown internationally, even as the book was being published in eight other languages. The film uncovered enslaved workers, many of them children, in cocoa farming in West Africa, children enslaved to weave carpets in India, as well as instances of domestic slavery in Britain and the United States. Subtitled in several languages and shown around the world, the result was both new laws and major interventions on the ground. For example, chocolate companies and antislavery groups formed the International Cocoa Initiative[12] to address the problem of slavery in chocolate. Together the book and film demonstrated the reality of modern slavery and publicized and legitimized the issue. National governments began to consider new antitrafficking and antislavery laws.

With greater public awareness, NGOs proliferated and the debates over which were the "worst" forms of slavery faded. In 2000 a branch of the original 1786 British antislavery group (now called Anti-Slavery International) opened its doors as Free the Slaves in Washington, DC. In the same year, the United States Congress passed into law the Trafficking Victims Protection Act, and set up a Trafficking in Persons (TiP) Office, headed by an ambassador, within the US State Department. The TiP Office was charged with investigating and reporting yearly on the state of trafficking and slavery in all countries.

Religious groups were keen and early supporters of antitrafficking and antislavery initiatives. Today, there are some twenty faith-based

---

[9] Luckoo and Tzvetkova, *Combating Trafficking in Persons: A Directory of Organizations.*

[10] The first edition was Kevin Bales, *Disposable People: New Slavery in the Global Economy* (Berkeley: University of California Press, 1999). A revised edition was published in 2004.

[11] True Vision, Producer/Directors Kate Blewitt and Brian Woods, released 2000. The film won the Peabody Award and two Emmy Awards. The documentary may be found at www.youtube.com/watch?v=WfdibtC4RYg&t=9s or at www.truevisiontv.com/films/slavery-a-global-investigation.

[12] International Cocoa Initiative: www.cocoainitiative.org/.

antislavery groups in Great Britain, and likely a larger number in the United States, though it is difficult to find precise numbers for North America. In the early 2000s, in Britain and the United States, there was also a parallel upsurge of interest in the history of William Wilberforce who had been a key religious commentator and political supporter in the Second Antislavery Movement.

8.3 THE EMERGENCE OF SURVIVOR LEADERSHIP

If there is a subplot constantly repeated since the beginning of the fifth movement in 1989, it is the struggle between slavery survivors demanding their autonomy and the practices of some antitrafficking groups insisting on infantilizing and exploiting them. In particular, this has been the case with a number of groups linked to Christian, especially fundamentalist, denominations, whose antislavery activity often begins with a focus on salvation – both in the metaphysical religious sense and in the practical sense that enslaved people must be saved from exploitation, especially sexual exploitation. From the early 1990s survivors of slavery were "saved" and/or "adopted" by several emerging antislavery groups, all of which had a religious foundation. Sudanese children, African children, girls, and women enslaved in commercial exploitation in several countries including the United States, were all used in ways that infantilized them and made for heart-wrenching, if exploitative, emotional appeals for support and funding.

By the early 2000s, slavery survivors, and a number of antislavery groups, repudiated this exploitation and opened the door to survivor voices, presence, and participation. For example, one book of authentic survivor narratives[13] was published in order to answer and challenge published narratives that had been doctored, often by groups with religious ties, in order to increase emotional appeal. That practice of infantilizing and exploiting still goes on but is much more likely to be answered and refuted by survivor scholars and leaders. This is especially the case with the Survivor Alliance[14] – a key organization, launched in 2018, now with nearly 1,000 survivor members in thirty-nine countries. The very fact that hundreds of survivors of enslavement are operating at a global level to train, support, and assist other survivors is historic. The handful of survivor leaders in past movements (Frederick Douglass, Harriet

---

[13] Bales and Trodd (eds.), *To Plead Our Own Cause.*
[14] Survivor Alliance: www.survivoralliance.org/.

Tubman, Olaudah Equiano, and Sojourner Truth, to name just a few) often lived and worked with constant challenges and little support. The advent of the Survivor Alliance – global, operating to the highest levels of support and sensitivity, and constantly renewing its training and content to better serve those who come to freedom – is historic though rarely noted.

8.4 THE CHALLENGE OF MEASUREMENT

A key challenge faced by all antitrafficking/antislavery groups (as well as law enforcement and governments) is the hidden nature of slavery crime and the difficulty of measuring or estimating the size of the problem. In the past, in several countries, politicians were unwilling to make significant changes to law, or to provide needed funding, to address a problem that could not be measured and verified. Anecdotes were plentiful, reliable measurement was difficult and rare. The first social scientific estimate in the late 1990s,[15] ringed with caveats,[16] suggested a conservative global total of 27 million in slavery. In 2013, the Walk Free Foundation, working with the Wilberforce Institute in Hull, UK, published its first Global Slavery Index report with an estimate of 29.8 million in slavery worldwide. In subsequent years the estimate has grown to 50 million people in slavery in 2024. Slavery, however, is normally a hidden crime and for that reason has proved difficult to measure.[17]

If the precise numbers in slavery are hard to obtain, the impact of enslavement on societies and communities is much clearer – particularly in the ways that slavery and trafficking are entangled with other pressing problems such as conflict and genocide, with environmental destruction and climate change, and within various discriminatory religious practices. For example, we now know that slavery, in different forms, occurred in 87 percent of 171 conflicts around the world between 1989 and 2016 (amounting to 1,113 "conflict years").[18]

---

[15] Bales, *Disposable People*, 1st ed. (1999).

[16] Kevin Bales, "International labor standards: quality of information and measures of progress in combating forced labor," *Comparative Labor Law and Policy Journal*, 24:2 (Winter 2003), 321–364.

[17] Kevin Bales and Monti Datta, "Slavery in Europe: Part 1, estimating the dark figure," *Human Rights Quarterly*, 35:3 (2013), 817–829; see also Kevin Bales, "Unlocking the statistics of slavery," *Chance* (Journal of the American Statistical Association), 30:3 (2017), 5–12.

[18] Smith, Datta, and Bales, "Contemporary slavery in armed conflict."

In many of these conflicts, enslavement was a precursor to genocide, as in the well-documented case of the ISIS assault on the Yazidi communities and culture in northern Iraq from 2014 to 2017.[19] Slavery has also been shown to be used in types of work and production that are extremely damaging to the environment, illustrated by the estimate that if slavery were treated as a country, it would be the third largest emitter of CO_2 in the world after China and the United States.[20] This intersectionality with slavery clearly occurs with religious groups as well – as explored in this volume. Especially troubling, in 2024 half of the countries in the world were found to not have a law against slavery; and 58 percent of countries had no law against forced labor.[21] In spite of the promulgation of the Bellagio-Harvard Guidelines described above, it is clear that the world is far from achieving a coherent legal or policy response to slavery.

8.5 CHALLENGES, AND OPPORTUNITIES, OF THE TWENTY-FIRST CENTURY

As the twenty-first century unfolds we can state several key facts about slavery in our world. The first is that slavery is pervasive, present in all countries and regions. Second, it appears to be growing in parallel with the increase in the global population. A third theme is that while slaves are a very small part of the global population (an estimated six out of every 1,000 people on the planet), their situation results in a significant, negative, and outsized impact on climate and the environment through their use by criminals in destructive crimes such as pervasive and illegal deforestation and mining.

A key fourth theme is that religious groups are central to addressing slavery and human trafficking in the twenty-first century, often exerting influence beyond that of national governments. Some of these, like the Roman Catholic group Talitha Cum, work worldwide and mobilize thousands of Religious Sisters in freeing and supporting the enslaved. Others, though fewer and on the fringes, practice and exploit enslavement, as we discussed in Chapter 7.

---

[19] See Chapter 7, and Al-Dayel, Mumford, and Bales, "Not yet dead."

[20] Kevin Bales and Benjamin Sovacool, "From forests to factories: how modern slavery deepens the crisis of climate change," *Energy Research & Social Science* 77 (2021), 1–9: doi.org/10.1016/j.erss.2021.102096.

[21] See Antislavery in Domestic Legislation Database, Rights Lab, University of Nottingham.

While the global situation is mixed and lacking wider consensus and action, religious groups continue to make headway in addressing contemporary slavery. Religious groups were keen and early supporters of anti-trafficking and antislavery initiatives. The American group International Justice Mission (IJM), using a law-based approach to addressing human trafficking globally, was founded in 1997. Set up by Christian lawyers, IJM focused on the key area of legal research and action, using the law to liberate those caught up in slavery and, crucially, to charge and convict slaveholders. With significant support from a wide range of primarily Protestant churches, IJM opened offices in India, the Philippines, Thailand, and Kenya – supporting legal action against enslavement within national legal systems. In Cambodia, IJM worked closely with the government to enact new laws that addressed the enslavement into commercial sexual exploitation of young women and girls. By 2005, IJM had also opened offices in Latin America.

The online sexual exploitation of children became a key area of work for IJM in 2016, and led to both exposing and raising this issue globally (being online the exploiters could be anywhere, with many logging in from Europe and North America). This led to the legal convictions of perpetrators and abusers in the Philippines. In 2021, IJM led a successful campaign to end legal grounds for child marriage in the Dominican Republic. There are now thirty-nine IJM offices in twenty-six countries, and some 1,200 people on staff. IJM has a strong religious basis – as noted on their website: "Each staff member, spread across 26 countries in 39 offices, communes with God and prays at least one hour each workday."[22]

A much smaller but still impactful nonprofit, Love146, was founded in 2002 by Rob Morris, an evangelical Protestant who had previously worked in youth ministry and an international medical charity. While living in an intentional Christian community in New Haven, Connecticut, Morris and several coreligionists learned about the phenomenon of child sex trafficking and eventually founded Love 146, which combats child trafficking and exploitation, focusing on survivor care and prevention.[23]

Unseen, a UK charity founded by Protestant pastor Andrew Wallis, also provides support for survivors of slavery. In a chance encounter while on a trip to Ukraine in 2008, Wallis and colleagues from his church

---

[22] International Justice Mission: www.ijm.org/.
[23] Cf. the organization's website at love146.org, and a podcast with Rob Morris at: vineyardusa.org/podcast/love-146-telling-the-whole-story-with-rob-morris/.

intervened to prevent a Ukrainian girl from being tricked by traffickers. Wallis' subsequent collaboration with cofounder Kate Garbers and local UK police led to Unseen's founding. Their organization's investigative work was a key catalyst for the development and passing of the UK's 2015 Modern Slavery Act.[24]

Another UK charity, the Medaille Trust, was founded by the Catholic Religious Sr. Ann Teresa, who had spent many years working with women caught up in commercial sexual exploitation in Southampton, England:

She helped many of them find work at nearby Bed and Breakfasts and even invited them to share meals at the convent. Reflecting on that period, Sr Ann Teresa said: "The convent became a second home for some. We celebrated Christmas and birthdays with them, took them to the theatre; anything that gave them a bit of happiness." In 2005, after listening to a talk on human trafficking that she gave at a church, a couple offered Sr. Ann Teresa a house to be used as a safe house for victims of human trafficking.[25]

Thanks to funds from generous donors and several Catholic Religious Congregations, the Medaille Trust was formed in 2006, and now operates ten safe houses for survivors of slavery. Sr. Ann Teresa is just one of hundreds of Catholic sisters engaged in antislavery work.

8.6 THE UNIQUE ROLE OF CATHOLIC RELIGIOUS SISTERS

While religious antislavery and antitrafficking groups exist in most countries, little is generally known about one of the very largest groups. Talitha Kum[26] is a global organization and alliance of Roman Catholic Religious Sisters with sixteen offices/projects in Africa, eighteen in the Americas, twenty-two in Asia, eight in Europe, and two in Australia/New Zealand. Groups of Religious Sisters are organized in a global network that combines 5,871 active members and collaborators, including 777 congregations of Women Religious. A congregation of Women Religious is a group of women belonging to a specific organized theological group who profess the simple vows of poverty, chastity, and obedience, living a common life and engaging in ministering to the needs

---

[24] See Unseen: www.unseenuk.org/about-us/unseen-history/ and Ingrid Barratt, "I am not your slave," *War Cry Magazine*, Sep. 23, 2017, 6–9: www.salvationarmy.org.nz/our-community/faith-in-life/soul-food/im-not-your-slave.

[25] Medaille Trust, "Our History": www.medaille-trust.org.uk/about-us/our-history.

[26] Talitha Kum: www.talithakum.info/en.

of the wider society. Religious Sisters are not paid salaries, and they normally live all together, sharing meals and household chores.

There is one way in which Talitha Kum is almost unique among antislavery organizations – their fearlessness when conflicts emerge. While the wider antislavery movement has been slow to realize the steep increase in slavery and exploitation in conflict zones (such as the occupation of Yazidi areas by ISIS described above), Talitha Kum has been quick to move toward, rather than away from, armed conflicts. In 2022 they moved Sisters from India into Myanmar as the civil war there worsened, and over the same period extended work into conflict zones in Sri Lanka, Burkina Faso, Mali, the Democratic Republic of the Congo (DRC), Syria, Venezuela, and more recently Ukraine. Conflict increases vulnerability to slavery and trafficking; Talitha Kum responds with care for victims and displaced people affected by conflict.

In 2024 Talitha Kum reported sixty intercongregational networks in 107 countries having served 753,392 people in the previous year, some of whom were victims of trafficking or enslavement. To the best of our knowledge, given the lack of centralized information about antislavery groups, we believe Talitha Kum to be the largest nongovernmental organization in the world working against slavery and trafficking. While Talitha Kum has a digital presence, its breadth and depth of on-the-ground projects and interventions is not widely understood. This is not surprising, because Religious Sisters do not operate like nongovernmental organizations, which have paid employees working set hours in specific occupational roles, or special teams that do research, fundraising, and publicity. Indeed, Religious Sisters operate within a culture and structure very far removed from that of nongovernmental and charity organizations, and even further removed from the world of government or business. "[R]ecruitment procedures" for Sisters, as noted in a recent study of Religious Sisters:

do not include any type of formal skills assessment or required training, except for one key expectation – that a Religious Sister will "have a vocation." For Women Religious *vocation* means "to be called by God to service," and no other characteristic or skill is sufficient to enable a person who does not have a vocation to be a Woman Religious. A key organising concept is that whatever skill sets, training, or personal characteristics a woman might have, she can only be truly mobilised through her vocation, being personally called by God to service.[27]

---

[27] Bidisha Saikia and Kevin Bales, "Monitoring and measuring the ineffable: religious Sisters and the Adavasi peoples in Assam," *International Journal of Asian Christianity*, 6:1 (2023), 122–143, 132.

This orientation to work, and the way that human rights and antislavery work is carried out by Women Religious, is very different from that of governmental or nongovernmental organizations, and it is little publicized or understood. Women Religious bring something unique to their antislavery work:

Women Religious are not hired according to a set job description. Their vocation is more a surrender of self, the extinguishing of their ego in service to others. While conventional workers exchange their hours and energy for remuneration and, hopefully, fulfilment, Women Religious begin their "employment" by actively giving away their lives, offering it to be used in whatever way decided by their Congregation. This is a profound and alternative economic, social, psychological, and fundamentally political, philosophical orientation to human existence. For the Sister, it is both a diminution of self and an aggrandizement of the soul as part of a larger, eternal, effort.

The unique "skill-set" of Women Religious flows from renouncing self and the acceptance of a life of service to others. It is altruism writ large, requiring the sacrifice of a "worldly existence." It is expected that there should be no self-serving component to work, though this is paradoxical in that self-sacrifice is also seen as a positive attribute. A vocation also leads to, in most instances, a lifetime of subsistence support. Food, clothing, and shelter are provided to Women Religious, though with an expectation that subsistence may be minimal, and that they will be expected to work in preparation – cooking, sewing, cleaning, building, gardening, any work that may be necessary to support the material life of the Sisters in a House or the larger Congregation.[28]

In the ethnographic study quoted above, Sisters were asked about what they felt were the key skills and orientation to their work. Again, the responses were markedly different to that of workers within nongovernmental organizations. In addition to having a *vocation*, Sisters named their key skills, some of which are orientational and others functional, as: first, "*being pure at heart*" – something like an active altruism that rejects any self-serving actions; second, an "*adherence to a shared moral structure*" – meaning the foundational beliefs, rules, and practices of their Congregation and the wider Church; third, a "*focus on justice and mercy*" – the *functional* use of this skill is to act in ways that support justice, expressed with mercy. The range of actions to be taken within that aim are potentially infinite, hence the skill needed in their interpretation and functional mobilization. Fourth, "*empathy*" – "the dynamic act of compassion and sympathy, and equally important is the functional and active *responsiveness* to individuals and groups that empathy has

---

[28] Ibid., 132.

identified as needing support and care"; and, fifth, all work and service is to be carried out with *"grace or gentleness"* – a gentleness of spirit and action, reflecting an inner peace, a reverence, and a pervasive hospitality.

If there is a specific skill set that transcends and includes these orientations it is the methodology of response and action termed *"accompaniment"* within the work of the Sisters. The ethnographic study explains:

It [accompaniment] means, literally, moving into the immediate physical space, work, and lives of that constituency [of need] – sharing virtually all daily acts of domestic and economic life. It is an entry into the lives of others that is whole and persistent. Children, the elderly, and the unwell are cared for, food is cooked and shared, when night brings an end to the struggle for subsistence, the Sisters sleep nearby and wake early to begin again their accompaniment. If young people are working in factories or fields, Sisters accompany them there, to understand the benefits and dangers of their work, helping those they accompany to see alternatives, or reminding employers of their responsibilities for worker safety. As they get to know those they accompany, Sisters may help them toward a training program, medical care, basic education, or the forming of a village credit union.[29]

What is crucial here is that these tools of intervention and support are broad-based and generally applicable in all situations of need – from public health challenges, to extreme poverty, to extreme forms of discrimination and to those who are caught in trafficking and enslavement.

In a second study of the same group of Religious Sisters they were asked to complete an attitudinal scale that explored orientations to voluntarism and altruism. Their responses were then compared to a national (UK) sample of active charity supporters. The British charity supporters reported clearly defined attitudes toward their charitable acts: "The charity supporters/volunteers held attitudes that were described by four factors: *a sense of effectiveness; a sense of sociability or generalism; an idealism or philosophical commitment;* and a *'feel good' factor.*"[30] The results of the analysis of the responses of the Religious Sisters to the attitudinal scale presented a significantly different picture and orientation.

Where the sample of charity supporters expressed a strong "sense of effectiveness," the Religious Sisters strongly expressed *humility*. Where charity supporters were proud of their charity work, the Sisters humbly shifted the appreciation and centre of gravity for their work to the *larger Congregation* and *divine guidance*. Where charity supporters acted as

---

[29] Ibid., 134.

[30] Bidisha Saikia, Monti Datta, Luke De Pulford and Kevin Bales, "Exploring the worldview of Religious Sisters: A comparative empirical analysis of altruistic/voluntaristic attitudes," *Intercultural Human Rights Law Review*, 17 (2022), 227–250, 243.

independent (if collaborative) agents, the Sisters expressed strong *deference* to their leaders and ultimately God's guidance. While charity supporters expressed great sympathy, normally at a distance, for those in need, the Religious Sisters expressed deep *empathy* with those with whom they are working directly. Where charity supporters named and acted upon their good intentions, the Sisters expressed a *realism blended with humility* in the face of human suffering. Finally, while charity supporters exercised free choice in the people or causes they chose to help, the Religious Sisters focused on, and were led by, the *discipline* and leadership of their vocation and the larger Congregation.

While those differences existed, there were also areas of strong agreement between the two groups. The article explains that there is:

[A]n area of positive philosophical alignment, a deep expression of what are felt to be fundamental truths. Both groups strongly agree with the assertion that "There will be peace only when there is justice." Both groups strongly agree with the statements that: "The more you put into life the more you will get out of it," "Some issues are much more important than my personal life," and "It's not enough to just *talk* about what's wrong – you've got to *do* something." Both groups are carried along by a strong belief in the ultimate good they seek to support and expand.[31]

In terms of direct action by Religious Sisters against human trafficking and slavery, the breadth of their work is global, but also sometimes difficult to pinpoint. For the Sisters based in the Indian state of Assam and studied in the research described above, one of their most significant interventions is their constant monitoring of the flow of young people within the Indian rail system, and the direct accompaniment with agricultural workers on tea plantations and other rural jobs who are caught in debt bondage, often hereditary bondage. The flow of poor young people (often lower caste and suffering from discrimination) seeking work through migration creates a significant flow of impressionable young people who are easily lured, tricked, and enslaved. The Sisters' key aim is to intercede with refugee young people before traffickers can lure them into a situation in which they will be assaulted and brutalized and, potentially, forced into enslavement in commercial sexual exploitation. It is the practice of *accompaniment*, described above, that separates these Sisters' working practices from those of most nongovernmental organizations. When the Sisters have found a vulnerable person who needs

---

[31] Ibid., 246.

protection and support, they build a bond through physically staying with and near them until they are out of danger and their situation is no longer precarious. For much of the charity, human rights, and governmental world there is little clear understanding of the methods and outcomes achieved by Religious Sisters. Clearly, more sharing and dialogue is in order.

8.7 MORE CONTEMPORARY ANTISLAVERY GROUPS AND LEADERS WITH RELIGIOUS LINKS

One aspect of the contemporary global antislavery movement is the remarkable mosaic of the organizations that work to end slavery. There are so many nonprofit and faith-based organizations, some just beginning, others evolving into new groups, still others fading and disappearing, that obtaining an accurate count would be a monumental task. The fluid worldwide total is certainly in the high hundreds, if not the low thousands. Nearly all groups have clear and specific goals, areas of focus, and programs of communication and liberation – but, of course, there are always a few NGOs and groups closing down, and a few others being set up every year. The Global Modern Slavery Directory[32] provides an interactive map and database of antislavery groups worldwide with significant detail of their aims, constituencies, populations served, types of trafficking and slavery they work on, and much more. The Global Modern Slavery Directory was set up and is run by the Polaris Project, based in Washington, DC, with the collaboration of many other anti-trafficking/antislavery groups.

While not specifically a religious organization, the United States-based group Free the Slaves maintains a broad program supporting religious responses to slavery and human trafficking. Free the Slaves was set up in 2000 as the American wing of Anti-Slavery International in the UK (the world's oldest and original antislavery group, dating from the eighteenth century). Uniquely, Free the Slaves has organized a broad coalition of religious groups in its "Faith in Action Ending Slavery" program. Judaism, Christianity, Islam, Hinduism, Buddhism, and the Baha'i Faith are represented and contribute faith-based responses to the issues of modern slavery. One extensive program is the Passover Project,[33] which provides discussion and reflection materials that focus on the Passover

---

[32] Global Modern Slavery Directory: globalmodernslavery.org/directory.
[33] Free the slaves: freetheslaves.net/take-action/faith-in-action-ending-slavery/.

Seder (an annual shared meal and time of reflection) based on the Bible verse that orders Jews to retell the story of the "Exodus" from Egypt: "You shall tell your child on that day, saying, 'It is because of what the Lord did for me when I came out of Egypt.'" (Exod 13:8); and further that: "Remember that you were a slave in Egypt and that the Lord your God redeemed you from there. Therefore, I command you to do [justice]." (Deut 24:18). The Project aims to mobilize Jewish communities to take strong advocacy positions against modern slavery, and to inspire synagogues, Jewish schools and other Jewish institutions to be careful consumers and investors to be sure the products they buy, or the companies in which they invest, are not tainted by slavery.

From the Hindu tradition, a key actor in both the South Asian and the global antislavery movement, until his death in 2020 at the age of eighty, was Swami Agnivesh. Agnivesh was born to a Brahmin family and named Shyam Vepa Rao. At university he took degrees in law and economics, but after graduation he renounced his family caste status and became a "priest," taking vows of chastity and poverty, and leaving behind his birth name. He joined the monotheistic Hindu reform movement known as Arya Samaj. In contrast to the many gods in Hinduism, a key principle of Arya Samaj belief is that: "God is Truth-consciousness – Bliss personified, Formless, Omnipotent, Just, Merciful, Unborn, Infinite, Unchangeable, Beginningless, Incomparable, Support of all, Lord of all, Omnipresent, Internal, Undecaying, Immortal, Fearless, Eternal, Holy, and creator of the universe. He alone deserves worship."[34] A prime object of Arya Samaj is to do good to the whole world, and to achieve physical, spiritual, and social prosperity for all – clearly a highly inclusive faith with a strong social action orientation.

Swami Agnivesh first became a teacher, then was named the Minister for Education in his native state in 1979. In the same year, police shot down protesting bonded laborers. When Agnivesh confronted the government, he was told to "shut up and stick to education." In response, he quit his government post and devoted himself to work with those trapped in bonded labor – and he was soon arrested and imprisoned as a "subversive." As the Bonded Labour Law was being passed in the Indian Congress, Agnivesh was in prison. On his release he began to focus on workers enslaved in stone quarries, uncovering extensive debt bondage and violence. In 1981 he founded the Bonded Labour Liberation Front

---

[34] "10 Principles of Arya Samaj": aryasamajindia.org/read/10-principles-of-arya-samaj.

(BLLF), working through both direct action and the courts. After liberating bonded laborers, the BLLF provided education, skills training, and social and legal support. Agnivesh suffered two assassination attempts, but the BLLF has freed, and continues to free, enslaved workers from agriculture, brick kilns, and quarries, as well as children enslaved in carpet weaving. It is estimated that there are some 200,000 to 300,000 children enslaved in the carpet industry in South Asia, most in Uttar Pradesh in central India.[35] For more than forty years, Agnivesh took no salary, owned no property at all, and lived in the utmost simplicity.

In North America many evangelical and fundamentalist Christian churches and groups have chosen to work together in coalitions and collaborations on the issues of human trafficking and modern slavery. A good example is the group FAAST (Faith Alliance Against Slavery and Trafficking) in the United States, that brings together two Christian universities (of the Nazarene denomination), three charitable groups working globally, and the Salvation Army. With its long history of working closely with the very poor and the displaced, the Salvation Army has specialized in responding to refugee crises in several parts of the world. For example, its highly mobile staff moved onto the beaches and into the towns of southern Greece when large numbers of refugees began to make dangerous boat crossings fleeing Lebanon and other warzones in the Middle East. Not surprisingly, human traffickers also tried to intercept desperate asylum seekers, requiring close cooperation between the Salvation Army teams and the Greek police and army.

There are also groups that work quietly and receive little public attention; we shall finish our broad sampling with three of these: the Santa Marta Group, Stella Maris, and the Coalition of Immokalee Workers. The Santa Marta Group is a coalition that brings together the Roman Catholic Church, police and law enforcement, politicians and government offices, and antislavery NGOs, in a number of countries. Their key aim is to mobilize across institutional boundaries, to link groups and move quickly when there is a chance of trafficking and enslavement emerging in the constant change of modern economies. The Group began as a partnership between the UK Metropolitan Police and Religious Sisters during the 2012 London Olympic and Paralympic Games. Criminal gangs see the influx of spectators and workers to large-scale public events

---

[35] See "Child labour in the carpet industry": vkioupi.github.io/sustainability/carpets.html#:~:text=Child%20weavers%20in%20South%20Asia&text=The%20total%20number%20of%20children,Uttar%20Pradesh%20in%20central%20India.

like the Olympics as a business opportunity. They move women they have trafficked into prostitution to these events. Religious sisters who had worked with trafficked people collaborated with the Metropolitan Police Human Trafficking Unit to introduce an outreach and support facility for those enslaved in commercial sexual exploitation. This collaboration during a major event proved successful and brought greater recognition of how these partnerships across London offered a model to be developed further. Victims were provided with safety and protection and, while there were no pre-conditions that they would assist or cooperate with a police investigation, often in doing so these women were able to provide the police with intelligence and to be powerful witnesses leading to increased prosecutions and convictions of traffickers. This partnership was so successful that the emerging Santa Marta Group began to duplicate the process in other countries. In many ways the Santa Marta Group is a global umbrella organization. The US Government's Head of Homeland Security investigations explained that, "Through Santa Marta Group I can now get on the phone to the relevant people on trafficking around the world."[36] The global spread of linked religious bodies provides research and information support to individual countries confronting a global and often hidden crime. According to Dr. David Ryall, Director of the Santa Marta Group, "only a very small number of all estimated trafficking offences around the world results in a criminal conviction."[37] The Group's central premise, accordingly, is that societies and governments must together take decisive action against the criminal networks that engage in trafficking.

The Coalition of Immokalee Workers (CIW) was quietly formed through community organizing of itinerant farmer workers in 1993.[38] In the vast tomato and fruit fields of the American state of Florida, many workers, especially those who had immigrated from Central America, found they were coming under the control, often violent, of local labor "recruiters." The violence and abuse of workers was happening far from law enforcement in nearby cities. It was labor activists, often driven by an understanding of "liberation theology," that began monitoring, organizing, and consolidating the mutual support and protection afforded by a wider worker coalition. Once organized, CIW investigations found numerous multi-state farm slavery operations across the Southeastern

---

[36] Santa Marta Group: santamartagroup.org/about/the-santa-marta-group.
[37] Dr. David Ryall, personal correspondence with the authors, Oct. 29, 2024.
[38] Coalition of Immokalee Workers: ciw-online.org/.

United States. From the early 1990s, CIW-led legal prosecutions helped liberate over 1,200 workers held against their will. This work of liberation was so successful that their model has been adapted to fight worker exploitation in settings as diverse as dairy farms in Vermont, tomato fields in Morocco, and apparel sweatshops in Bangladesh. In addition to liberating enslaved workers, CIW also initiated an innovative campaign to bring some of the world's largest food processing companies into a relationship with workers on the ground. This Campaign for Fair Food led to Fair Food Agreements with fourteen multi-billion-dollar food retailers, establishing more humane farm labor standards and fairer and dependable wages for farmworkers.

Stella Maris is a large and global antislavery religious organization that most people, including human rights workers, have never heard of. In October 1920, the first meeting of a group called the Apostleship of the Sea took place in Glasgow, Scotland. Fundamentally a support service for Catholic sailors, it has grown over time to support all seafarers. While the early years were focused in providing decent housing for sailors while in port, the organization evolved rapidly as the nature of international shipping changed in the late twentieth century. As the organization notes:

[G]lobalisation and the drive for greater profit margins, combined with technological advances, changed the face of international shipping forever. Ships became larger, ports moved down river, and turnaround times for ships in port were reduced dramatically. Crews also became smaller, and were increasingly recruited from developing world countries where wages were lower. Owners registered their ships under so-called flags of convenience to avoid stringent regulatory controls.[39]

The result is that around the world jobs are offered to young men that, once out at sea, sometimes turn into situations of enslavement and abuse. An article in the trade journal *Seatrade Maritime News* highlighted the need to address

the illegal, unreported and unregulated fishing that has spread like a virus across the world's oceans and clearly identify where this criminality emerges. Korea, Thailand, Myanmar, Cambodia, Indonesia, Taiwan, Russia and the Ukraine are all states where these vessels are owned, although they sail under many other accommodating flags, and none. The crews can be found from the unemployed and desperate in the developing world, tricked and robbed, beaten and brutalised by their officers, on their long, dreadful voyages.[40]

---

[39] "Our History": stellamaris.org.uk/our-history/.

[40] Michael Grey, "Slaves at sea," *Seatrade Maritime News*, Aug. 15, 2016: www.seatrade-maritime.com/ship-operations/slaves-at-sea. Grey references Alastair Gouper, Hance

Brutality and murder are common on unregulated and criminal ships, and crew members are often "disposed of" if they become injured or attempt escape or resistance.

Given that most of the violations of human rights occurring on ships are outside the jurisdiction of nations, the work of Stella Maris is crucial. Stella Maris workers reach out to recently landed sailors, provide safe places to sleep, and make available modern drop-in centers inside the docks, equipped with email terminals and telephones to provide contact with loved ones back home whom they may not have seen for nine or even twelve months. Remarkably, as the antislavery NGO most of us have never heard of, they are operating with an international staff of 1,000 chaplains and volunteers in 330 ports across 60 countries from Australia to the United States.

The groups just discussed represent the breadth and commitment of a wide spectrum of faith in action. The vast reach of global slavery means that a wide spectrum of responses is necessary, as well as a certain agility and responsiveness necessitated by political shifts, changing economic trends, the eruption or cessation of conflicts, and the slow but currently ineluctable transformation and destruction of the global ecosystem.

8.8　THE FUTURE OF FAITH, THE FUTURE OF SLAVERY

Who, then, can effectively address the plight of the millions of enslaved people around the world? It would be reasonable to look to nation states that have laws against slavery, and to the international organizations, such as the United Nations, that have a clear remit to both study and confront slavery in its various manifestations. But even a cursory study of these national and international actors shows a lack of cooperation, resources, and commitment devoted to the on-the-ground work of liberation. Effective cooperation in liberation is hampered by the fact that many nations, as noted earlier, still have no clear legal prohibition of slavery, and the fact that the laws that do exist within nations are a patchwork of provisions that reach only to the edge of national borders, and there meet other legal systems that are unaligned and often contradictory.

That said, there are a handful of countries – the United States, China, Japan, Germany, India, United Kingdom, France – whose governments

Smith, and Bruno Ciceri, *Fishers and Plunderers: Theft, Slavery, and Violence at Sea* (London: Pluto Press, 2015).

could afford the cost in money and human effort to end global slavery - much in the way that the United States established the Marshall Plan to rebuild Europe after World War II. Beginning in 1948 the United States spent $150 billion (in 2024 dollars) over a four-year period and rapidly rebuilt the European economies and infrastructure – a transformative accomplishment equivalent to eradicating slavery and with the same effect of unleashing what can appropriately called a "freedom dividend."[41] Today, however, there is no discussion, no movement, no intellectual leadership, no broad campaigns (with the exception of the scattered antislavery groups) calling for global liberation led by nation-states and international bodies.

In the world of the twenty-first century, there is another constituency with the power to interdict and dramatically reduce global slavery: the 3,000 to 4,000 billionaires on the planet. The power of this elite class of capitalists is, simply, their purchasing power. One estimate of the cost of freeing all of the approximately 50 million people enslaved today, with rehabilitative support included, is £17 billion/$23 billion.[42] Meanwhile, there are some 3,500 billionaires in the world with a combined wealth of £11.3 trillion/$14.5 trillion. That works out to the full cost of global liberation equalling 0.16 percent of the wealth of the world's super-rich. But the chance of getting the world's billionaires to cooperate to end slavery is tiny – even though liberation would benefit the global economy which would in turn create even more riches for the elite. It needs to be said that there *are* billionaires, like the Australian philanthropist Andrew Forrest, who support the liberation of slaves. But they are a tiny handful out of thousands. As with the nation-states and the international community, we cannot wash our hands and leave it to the super-rich to bring slavery to an end.

To find a way to radically diminish slavery it may be that we should look back, not forward. As described earlier, at the end of the eighteenth century, two religious groups combined their insights and efforts to end legal slavery within Great Britain and more broadly. They were two faith groups that stood near opposite ends of Christian expression, organization, and dogma, but they were in agreement that slavery must come to an end. In 1786, the year these two groups founded the world's first human

---

[41] See Bales and Sovacool, "From forests to factories."

[42] Kevin Bales, "Slavery in the economy of the Anthropocene," Barbara Weinstock Lectures on the Morals of Trade, Mar. 2023, online video clip: www.youtube.com/watch?v=7iFKUOlG3nw.

rights campaign, the Church of England was only some 200 years old following its split with the Roman Catholic Church in 1534. The Religious Society of Friends, the Quakers, was about 100 years old after emerging in relatively large numbers around 1652 as the religious conflict of the English Civil War came to an end.

We have described in Chapter 5 how this joint antislavery campaign mobilized significant parts of the British population at the end of the eighteenth century. It was a movement of innovations. The first-ever popular and national boycotts of slave-made goods were instituted. Women, especially Quaker women, normally excluded from any political involvement, organized large groups to gather petitions, teach and campaign for emancipation, and serve as the backbone of the national movement. Members of the Church of England such as William Wilberforce, Granville Sharp, Hannah Moore, Zachery Macaulay, Thomas Fowell Buxton, and Thomas Clarkson provided a solid foundation of abolition within the more conservative Established Anglican Church and were able to hold political positions that were forbidden to dissident Quakers.[43]

The organizing and political outcomes accomplished by this somewhat curious religious partnership went far beyond the abolition of the slave trade (1807) and the abolition of legal slavery throughout much of the British Empire in 1833. As noted earlier, from 1807 until 1867 the Royal Navy was ordered to suppress the slave trade, first the transatlantic trade and then more widely. No other country or group has mounted such an extensive campaign to bring slavery to an end as this extension of military and diplomatic efforts lasting more than 100 years. And for all that time, religiously based antislavery groups and individuals served the effort at all levels. If there were ever a truly global movement that also made dramatic inroads into the numbers of men, women, and children held in slavery, it was this movement that spanned most of the nineteenth century.

For reasons that are relatively well understood, by the end of the nineteenth century there was a common assumption that slavery was fundamentally ended. The great conflagration of the twentieth century, its world wars, the ultimate collapse of colonial imperialism, and the emergence of a truly global economy worked together to distract public attention from ongoing forms of slavery around the world, both ancient and new. By the mid-twentieth century slavery was generally assumed to be a thing of the past and only a tiny handful of people and groups knew

---

[43] The first Quaker allowed to sit in Parliament was Joseph Pease in 1832.

otherwise. In fact, there were significant pockets of slavery in countries like Mauritania that had never ended. Likewise, the extensive enslavement in armed conflicts – the millions enslaved during World War II, for example – also seemed to fade from popular consciousness after 1945. While groups like Anti-Slavery International in the UK, reduced to a tiny handful of staff by the 1970s, did their best to raise the issue, their efforts tended to fall upon deaf ears. Only at the end of the twentieth century did the level of public recognition and some slight governmental responses emerge.

From the 1990s, antislavery groups, and especially religiously based antislavery groups began to emerge. Plan International[44], Anti-Slavery International[45], ActionAid[46], World Vision[47], BRAC[48], and Save the Children[49] are all among the largest fifteen non-governmental organizations in the world and all devote some or all of their work to antislavery and liberation. Likewise, as described above, there are many faith-based antislavery groups with a global reach, like Stella Maris and the remarkable and sizable global organization Talitha Kum. And each of these global players are surrounded by smaller local groups, as was the case in the first antislavery movement in 1787. Local churches in many countries support small actions of liberation in the developing world. Some local religious groups link to even larger groups such as International Justice Mission. This global coverage of faith groups that seek to end slavery, this common cause, this phenomenal collection of experience and knowledge of both global and local slavery and human trafficking may be the true future of liberation.

It is clear that individual governments and international bodies, or the strength of businesses, or the largesse of billionaires, will likely never rise to the challenge of global slavery without the impetus of a mass movement. A coalition formed of religious groups, combining moral, economic, and political power and expertise, could drive such a movement. Are the faith groups of the world, distracted by so many needs and issues, ready to act? Possibly. The linkages of instantaneous global communication provide the tools of coordination and intelligence gathering. The goal is perfectly clear: liberation of those in slavery. A deep understanding of slavery crime and practice is possessed by faith-based organizations already working on the issue. And the religious motivation to act is

---

44 Plan International: plan-international.org.   45 Antislavery: www.antislavery.org.
46 ActionAid: actionaid.org/who-we-are.   47 WorldVision: www.worldvision.org.
48 BRAC: www.brac.net.   49 Save the Children: www.savethechildren.net.

fundamental, even if its nuances vary from group to group. Is it possible for us to follow Thomas Clarkson in his moment of revelation, agreeing that the tragic facts of slavery are real, and that it is "time some person should see these calamities to their end"?[50]

[50] Clarkson, *The History of the Rise, Progress, and Accomplishment*, vol. 1, 161–162. Underlining added.

Bibliography

"10 Principles of Arya Samaj," (2024): aryasamajindia.org/read/10-principles-of-arya-samaj.

Aird, Sarah C., "Ghana's slaves to the gods," *Human Rights Brief*, 7:1 (1999): 6–8, 26.

Al-Dayel, Nadia, Andrew Mumford, and Kevin Bales, "Not yet dead: the establishment and regulation of slavery by the Islamic State," *Studies in Conflict & Terrorism*, 45:11 (2020): doi.org/10.1080/1057610X.2020.1711590.

al-Dawish, Ahmad 'Abd al-Razzaq (ed.), *Fatawa al-Lanja al-da'ima li'l-buhuth al-'ilmiyya wa'l-ifta*. 5th ed., vol. 16. (Riyadh: Dar al-Mu'ayyad, 2004).

Alexander VI, *Inter caetera*, May 4, 1493: https://www.papalencyclicals.net/alex06/alex06inter.htm.

Alford, Deann, "Sex slaves' slow freedom," *Christianity Today*, 49:2 (February 2005), 22.

al-Jabbār, 'Abd, *al-Mughnī fī abwāb al-tawḥīd wa al-'adl*, ed. A. F. al-Ahwānī and I. Madkūr, 15 vols. (Cairo: al-Mu'assasah al-Misrīyah al-Āmmah li al-Ta'līf wa al-Tarjamah wa al-Tibā'ah wa al-Nashr, 1960–1969).

Allain, Jean, *The Law and Slavery: Prohibiting Human Exploitation* (Leiden: Brill, 2015).

al-Nabhānī, Yūsuf, *Sa'ādat al-anām fī ittibā' dīn al-islām wa tawḍīḥ al-farq baynahu wa bayna dīn al-naṣara fī al-'aqā'id wa al-aḥkām [Happiness in Following the Religion of Islam and Clarifying the Difference between Islam and Christianity in Terms of Beliefs and Rules]* (no publisher, 1908).

Ambrose, *De officiis: Volume I, Introduction, Text, and Translation*, ed. and trans. Ivor J. Davidson (Oxford: Oxford University Press, 2001).

De officiis: Volume II, Commentary, ed. and trans. Ivor J. Davidson (Oxford: Oxford University Press, 2001).

Ambrosiaster, *Commentaries on Galatians-Philemon*, trans. and ed. Gerald L. Bray (Downers Grove, IL: InterVarsity Press, 2009).

Andreau, Jean and Raymond Descat, *The Slave in Greece and Rome*, trans. Marion Leopold (Madison, WI: University of Wisconsin Press, 2011).

Andujar, Eduardo, "Bartolome de Las Casas and Juan Gines de Sepulveda: moral theology versus political philosophy," in Kevin White (ed.), *Hispanic Philosophy in the Age of Discovery*, Studies in Philosophy and the History of Philosophy, vol. 29 (Washington, DC: The Catholic University of America Press, 1997).

Anonymous, *Arguments against Making Slaves of Men* (1715).

Anstey, Roger, *The Atlantic Slave Trade and British Abolition, 1760–1810* (London: MacMillan, 1975).

"The pattern of British abolitionism in the eighteenth and nineteenth centuries," in C. Bolt and S. Drescher (eds.), *Anti-Slavery, Religion, and Reform: Essays in Memory of Roger Anstey* (Folkestone, Kent: Wm Dawson & Sons, 1980), 19–42.

Aquinas, Thomas, *Commentaries on St. Paul's Epistles to Timothy, Titus, and Philemon*, trans. Chrysostom Baer (South Bend, IN: St. Augustine's Press, 2007).

Opera omnia sancti Thomae Aquinatis, tome 9 (Rome: Typographia Polyglotta, 1897).

Summa Theologica, trans. Fathers of the English Dominican Province (Westminster, MD: Christian Classics, 1981).

Augustine, *Augustine on Romans*, trans. Paula Fredriksen Landes (Chico, CA: Scholars Press, 1982).

The City of God against the Pagans, vol. 6, trans. William Chase Greene (Cambridge: Harvard University Press, 1960).

Expositions on the Psalms 124:7–8, in P. Schaff (ed.), *A Select Library of the Nicene and Post-Nicene Fathers of the Christian Church, Volume 8, Saint Augustine: Expositions on the Book of Psalms* (Buffalo, NY: Christian Literature Publishing Co., 1888).

The Works of Saint Augustine: Volume 14: Writings on the Old Testament, trans. Joseph T. Lienhard and Sean Doyle (New York: New City Press, 2016).

Auping, John A., *Religion and Social Justice: The Case of Christianity and the Abolition of Slavery in America* (Mexico City: Universidad Iberoamericana, 1994).

Avalos, Hector, "Pope Alexander VI, slavery and voluntary subjection: 'Ineffabilis et Summi Patris' in context," *Journal of Ecclesiastical History*, 65:4 (2014), 738–760.

Axson, Stockton, *Brother Woodrow: A Memoir of Woodrow Wilson*, ed. A. S. Link (Princeton: Princeton University Press, 1993).

Azevedo, Celia M., "Rocha's 'The Ethiopian Redeemed' and the circulation of anti-slavery ideas," *Slavery & Abolition*, 24:1 (2003), 101–126.

Bahadur, Dipendra, "Deuki Pratha in Nepal: problems and changing beliefs," *Tribhuvan University Journal*, 35:2 (2020), 89–102: doi.org/10.3126/tuj .v35i2.36194.

Baker, Ray Stannard *Woodrow Wilson: Life and Letters* (New York: Charles Scribner's Sons, 1946).

Bales, Kevin, *Blood and Earth: Modern Slavery, Ecocide, and the Secret to Saving the World* (New York: Spiegel & Grau, 2016).

Disposable People: New Slavery in the Global Economy, 1st ed. (Berkeley: University of California Press, 1999).

Disposable People: New Slavery in the Global Economy, rev. ed. (Berkeley: University of California Press, 2004).

Ending Slavery: How We Free Today's Slaves (Berkeley: University of California Press, 2007).

"International labor standards: quality of information and measures of progress in combating forced labor," *Comparative Labor Law and Policy Journal*, 24:2 (Winter 2003), 321–364.

"Slavery and the human right to evil," *Journal of Human Rights*, 3:1 (2004), 55–65.

"Slavery in the economy of the Anthropocene," Barbara Weinstock Lectures on the Morals of Trade, March 2023, online video clip: www.youtube.com/watch?v=7iFKUOlG3nw.

"Unlocking the statistics of slavery," *Chance (Journal of the American Statistical Association)*, 30:3 (2017), 5–12.

Bales, Kevin and Monti Datta, "Slavery in Europe: Part 1, estimating the dark figure," *Human Rights Quarterly*, 35:3 (2013), 817–829.

Bales, Kevin and Alison Gardner, "Free soil, free produce, free communities," in G. LeBaron, J. Pliley, and D. Blight (eds.), *Fighting Modern Slavery and Human Trafficking: History and Contemporary Policy* (Cambridge: Cambridge University Press, 2020), 73–96.

Bales, Kevin and Benjamin Sovacool, "From forests to factories: how modern slavery deepens the crisis of climate change," *Energy Research & Social Science* 77 (2021), 1–9: doi.org/10.1016/j.erss.2021.102096.

Bales, Kevin and Zoe Trodd (eds.), *To Plead Our Own Cause: Personal Stories by Today's Slaves* (Ithaca: Cornell University Press, 2008).

Barnhart, Michael, "Buddhist ethics and social justice," in R. Bontekoe and M. Stepaniants (eds.), *Justice and Democracy: Cross-Cultural Perspectives* (Honolulu: University of Hawai'i Press, 1997), 327–341.

Barratt, Ingrid, "I am not your slave," *War Cry Magazine*, Sept. 23, 2017, 6–9, www.salvationarmy.org.nz/our-community/faith-in-life/soul-food/im-not-your-slave.

Bartolus de Saxoferrato, *Commentaria: cum additionibus Thomae Diplovatatii aliorumque excellentissimorum doctorum, una cum amplissimo repertorio noviter elucubrato per dictum calrissimum doctorem dominum Thomam Diplovatatium*, ed. G. Polari (Venice, 1526; facsimile Rome 1996).

Baxter, Richard, *A Christian Directory: Or, a Sum of Practical Theology, and Cases of Conscience* (London: Thomas Parkhurst, 1673).

Beattie, James, *Elements of Moral Science* (Edinburgh: T. Cadell and William Creech, 1793).

Benezet, Anthony, *The Complete Antislavery Writings of Anthony Benezet, 1754–1783*, ed. D. L. Crosby (Baton Rouge, LA: Louisiana State University Press, 2013).

Blackburn, Robin, *The American Crucible: Slavery, Emancipation and Human Rights* (London: Verso, 2011).

Blackmon, Douglas A., *Slavery by Another Name: The Re-Enslavement of African-Americans from the Civil War to World War II* (London: Icon Books, 2012).

Bloch, Marc, "How and why ancient slavery came to an end," in *Slavery and Serfdom in the Middle Ages*, trans. William R. Beer (Berkeley: University of California Press, 1975), 1–31.

Bloom, Paul, *Against Empathy: The Case for Rational Compassion* (New York: Ecco, 2016).

  Just Babies: The Origins of Good and Evil (New York: Crown Publishers, 2013).

Bobzien, Susanne, *Determinism and Freedom in Stoic Philosophy* (Oxford: Oxford University Press, 1999).

Bodhi, Bhikku (ed.), *In the Buddha's Words: An Anthology of Discourses from the Pali Canon* (Somerville, MA: Wisdom Publications, 2015).

Bodin, Jean. *The Six Books of a Common-weale*, trans. Richard Knolles (London: Adam Islip, 1606).

Bonnassie, Pierre, *From Slavery to Feudalism in South-Western Europe* (Cambridge: Cambridge University Press, 1991).

Bostom, Andrew G. (ed.), *The Legacy of Jihad: Islamic Holy War and the Fate of Non-Muslims* (Amherst, NY: Prometheus Books, 2005).

Bourne, George, *The Book and Slavery Irreconcilable, with Animadversions upon Dr. Smith's Philosophy* (Philadelphia: J. M. Sanderson & Co., 1816).

Boyd, Doreen, Bethany Jackson, Jessica Wardlaw, Giles Foody, Stuart Marsh, and Kevin Bales, "Slavery from space: demonstrating the role for satellite remote sensing to inform evidence-based action related to UN SDG Number 8," *ISPRS Journal of Photogrammetry and Remote Sensing*, 142 (2018), 380–388.

Bradley, K. R., *Slaves and Masters in the Roman Empire: A Study in Social Control* (Oxford: Oxford University Press, 1987).

Brodman, James William, *Ransoming Captives in Crusader Spain: The Order of Merced on the Christian-Islamic Frontier* (Philadelphia: University of Pennsylvania Press, 1986).

Brown, Christopher Leslie, *Moral Capital: The Foundations of British Abolitionism* (Chapel Hill, NC: The University of North Carolina Press, 2006).

Brown, John, *A Dictionary of the Holy Bible … Forming a Sacred Commentary; a Body of Scripture History, Chronology, and Divinity* (Pittsburgh, 1807).

Brown, Jonathan A. C., *Slavery & Islam* (London: Oneworld Academic, 2019).

Bruns, Roger (ed.), *Am I Not a Man and a Brother: The Antislavery Crusade of Revolutionary America, 1688—1788* (New York: Chelsea House Publishers, 1983).

Brunschvig, R., "'Abd," in P. Bearman, Th. Bianquis, C. E. Bosworth, E. van Donzel, and W. P. Heinrichs (eds.), *Encyclopaedia of Islam, second edition* (Brill: 2012): dx.doi.org/10.1163/1573-3912_islam_COM_0003.

Calvin, John, *Calvin's New Testament Commentaries: A New Translation*, vol. 10, eds. D. Torrance and T. Torrance (Grand Rapids, MI: Eerdmans, 1972).

Cameron, Catherine M., *Captives: How Stolen People Changed the World* (Lincoln, NE: University of Nebraska Press, 2016).

Carey, Brycchan, *From Peace to Freedom: Quaker Rhetoric and the Birth of American Antislavery, 1657–1761* (New Haven: Yale University Press, 2012).

Carlyle, Robert W. and Alexander J. Carlyle, *A History of Mediaeval Political Theory in the West, Volume II: The Political Theory of the Roman Lawyers and the Canonists, from the Tenth Century to the Thirteenth Century* (New York: Barnes & Noble, 1909–1936).

Cassidy, Richard J., *Paul in Chains: Roman Imprisonment and the Letters of St. Paul* (New York: The Crossroad Publishing Company, 2001).

Cazden, Elizabeth, "Quakers, slavery, anti-slavery, and race," in S. W. Angell and B. P. Dandelion (eds.), *The Oxford Handbook of Quaker Studies* (Oxford: Oxford University Press, 2013), 347–362.

Chakravarti, Uma, "Of Dasas and Karmakaras: Servile labour in ancient India," in Utsa Patnaik and Manjari Dingwaney (eds.), *Chains of Servitude: Bondage and Slavery in India* (Madras: Sangam Books, 1985), 35–75.

Chanana, Dev Raj, *Slavery in Ancient India: As Depicted in Pali and Sanskrit Texts* (New Delhi: People's Publishing House, 1960).

Christie, John W. and Dwight L. Dumond (eds.), *George Bourne and the Book and Slavery Irreconcilable* (Wilmington, DE: The Historical Society of Delaware, 1969).

Clarence-Smith, William Gervase, *Islam and the Abolition of Slavery* (Oxford: Oxford University Press, 2006).

Clarkson, Thomas, *The History of the Rise, Progress, and Accomplishment of the Abolition of the African Slave-Trade by the British Parliament* (New York: J. S. Taylor, 1836).

Cline, Catherine Ann, "The Church and the movement for Congo reform," *Church History*, 32:1 (1963), 46–56.

Coleman-Norton, P. R., "Paul and the Roman law of slavery," in P. R. Coleman-Norton (ed.), *Studies in Roman Economic and Social History in Honor of Allan Chester Johnson* (Princeton: Princeton University Press, 1951), 155–177.

Columbus, Christopher, *Journal of First Voyage to America* (New York: Albert & Charles Boni, 1924).

Select Letters of Christopher Columbus, with Other Original Documents, Relating to His Four Voyages to the New World, trans. and ed. by R. H. Major (London: Hakluyt Society, 1870).

Conway, J. S., *The Nazi Persecution of the Churches: 1933–1945* (New York, Basic Books: 1968).

Cooper, Jr., John Milton, *Woodrow Wilson: A Biography* (New York: Alfred A. Knopf, 2009).

Corcoran, Gervase, *Saint Augustine on Slavery* (Rome: Institutum Patristicum Augustinianum, 1985).

Cowans, Jon, *Early Modern Spain: A Documentary History* (Philadelphia: University of Pennsylvania Press, 2003).

Crane, R. S., "Anglican apologetics and the idea of progress, 1699–1745," *Modern Philology* 31:3 (1934), 273–306.

Crofts, Daniel W., *Reluctant Confederates: Upper South Unionists in the Secession Crisis* (Chapel Hill, NC: The University of North Carolina Press, 1989).

Crouch, Andy, *Culture Making: Recovering Our Creative Calling* (Downers Grove, IL: InterVarsity Press, 2008).

Dandamaev, Muhammed, "Slavery: Ancient Near East," in D. N. Freedman (ed.), *Anchor Bible Dictionary* (New York: Doubleday, 1992).

Dandamaev, Muhammed and Vladimir G. Lukonin, *The Culture and Social Institutions of Ancient Iran* (Cambridge: Cambridge University Press, 1989).

d'Anjou, Leo, *Social Movements and Cultural Change: The First Abolition Campaign Revisited* (New York: Aldine de Gruyter, 1996).

Datta, Monti Narayan and Kevin Bales, "Slavery is bad for business: analyzing the impact of slavery on national economies," *The Brown Journal of World Affairs*, 19:2 (2013), 205–223.

Davenport, Frances Gardiner (ed.), *European Treaties bearing on the History of the United States and Its Dependencies to 1648* (Washington, DC: Carnegie Institution of Washington, 1917), 20–26.

Davies, Nigel, *Human Sacrifice: In History and Today* (New York: Dorset Press, 1981).

Davis, David Brion, "The emergence of immediatism in British and American antislavery thought," *The Mississippi Valley Historical Review*, 49:2 (1962), 209–230.

  Inhuman Bondage: The Rise and Fall of Slavery in the New World (Oxford: Oxford University Press, 2006).

  The Problem of Slavery in Western Culture (Ithaca: Cornell University Press, 1966).

  The Problem of Slavery in the Age of Revolution, 1770–1823 (Ithaca: Cornell University Press, 1975).

  Slavery and Human Progress (Oxford: Oxford University Press, 1984).

Davis, Robert C., *Holy War and Human Bondage: Tales of Christian-Muslim Slavery in the Early-Modern Mediterranean* (Santa Barbara, CA: ABC CLIO, 2009).

Denzinger, Heinrich and A. Schonmetzer (eds.), *Enchiridion Symbolorum Definitionem Et Declarationum De Rebus Fidei et Morum*, 35th ed. (Friburg in Br.: Herder, 1965).

Dew, Thomas R., "Abolition of Negro slavery," *American Quarterly Review*, 12 (1832), 189–265.

Dharmasutras: The Law Codes of Apastamba, Gautama, Baudhayana and Vasistha, trans. Patrick Olivelle (Oxford: Oxford University Press, 1999).

"Dhimmi," *New World Encyclopedia*: www.newworldencyclopedia.org/entry/Dhimmi.

Didache: The Teaching of the Twelve Apostles, trans. Clayton N. Jefford (Salem, OR: Polebridge Press, 2013).

Douglass, Frederick, *My Bondage and My Freedom*, ed. John Stauffer (New York: The Modern Library, 2003).

  "England should lead the cause of emancipation: an address delivered in Leeds, England, on December 23, 1846," *Leeds Times*, December 26, 1846.

The Frederick Douglass Papers: Series One – Speeches, Debates, and Interviews, eds. John Blassingame et al. (New Haven: Yale University Press, 1979).

Drake, Thomas E., *Quakers and Slavery in America* (New Haven: Yale University Press, 1950).

Drescher, Seymour, *Abolition: A History of Slavery and Antislavery* (Cambridge: Cambridge University Press, 2009).

Capitalism and Slavery: British Mobilization in Comparative Perspective (Oxford: Oxford University Press, 1987).

Dunning, David, "Motivated cognition in self and social thought," in M. Mikulincer and P. R. Shaver (eds.), *APA Handbook of Personality and Social Psychology. I. Attitudes and Social Cognition* (Washington, DC: American Psychological Association, 2015), 777–803.

Dunstan, William E., *The Ancient Near East* (Fort Worth, TX: Harcourt Brace, 1998).

Dzansi, D. Y. and Biga, P. "'Trokosi' – slave of a fetish: an empirical study," *Studies of Tribes and Tribals*, 12:1 (2014), 1–8.

Eadmer, *Eadmer's History of Recent Events in England: Historia Novorum in Anglia*, trans. Geoffrey Bosanquet (London: The Cresset Press, 1964).

The Edicts of Asoka, ed. and trans. by N. A. Nikam and Richard McKeon (Chicago: The University of Chicago Press, 1959).

Eltis, David, *The Rise of African Slavery in the Americas* (Cambridge: Cambridge University Press, 2000).

Eltis, David and Stanley Engerman, "Dependence, servility, and coerced labor in time and space," in D. Eltis and S. Engerman (eds.), *The Cambridge World History of Slavery: Volume 3, AD 1420–AD 1804* (Cambridge: Cambridge University Press, 2011), 1–21.

Eltis, David and Stanley Engerman (eds.), *The Cambridge World History of Slavery: Volume 3, AD 1420–AD 1804* (Cambridge: Cambridge University Press, 2011).

Erdem, Y. Hakan, *Slavery in the Ottoman Empire and Its Demise, 1800–1909* (New York: St. Martin's Press, 1996).

Faust, Drew Gilpin (ed.), *The Ideology of Slavery: Proslavery Thought in the Antebellum South, 1830–1860* (Baton Rouge, LA: Louisiana State University Press, 1981).

Fede, Andrew T., *Homicide Justified: The Legality of Killing Slaves in the United States and the Atlantic World* (Athens, GA: University of George Press, 2017).

Fernandez-Armesto, Felipe, *Columbus* (Oxford: Oxford University Press, 1991).

Finkelman, Paul (ed.), *Defending Slavery: Proslavery Thought in the Old South, A Brief History with Documents* (Boston: Bedford/St Martin's, 2003).

Finley, Moses, *Ancient Slavery and Modern Ideology* (New York: Viking Press, 1980).

Fisher, Siobhan K., "Occupation of the womb: forced impregnation as genocide," *Duke Law Journal*, 46:1 (1996), 91–133.

Fitzgerald, John T., "The Stoics and the early Christians on the treatment of slaves," in T. Rasimus, T. Engberg-Pedersen, and I. Dunderberg (eds.),

Stoicism in Early Christianity (Grand Rapids, MI: Baker Academic, 2010), 141–75.

Flournoy, J. J., *A reply, to a pamphlet, entitled "Bondage...* (Athens, Ga., 1838).

Foner, Eric, *Free Soil, Free Labor, Free Men: The Ideology of the Republican Party before the Civil War* (Oxford: Oxford University Press, 1995).

Ford, Lacy K., *Deliver Us from Evil: The Slavery Question in the Old South* (Oxford: Oxford University Press, 2009).

Foster, John, *Discourses on All the Principal Branches of Natural Religion and Social Virtue*, vol. 2 (London, 1752).

Fox, George, "Gospel family-order," in J. William Frost (ed.), *The Quaker Origins of Antislavery* (Norwood, PA: Norwood Editions, 1980), 35–55.

Freamon, Bernard, *Possessed by the Right Hand: The Problem of Slavery in Islamic Law and Muslim Cultures* (Leiden: Brill, 2019).

Frost, J. William (ed.), *The Quaker Origins of Antislavery* (Norwood, PA: Norwood Editions, 1980).

Fynn-Paul, Jeffrey, "Empire, monotheism and slavery in the greater Mediterranean region from antiquity to the early modern era," *Past & Present*, 205 (Nov 2009), 3–40.

Gardner, Jane F., "Slavery and Roman law," in K. Bradley and P. Cartledge (eds.), *The Cambridge World History of Slavery: Volume 1, The Ancient Mediterranean World* (Cambridge: Cambridge University Press, 2011), 414–437.

Garnsey, Peter, *Ideas of slavery from Aristotle to Augustine* (Cambridge: Cambridge University Press, 1996).

Gatta, Francesco and Giuseppe Plessi (eds.) *Liber Paradisus* (Bologna, 1956).

Guasco, Michael, *Slaves and Englishmen: Human Bondage in the Early Modern Atlantic World* (Philadelphia: University of Pennsylvania Press, 2014).

Gerbner, Katharine, "Antislavery in print: The Germantown protest, the 'Exhortation,' and the seventeenth-century Quaker debate on slavery," *Early American Studies*, 9:3 (Fall 2011), 552–575.

Ghazal, Amal N., "Debating slavery and abolition in the Arab Middle East," in Behnaz A. Mirzai, Ismael Musah Montana and Paul E. Lovejoy (eds.), *Slavery, Islam, and Diaspora* (Trenton, NJ/Asmara, Eritrea: Africa World Press, 2009), 139–154.

Glancy, Jennifer, *Slavery as Moral Problem: In the Early Church and Today* (Minneapolis: Fortress Press, 2011).

Goeschel, Christian and Nikolaus Wachsmann, "Before Auschwitz: The formation of the Nazi concentration camps, 1933–9," *Journal of Contemporary History*, 45:3 (2010), 515–534: www.jstor.org/stable/20753613.

Goldenberg, David M., *The Curse of Ham: Race and Slavery in Early Judaism, Christianity, and Islam* (Princeton: Princeton University Press, 2003).

Goltzman, Jonathan C., "Cultural relativism or cultural intrusion? Female ritual slavery in Western Africa and the international covenant on civil and political rights: Ghana as a case study," *New England International and Comparative Law Annual*, 4 (1998), 53–72.

Goody, Jack, "Slavery in time and space," in J. Watson (ed.), *Asian and African Systems of Slavery* (Berkeley: University of California Press, 1980), 16–42.

Gouper, Alastair, Hance Smith, and Bruno Ciceri, *Fishers and Plunderers: Theft, Slavery, and Violence at Sea* (London: Pluto Press, 2015).

Green, Beriah, *The Chattel Principle: The Abhorrence of Jesus Christ and the Apostles; Or, No Refuge for American Slavery in the New Testament* (New York: American Anti-Slavery Society, 1839).

Gregory of Nyssa, *Opera*, vol. 5, ed. J. McDonough and P. Alexander (Leiden, 1962).

Grey, Michael, "Slaves at sea," *Seatrade Maritime News*, Aug. 15, 2016: www.seatrade-maritime.com/ship-operations/slaves-at-sea.

Griffin, M. T., *Seneca: A Philosopher in Politics* (Oxford: Clarendon Press, 1976).

Gutierrez, Gustavo, *Las Casas: In Search of the Poor of Jesus Christ*, trans. Robert R. Barr (Maryknoll, NY: Orbis Books, 1993).

Haidt, Jonathan and Fredrik Bjorklund, "Social intuitionists answer six questions about moral psychology," in W. Sinnott-Armstrong (ed.), *Moral Psychology, Volume 2, The Cognitive Science of Morality: Intuition and Diversity* (Cambridge, MA: The MIT Press, 2008), 181–254.

Haleem, M. A. S. Abdel (ed. and trans.), *The Qur'an, English Translation and Parallel Arabic Text* (Oxford: Oxford University Press, 2010).

Hanke, Lewis, *The Spanish Struggle for Justice in the Conquest of America* (Philadelphia: University of Pennsylvania Press, 1949).

Hansen, Anne Ruth, *How to Behave: Buddhism and Modernity in Colonial Cambodia, 1860–1930* (Honolulu: University of Hawai'i Press, 2011).

Harrill, James Albert, *The Manumission of Slaves in Early Christianity* (Tubingen: Mohr-Sieback, 1995).

Harris, R., *Scriptural researches on the licitness of the slave-trade, shewing its conformity with the principles of natural and revealed religion, delineated in the sacred writings of the word of God* (London: John Stockdale, 1788).

Harris, Sam, *Letter to a Christian Nation* (New York: Alfred A. Knopf, 2006).

Harris, Sam and Maajid Nawaz, *Islam and the Future of Tolerance: A Dialogue* (Cambridge, MA: Harvard University Press, 2015).

Hart, David Bentley, *Atheist Delusions: The Christian Revolution and Its Fashionable Enemies* (New Haven: Yale University Press, 2009).

Haslam, Nick, "Dehumanization: an integrative review," *Personality and Social Psychology Review*, 10 (2006), 252–264.

Haynes, Stephen R., *Noah's Curse: The Biblical Justification of American Slavery* (Oxford: Oxford University Press, 2002).

Healey, Robynne Rogers, "History of Quaker faith and practice: 1650–1808," in S. W. Angell and P. Dandelion (eds.), *The Cambridge Companion to Quakerism* (Cambridge: Cambridge University Press, 2018), 13–30.

Hefele, Charles Joseph, *A History of the Councils of the Church, From the Original Documents*, vol. 3 (Edinburgh: T & T Clark, 1883)

  A History of the Councils of the Church, From the Original Documents, vol. 4 (Edinburgh, T & T Clark, 1895).

Hellie, Richard, "Slavery," *Encyclopedia Britannica*, Aug. 17, 2020: www.britannica.com/topic/slavery–sociology.

Hershbell, J. P., "Epictetus: a freedman on slavery," *Ancient Society*, 26 (1995), 185–204.

Hezser, Catherine, "Slavery and the Jews," in K. Bradley and P. Cartledge (eds.), *The Cambridge World History of Slavery: Volume 1, The Ancient Mediterranean World* (Cambridge: Cambridge University Press, 2011), 438–455.

Higman, B. W., "Demographic trends," in D. Eltis, S. Engerman, S. Drescher, and D. Richardson (eds.), *The Cambridge World History of Slavery: Volume 4, AD 1804–AD 2016* (Cambridge: Cambridge University Press, 2017), 20–48.

Hochschild, Adam, *Bury the Chains: Prophets and Rebels in the Fight to Free an Empire's Slaves* (Boston: Houghton Mifflin, 2005).

  King Leopold's Ghost: A Story of Greed, Terror, and Heroism in Colonial Africa (Boston: Houghton Mifflin, 1998).

  The Holy Bible: containing the Old and New Testaments, Revised Standard Version, Catholic Edition (San Francisco: Ignatius Press, n.d.).

Hopkins, Samuel, *A Dialogue Concerning the Slavery of the Africans* (Norwich: Judah P. Spooner, 1776).

Hughes, Derek (ed.), *Versions of Blackness: Key Texts on Slavery from the Seventeenth Century* (Cambridge: Cambridge University Pres, 2007).

Hunwick, John, "Islamic law and polemics over race and slavery in North and West Africa (16–19th Century)," in Shaun E. Marmon (ed.), *Slavery in the Islamic Middle East* (Princeton: Markus Wiener Publishers, 1999), 43–68.

Hunwick, John and Eve Troutt Powell (eds.), *The African Diaspora in the Mediterranean Lands of Islam* (Princeton: Markus Wiener Publishers, 2002).

Hutcheson, Francis, *A System of Moral Philosophy, In Three Books* (London: A. Millar, 1755).

Ibn Ishaq, Muhammad, *The Life of Muhammad: A Translation of Ibn Ishaq's Sirat Rasul Allah*, trans. A. Guillaume (Oxford: Oxford University Press, 1967).

ibn Rashid, Ma'mar, *The Expeditions: An Early Biography of Muhammad*, trans. Sean W. Anthony (New York: NYU Press, 2015).

International Justice Mission, "What is Bonded Labor?": www.ijm.org/news/what-is-bonded-labor.

Jackson, Sherman A., *Islam and the Problem of Black Suffering* (Oxford: Oxford University Press, 2009).

Jakobsen, Siw Ellen, "Out on a limb after forced marriage," *Sciencenorway.no*, Mar. 10, 2015: sciencenorway.no/forskningno-immigration-norway/out-on-a-limb-after-forced-marriage/1415065.

The Jataka, Or: Stories of the Buddha's Former Births, vol. 6, trans. E. B. Cowell and W. H. D. Rouse (Cambridge: Cambridge University Press, 1907).

Jennings, Judith, *The Business of Abolishing the British Slave Trade, 1783-1807* (London: Frank Cass, 1997).

Joner, Henrique, "Impressions of Luis de Molina about the trade of African slaves," *Patristica et Mediaevalia*, 36 (2015), 39–50.

Kadıoğlu, Ahmet Murat, "The use of Shinto for the legitimization of Japanese aggression in East Asia," *Nevşehir Hacı Bektaş Veli Üniversitesi SBE Dergisi*, 11:2 (2021), 492–500.

Kadivar, Mohsen, *Human Rights and Reformist Islam* (Edinburgh: Edinburgh University Press, 2021).

Kautilya, *Kautilya's Arthasastra*, trans. R. Shamasastry (Mysore: Mysore Printing and Publishing House, 1960).

Kellerman, Christopher J., *All Oppression Shall Cease: A History of Slavery, Abolitionism, and the Catholic Church* (New York: Orbis Books, 2022).

Kelsey, Rayner W., "Early Books of Discipline of the Philadelphia yearly meeting," *Bulletin of Friends Historical Association*, 24:1 (1935), 12–23.

Kennedy, A. G., "Cnut's law code of 1018," *Anglo-Saxon England*, 11 (1983), 57–81.

Kim, Sung-Eun Thomas, "Perception of monastic slaves by scholar-officials and monks in the late Koryo and early Choson Periods," *Journal of Korean Religions*, 7:1 (2016), 5–34.

Kulikoff, Allan, *Abraham Lincoln and Karl Marx in Dialogue* (Oxford: Oxford University Press, 2018).

Kumar, Dharma, "Colonialism, bondage, and caste in British India," in Martin A. Klein (ed.), *Breaking the Chains: Slavery, Bondage, and Emancipation in Modern Africa and Asia* (Madison, WI: The University of Wisconsin Press, 1993), 112–130.

Lactantius, *Divine Institutes*, trans. Anthony Bowen and Peter Garnsey (Liverpool: Liverpool University Press, 2003).

Lagergren, David, *Mission and State in the Congo: A Study of the Relations between Protestant Missions and the Congo Independent State Authorities with Special Reference to the Equator District, 1885–1903* (Uppsala, Sweden: Gleerup, 1970).

Las Siete Partidas, Volume 4: Family, Commerce, and the Sea: The Worlds of Women and Merchants, trans. Samuel Parsons Scott, ed. R. I. Burns, S. J. (Philadelphia: University of Pennsylvania Press, 2001).

Lawrence, George, *An Oration on the Abolition of the Slave Trade* (New York: Hardcastle and Van Pelt, 1813).

The Laws of Manu: Translated with Extracts from Seven Commentaries, trans. G. Buhler (Oxford: Clarendon Press, 1886).

Lewis, Alexandra and Brad K. Blitz, "The Ru.Lag: the Kremlin's new empire of forced labor," *Journal of Modern Slavery*, 8:1 (2023): slavefreetoday.org/journal_of_modern_slavery/v8i1a9-the-ru-lag-the-kremlins-new-empire-of-forced-labor.pdf.

Lewis, Bernard, *Race and Slavery in the Middle East: An Historical Enquiry* (Oxford: Oxford University Press, 1990).

Leyens, Jacque-Philippe, Paola M. Paladino, Ramon Rodriquez-Torres et al., "The emotional side of prejudice: the attribution of secondary emotions to ingroups and outgroups," *Personality and Social Psychology Review*, 4 (2000), 186–197.

Lind, Joan Dyste, "The ending of slavery in Sweden: social structure and decision making," *Scandinavian Studies*, 50:1 (Winter 1978), 57–71.

Locke, Robynne A., "Rescued, rehabilitated, returned: Institutional approaches to the rehabilitation of survivors of sex trafficking in India and Nepal," Master's thesis, University of Denver (2010): digitalcommons.du.edu/etd/378.

Long Discourses: A faithful translation of the Digha Nikaya, vol. 3, trans. Bhikkhu Sujato (Eastwood, Australia: SuttaCentral, 2018).

Lovejoy, Paul E., *Transformations in Slavery: A History of Slavery in Africa* (Cambridge: Cambridge University Press, 1983).

Luckoo, F. and M. Tzvetkova, *Combating Trafficking in Persons: A Directory of Organizations* (London: CHANGE/Anti-Trafficking Programme, 2002).

Mabee, Carleton, *Black Freedom: The Nonviolent Abolitionists from 1830 Through the Civil War* (London: Collier-Macmillan Limited, 1970).

Macuch, M., "Barda and Bardadari, ii, in the Sasanian period," in E. Yar-shater (ed.), *Encyclopedia Iranica* (London and New York: Routledge & Kegan Paul, 1989).

The Mahabharata of Krishna-Dwaipayana Vyasa, Book 3, trans. Pratap Chandra Roy (Calcutta: Oriental Publishing Co., no date).

Mansi, G. D. (ed.) *Sacrorum conciliorum nova et amplissima collectio* (Florence, 1759–1767; Venice, 1769–1798).

Martinez, Rhonda, "The Trokosi tradition in Ghana: the silencing of a religion," *History in the Making*, 4:5 (2011): scholarworks.lib.csusb.edu/history-in-the-making/vol4/iss1/5.

Martyn, John R. C. (trans. and ed.), *The Letters of Gregory the Great*, vol. 2 (Toronto: Pontifical Institute of Mediaeval Studies, 2004).

Maxwell, John Francis, *Slavery and the Catholic Church: The History of Catholic Teaching Concerning the Moral Legitimacy of the Institution of Slavery* (Chicester and London: Barry Rose Publishers, 1975).

McCormick, Michael, *Origins of the European Economy: Communications and Commerce, A. D. 300-900* (Cambridge: Cambridge University Press, 2001).

Mendelsohn, Isaac, *Slavery in the Ancient Near East: A Comparative Study of Slavery in Babylonia, Assyria, Syria and Palestine from the Middle of the Third Millennium to the End of the First Millennium* (New York: Oxford University Press, 1949).

Mensah, Wisdom, "Girls in West Africa offered into sexual slavery as 'wives of gods,'" *The Conversation*, Oct. 29, 2018: theconversation.com/girls-in-west-africa-offered-into-sexual-slavery-as-wives-of-gods-105400.

Miers, Suzanne, *Slavery in the Twentieth Century: The Evolution of a Global Problem* (New York: AltaMira Press, 2003).

Migne, J. P. (ed.), *Patrologia cursus completes, series Latina*, vol. 102 (Paris, 1851).

Miller, Joseph C., *The Problem of Slaving as History: A Global Approach* (New Haven: Yale University Press, 2012).

Minkema, Kenneth P., "Jonathan Edwards on slavery and the slave trade," *The William and Mary Quarterly* 54:4 (Oct 1997), 823–834.

The Minor Law-Books, Part I: Narada, Brihaspati, trans. Julius Jolly (Oxford: Clarendon Press, 1889).

Montesquieu, M. De Secondat, Baron de, *The Spirit of Laws* (Dublin: G. and A. Ewing, 1751).

Morris, Marc, *The Norman Conquest: The Battle of Hastings and the Fall of Anglo-Saxon England* (New York: Pegasus Books, 2013).

Morris, Rosemary, "Emancipation in Byzantium: Roman law in a medieval society," in M. L. Bush (ed.), *Serfdom and Slavery: Studies in Legal Bondage* (London and New York: Longman, 1996), 130–143.

Moses Maimonides, *Mishneh Torah*, trans. Eliyahu Touger: www.chabad.org/library/article_cdo/aid/682956/jewish/Mishneh-Torah-Rambam.htm

Muldoon, James, *Popes, Lawyers, and Infidels* (Philadelphia: University of Pennsylvania Press, 1996).

Nasr, Seyyed Hossein (ed.), *The Study Quran: A New Translation and Commentary* (New York: HarperOne, 2015).

Nathan, Geoffrey, *The Family in Late Antiquity: The Rise of Christianity and the Endurance of Tradition* (London: Routledge, 2000).

National Human Rights Commission, India, *The Bonded Labour System (Abolition) Act, 1976 And the Prohibition of Employment as Manual Scavengers and their Rehabilitation Act, 2013* (New Delhi: National Human Rights Commission, 2021): nhrc.nic.in/sites/default/files/Bonded%20Labour.pdf.

Niehoff, Maren E., *Philo of Alexandria: An Intellectual Biography* (New Haven: Yale University Press, 2018).

Nolan, Patrick and Gerhard Lenski, *Human Societies: An Introduction to Macrosociology*, 11th ed. (Boulder: Paradigm Publishers, 2011).

Noonan, John T., Jr., *A Church That Can and Cannot Change: The Development of Catholic Moral Teaching* (Notre Dame, IN: University of Notre Dame Press, 2005).

Nordholt, Jan Willem Schulte, *Woodrow Wilson: A Life for Peace* (Berkeley: University of California Press, 1991).

Nordling, John G., "Onesimus fugitivus: a defense of the runaway slave hypothesis in Philemon," *Journal for the Study of the New Testament*, 41 (1991), 97–119.

Northrup, David, "Overseas movements of slaves and indentured workers," in D. Eltis, S. Engerman, S. Drescher, and D. Richardson (eds.), *The Cambridge World History of Slavery: Volume 4, AD 1804–AD 2016* (Cambridge: Cambridge University Press, 2017), 49–70.

Numbered Discourses: A sensible translation of the Anguttara Nikaya, vol. 3, trans. Bhikkhu Sujato (Eastwood, Australia: SuttaCentral, 2018).

Oldfield, J. R., *Popular Politics and British Anti-Slavery: The Mobilisation of Public Opinion against the Slave Trade, 1787 – 1807* (London: Frank Cass, 1998).

Origo, Iris, "The domestic enemy: the Eastern slaves in Tuscany in the fourteenth and fifteenth centuries," *Speculum*, 30 (July 1955), 321–366.

Osborn, George C., *Woodrow Wilson: The Early Years* (Baton Rouge, LA: Louisiana State Press, 1968).

Palais, James B., *Confucian Statecraft and Korean Institutions* (Seattle: University of Washington Press, 1996).

Paley, William, *The Principles of Moral and Political Philosophy* (London, 1785).

Panzer, Joel S., *The Popes and Slavery* (New York: Alba House, 1996).

Pao, David W., *Colossians and Philemon: Zondervan Exegetical Commentary Series on the New Testament* (Grand Rapids, MI: Zondervan, 2012).

Parker, Geoffrey, *Emperor: A New Life of Charles V* (New Haven: Yale University Press, 2019).

Patterson, Stephen J., *The Forgotten Creed: Christianity's Original Struggle against Bigotry, Slavery, & Sexism* (New York: Oxford University Press, 2018).

Peters, Rudolph (ed. and trans.), *Jihad in Mediaeval and Modern Islam: The Chapter on Jihad from Averroes' Legal Handbook "Bidayat al-mudjtahid"* (Leiden: Brill, 1977).

Pharr, Clyde (trans. and ed.), *The Theodosian Code: And Novels and the Sirmondian Constitutions* (Princeton: Princeton University Press, 1952).

Phillips, William D., Jr., "Slavery in the Atlantic islands and the early modern Spanish Atlantic world," in D. Eltis and S. Engerman (eds.), *The Cambridge World History of Slavery: Volume 3, AD 1420–AD 1804* (Cambridge: Cambridge University Press, 2011), 325–349.

Philo, *Philo: Volume VII, On the Decalogue. On the Special Laws, Books 1–3, Loeb Classical Library 320*, trans. F. H. Colson (Cambridge, MA: Harvard University Press, 1937).

Quirk, Joel, *The Anti-Slavery Project: From the Slave Trade to Human Trafficking* (Philadelphia: University of Pennsylvania Press, 2011).

Qutb, Sayyed, *In the Shade of the Qur'an*, 30 vols. (Malaysia: Muslim Welfare House, 1992).

Raphall, Morris J., "Bible view of slavery: a discourse," (New York: Rudd & Carleton, 1861): www.jewish-history.com/civilwar/raphall.html.

Ramelli, Ilaria L. E., *Social Justice and Legitimacy of Slavery: The Role of Philosophical Asceticism from Ancient Judaism to Late Antiquity* (Oxford: Oxford University Press, 2016).

Rawson, B. (ed.), *Marriage, Divorce, and Children in Ancient Rome* (Oxford: Clarendon Press, 1991).

Rediker, Marcus, *The Fearless Benjamin Lay: The Quaker Dwarf Who became the First Revolutionary Abolitionist* (Boston: Beacon Press, 2017).

Reiss, Fraidy, "Child marriage in the United States: prevalence and implications," *Journal of Adolescent Health*, 69:6, Supplement (2021), S8–S10: doi.org/10 .1016/j.jadohealth.2021.07.001.

Research Network on the Legal Parameters of Slavery, "Bellagio-Harvard Guidelines on the Legal Parameters of Slavery," (2012).

Reséndez, Andrés *The Other Slavery: The Uncovered Story of Indian Enslavement in America* (Boston: Houghton Mifflin Harcourt, 2016).

Rice, David, *Slavery Inconsistent with Justice and Good Policy* (Lexington, KY, 1792).

Roberts, Alexander and James Donaldson (eds.), *The Ante-Nicene Fathers, Volume I*, rev. A. C. Coxe (New York: Charles Scribner's Sons, 1913).

The Ante-Nicene Fathers, Volume VII, rev. A. C. Coxe (Grand Rapids, MI: Eerdmans, 1982).

Robertson, Ritchie, *The Enlightenment: The Pursuit of Happiness, 1680-1790* (New York: Harper Collins, 2021).

Robinson, Charles H., *Anskar: The Apostle of the North, 801–895* (London: 1921).

Rodrigues, Hillary P., *Introducing Hinduism*, 2nd ed. (New York: Routledge, 2017).

Rota, Michael, "Moral psychology and social change: the case of abolition," *The Journal of Interdisciplinary History*, 49:4 (2019), 567–590.

"On the definition of slavery," *Theoria (Stockholm)*, 86:5 (2020), 543–564.

Rotman, Youval, *Byzantine Slavery and the Mediterranean World* (Cambridge, MA: Harvard University Press, 2009).

Ryan, Maeve, *Humanitarian Governance and the British Antislavery World System* (New Haven: Yale University Press, 2022).

Saffin, John, *A Brief and Candid Answer to a Late Printed Sheet, Entitled, The Selling of Joseph*, partially available in George H. Moore, *Notes on the History of Slavery in Massachusetts* (New York: Appleton & Co., 1866), 251–256: nationalhumanitiescenter.org/pds/becomingamer/ideas/text3/slaverychristian.pdf.

Sahih al-Bukhari: sunnah.com/bukhari.

Saikia, Bidisha and Kevin Bales, "Monitoring and measuring the ineffable: religious Sisters and the Adavasi peoples in Assam," *International Journal of Asian Christianity*, 6:1 (2023), 122–143.

Saikia, Bidisha, Monti Datta, Luke De Pulford, and Kevin Bales, "Exploring the worldview of Religious Sisters: a comparative empirical analysis of altruistic/voluntaristic attitudes," *Intercultural Human Rights Law Review*, 17 (2022), 227–250.

Saller, Richard, "Corporal punishment, authority, and obedience in the Roman household," in B. Rawson (ed.), *Marriage, Divorce, and Children in Ancient Rome* (Oxford: Clarendon Press, 1991), 144–165.

Samson, Ross, "The end of early medieval slavery," in A. J. Frantzen and D. Moffat (eds.), *The Work of Work: Servitude, Slavery, and Labor in Medieval England* (Glasgow: Cruithne Press, 1994), 95–124.

Samuels, Harriet, "A human rights campaign? The campaign to abolish child slavery in Hong Kong 1919–1938," *Journal of Human Rights*, 6:3 (2007), 361–384: doi.org/10.1080/14754830701560764.

Sanderlin, George, "Introduction," in George Sanderlin (ed.), *Witness: Writings of Bartolome de Las Casas* (Maryknoll, NY: Orbis Books, 1992), 1–19.

Sanneh, Lamin O., *The Jakhanke Muslim clerics: a religious and historical study of Islam in Senegambia* (Lanham, MD: University Press of America, 1989).

Sarich, Jody, Michele Olivier, and Kevin Bales, "Forced marriage, slavery, and plural legal systems: an African example," *Human Rights Quarterly*, 38:2 (2016), 450–476: doi.org/10.1353/hrq.2016.0030.

Schaff, Philip (ed.), *A Select Library of the Nicene and Post-Nicene Fathers of the Christian Church, Volume XII: Saint Chrysostom: Homilies on the Epistles of Paul to the Corinthians* (Grand Rapids, MI: Eerdmans, 1979).

A Select Library of the Nicene and Post-Nicene Fathers of the Christian Church, Volume XIII: Saint Chrysostom: Homilies on Galatians, Ephesians, Philippians, Colossians, Thessalonians, Timothy, Titus, and Philemon (Grand Rapids, MI: Eerdmans, 1979).

Schopen, Gregory, "Liberation is only for those already free: Reflections on debts to slavery and enslavement to debt in an early Indian Buddhist monasticism," *Journal of the American Academy of Religion*, 82:3 (2014), 606–635.

"The monastic ownership of servants or slaves: local and legal factors in the redactional history of two *Vinayas*," *Journal of the International Association of Buddhist Studies*, 17:2 (1994), 145–174.

Scott, Thomas, *The Holy Bible Containing the Old and New Testaments with Original Notes, Practical Observations and Copious Marginal References* (Philadelphia, 1805).

Scotus, John Duns, *Duns Scotus on the Will and Morality*, trans. Allan B. Wolter (Washington, DC: Catholic University of America Press, 1986).

Segal, Ronald, *Islam's Black Slaves: The Other Black Diaspora* (New York: Farrar, Straus and Giroux, 2001).

Seneca, *Epistles 1–65*, Loeb Classical Library 75, trans. Richard M. Gummere (Cambridge, MA: Harvard University Press, 1917).

Sewall, Samuel, *The Selling of Joseph a Memorial* (Boston: 1700).

Sharp, Granville, *An Essay on Slavery, Proving from Scripture Its Inconsistency with Humanity and Religion* (Burlington: Isaac Collins, 1773).

Sheth, Surabhi, "Equality and inequality in the Hindu Scriptures," in R. Siriwardena (ed.), *Equality and the Religious Traditions of Asia* (New York: St. Martin's Press, 1987), 21–50.

Shmalo, Gamliel, "Orthodox approaches to Biblical slavery," *The Torah U–Madda Journal*, 16 (2012–2013), 1–20.

Siedentop, Larry, *Inventing the Individual: The Origins of Western Liberalism* (Cambridge, MA: Harvard University Press, 2014).

Silk, Jonathan A., "Slavery," in R. E. Buswell (ed.), *The Encyclopedia of Buddhism*, (New York: Thomson Gale, 2004).

Simpson, Lesley Byrd, *The Encomienda in New Spain: The Beginning of Spanish Mexico* (Berkeley: University of California Press, 1966).

"Slavery and the Bible," *De Bow's Review*, 9 (Sept. 1850), 281–286.

Smaragdus of Saint-Mihiel, *Via Regia*, ed. Matthew Ponesse, trans. James F. LePree (Leuven: Peeters, 2023).

Smith, Adam, *An Inquiry into the Nature and Causes of the Wealth of Nations* (New York: The Modern Library, 1937).

Lectures on Jurisprudence, ed. R. L. Meek, D. D. Raphael, and P. G. Stein (Oxford: Clarendon Press, 1978).

Smith, Angharad, Monti Narayan Datta, and Kevin Bales, "Contemporary slavery in armed conflict: introducing the CSAC dataset, 1989–2016," *Journal of Peace Research*, 60:2 (2022): doi.org/10.1177/002234332110 65649.

Smith, David Livingstone, *Less Than Human: Why We Demean, Enslave, and Exterminate Others* (New York: Macmillan, 2011).

Snell, Daniel C., "Slavery in the ancient Near East," in K. Bradley and P. Cartledge (eds.), *The Cambridge World History of Slavery: Volume 1, The Ancient Mediterranean World* (Cambridge: Cambridge University Press, 2011), 4–21.

Sokolow, Jayme A., "Revolution and reform: the antebellum Jewish abolitionists," *Journal of Ethnic Studies*, 9 (1981), 27–43.

Stark, Rodney, *For the Glory of God: How Monotheism Led to Reformations, Science, Witch-Hunts, and the End of Slavery* (Princeton: Princeton University Press, 2003).

Stewart, James Brewer, "Antislavery and abolitionism in the United States, 1776–1870," in D. Eltis, S. Engerman, S. Drescher, and D. Richardson (eds.), *The Cambridge World History of Slavery: Volume 4, AD 1804—AD 2016* (Cambridge: Cambridge University Press, 2017), 399–421.

Holy Warriors: The Abolitionists and American Slavery (New York: Hill and Wang, 1976).

Stringfellow, Thornton, "A brief examination of Scripture testimony on the institution of slavery," *Religious Herald* (1841).

Scriptural and Statistical Views in Favor of Slavery, 4th ed. (Richmond, VA: J. W. Randolph, 1856).

Sunan Abi Dawud: sunnah.com/abudawud.

Sutherland, Samuel S., "The study of slavery in the early and central Middle Ages: old problems and new approaches," *History Compass* 18:11 (2020): doi.org/10.1111/hic3.12633.

The Sutra on Upasaka Precepts: Translated from the Chinese of Dharmaraksa, trans. Bhiksuni Shih Heng-ching (Berkeley: Numata Center for Buddhist Translation and Research, 1994).

Tatara, Christopher, "Hitler, Himmler, and Christianity in the early Third Reich," *Constructing the Past*, 14:1, article 10: digitalcommons.iwu.edu/constructing/vol14/iss1/10.

Taylor, Joan E., *The Essenes, the Scrolls, and the Dead Sea* (Oxford: Oxford University Press, 2012).

Taylor, Michael, "British proslavery arguments and the Bible, 1823–1833," *Slavery & Abolition*, 37:1 (2016), 139–158.

Thapar, Romila, *Asoka and the Decline of the Mauryas* (London: Oxford University Press, 1961).

Tise, Larry E., *Proslavery: A History of the Defense of Slavery in America, 1701–1840* (Athens: The University of Georgia Press, 1987).

Turton, Andrew, "Thai institutions of slavery," in J. L. Watson (ed)., *Asian & African Systems of Slavery* (Berkeley: University of California Press, 1980), 251–92.

United States Holocaust Memorial Museum, "Concentration camp system: In depth," Aug. 22 2023, in *Holocaust Encyclopedia*: encyclopedia.ushmm.org/content/en/article/concentration-camp-system-in-depth.

Upadhyaya, Krishna Prasad, *Poverty, Discrimination and Slavery: The reality of bonded labour in India, Nepal and Pakistan* (London: Anti-Slavery International, 2008): www.antislavery.org/reports/poverty-discrimination-and-slavery-the-reality-of-bonded-labour-in-india-nepal-and-pakistan/.

The Upanishads, 2nd ed., trans. Eknath Easwaran (Tomales, CA: Nilgiri Press, 2007).

Uziel, R. Ben-Zion Meir Hai, *Mikhmannei Uziel* (Tel Aviv, 1939).

Venters, Laurie, "Recovering runaways: Slave catching in the Roman world," Master's thesis, (Leiden University: 2019): studenttheses.universiteitleiden.nl/handle/1887/74843.

Vermes, Geza and Martin Goodman (eds.), *The Essenes according to the Classical Sources* (Sheffield: JSOT Press, 1989).

Vita Sanctae Balthildis, Scriptores Rerum Merovingicarum (Hannover, 1888).

Walvin, James, "The rise of British popular sentiment for abolition, 1787–1832," in C. Bolt and S. Drescher (eds.), *Anti-Slavery, Religion, and Reform: Essays in Memory of Roger Anstey* (Kent: Wm Dawson & Sons, 1980), 149–162.

England, Slaves, and Freedom, 1776–1838 (London: MacMillan Press, 1986).

Watson, James L. (ed.), *Asian & African Systems of Slavery* (Berkeley: University of California Press, 1980).

Watson, Richard, *Anecdotes of the Life of Richard Watson, Bishop of Llandaff; Written by Himself at Different Intervals and Revised in 1814* (London, 1817).

Weld, Theodore Dwight, *The Bible against Slavery: An Inquiry into the Patriarchal and Mosaic Systems on the Subject of Human Rights* (New York: American Anti-Slavery Society, 1838).

Letters of Theodore Dwight Weld, Angelina Grimke and Sarah Grimke 1822–1844, eds. G. H. Barnes and D. L. Dumond (New York: Da Capo Press, 1970).

Westermann, William L., *The Slave Systems of Greek and Roman Antiquity* (Philadelphia: The American Philosophical Society, 1955).

Wickham, Chris, *Framing the Early Middle Ages: Europe and the Mediterranean, 400–800* (Oxford: Oxford University Press, 2005).

Wijesekera, Nandadeva, "Slavery in Sri Lanka: Presidential address delivered on 20-12-74," *Journal of the Sri Lanka Branch of the Royal Asiatic Society* 18 (1974), 1–22.

Wiking, Sofia, "From slave wife of the gods to 'ke te pam tem eng': Trokosi seen through the eyes of the participants," unpublished Master's thesis, Malmo University, Sweden (2009).

Wilson, Andrew, "The best argument for a trajectory hermeneutic – and where it goes wrong," *Think*, Mar. 6, 2013: thinktheology.co.uk/blog/article/the_best_argument_for_a_trajectory_hermeneutic_and_where_it_goes_wrong.

Wilson, Ellen Gibson, *Thomas Clarkson: A Biography* (New York: St. Martin's Press, 1990).

Wilson, Joseph R., *Mutual Relation of Masters and Slaves as Taught in the Bible* (*Augusta*, Georgia: Steam Press of Chronicle and Sentinel, 1861): docsouth.unc.edu/imls/wilson/wilson.html.

Woolman, John, *The Journal and Major Essays of John Woolman*, ed. P. P. Moulton (Oxford: Oxford University Press, 1971).

Wolter, Allan B. "Introduction," in John Duns Scotus, *Duns Scotus on the Will and Morality*, trans. Allan B. Wolter (Washington, DC: Catholic University of America Press, 1986).

Wyatt-Brown, Bertram, *Yankee Saints and Southern Sinners* (Baton Rouge, LA: Louisiana State University Press, 1985).

Yogi, Anju Gautam, "Women sacrificed to gods struggle to rehabilitate, Deuki tradition wanes in Nepal," Sep. 10, 2012, *Global Press Journal*: globalpressjournal.com/asia/nepal/women-sacrificed-to-gods-struggle-to-rehabilitate-deuki-tradition-wanes-in-nepal/.

Yoshimi, Yoshiaki, *Comfort Women: Sexual Slavery in the Japanese Military During World War II*, rev. ed., trans. Suzanne O'Brien (New York: Columbia University Press, 2002).

Index

Printed by Integrated Books International,
United States of America